Las Vegas

WHAT'S NEW | WHAT'S ON | WHAT'S BEST

www.timeout.com/lasvegas

Contents

Las Vegas by Area

Essentials

Published by Time Out Guides Ltd
Universal House
251 Tottenham Court Road
London W1T 7AB
Tel: + 44 (0)20 7813 3000
Fax: + 44 (0)20 7813 6001
Email: guides@timeout.com
www.timeout.com

Managing Director Peter Fiennes
Editorial Director Ruth Jarvis
Deputy Series Editor Dominic Earle
Business Manager Gareth Garner
Editorial Manager Holly Pick
Assistant Management Accountant Ija Krasnikova

Time Out Guides is a wholly owned subsidiary of Time Out Group Ltd.

© Time Out Group Ltd
Chairman Tony Elliott
Financial Director Richard Waterlow
Group General Manager/Director Nichola Coulthard
Time Out Magazine Ltd MD Richard Waterlow
Time Out Communications Ltd MD David Pepper
Time Out International MD Cathy Runciman
Production Director Mark Lamond
Group Marketing Director John Luck
Group Art Director John Oakey
Group IT Director Simon Chappell

Time Out and the Time Out logo are trademarks of Time Out Group Ltd.

This edition first published in Great Britain in 2007 by Ebury Publishing
A Random House Group Company
Company information can be found on www.randomhouse.co.uk
10 9 8 7 6 5 4 3 2 1

For further distribution details, see www.timeout.com

ISBN 10: 1-84670-043-4
ISBN 13: 978184670 0439

A CIP catalogue record for this book is available from the British Library

Printed and bound by Firmengruppe APPL, aprinta druck, Wemding, Germany

The Random House Group Limited makes every effort to ensure that the papers used
in our books are made from trees that have been legally sourced from well-managed
and credibly certified forests. Our paper procurement policy can be found on
www.rbooks.co.uk/environment.

Las Vegas Shortlist

The **Time Out Las Vegas Shortlist** is one of a new series of guides that draws on Time Out's background as a magazine publisher to keep you current with what's going on in town. As well as Las Vegas's key casinos and sights, and the best of its eating, drinking and leisure options, the guide picks out the most exciting venues to have recently opened and gives a full calendar of annual events. It also includes features on the important news, trends and openings, all compiled by locally based editors and writers. Whether you're visiting for the first time or you're a regular, you'll find the *Time Out Las Vegas Shortlist* contains all you need to know, in a portable and easy-to-use format.

The guide divides central Las Vegas into six areas, each contained in a separate chapter with its own map. These chapters are organised by casino. Within each casino section, we have detailed the various Sights & museums, Eating & drinking, Shopping, Nightlife and Arts & leisure venues; non-casino venues are listed at the end of each chapter. The front of the book contains chapters rounding up these scenes around the city, and giving a shortlist of our overall picks in a variety of categories. We also include itineraries for days out, plus essentials such as transport information and hotels.

Our listings give phone numbers as dialled within Las Vegas. When dialling from elsewhere in the US, prefix all seven-digit numbers with 1-702, the city's area code, to make an 11-digit number. Calls to numbers listed with the prefixes 1-800, 1-866, 1-877 or 1-888 will be free. From outside the US, dial your country's international access code, then the 11-digit number. Some venues within casinos do not have separate numbers; where this is the case, use the main casino number.

We have noted price categories by using one to four dollar signs ($-$$$$), representing budget, moderate, expensive and luxury. Major credit cards are accepted unless otherwise stated. We also indicate when a venue is **NEW**.

All our listings are double-checked. However, venues do sometimes close or change their hours or prices, so it's a good idea to call before visiting. While every effort has been made to ensure accuracy, the publishers cannot accept responsibility for any errors that this guide may contain.

Venues are marked on the maps using symbols numbered according to their order within the chapter and colour-coded according to the type of venue they represent:

❶ Sights & museums
❶ Eating & drinking
❶ Shopping
❶ Nightlife
❶ Arts & leisure

Map key	
Major sight or landmark	
Major casino & resort	
Park or forest	
Pedestrianised street	
One-way street	→
Interstate highway	(80)
US highway	(95)
State or provincial highway	(75)

Time Out Las Vegas Shortlist

EDITORIAL
Editor Will Fulford-Jones
Deputy Editor Charlotte Thomas
Researcher Miranda Morton
Proofreader Tamsin Shelton

DESIGN
Art Director Scott Moore
Art Editor Pinelope Kourmouzoglou
Senior Designer Henry Elphick
Graphic Designer Gemma Doyle
Junior Graphic Designer Kei Ishimaru
Digital Imaging Simon Foster
Ad Make-up Jodi Sher
Picture Editor Jael Marschner
Deputy Picture Editor Tracey Kerrigan
Picture Researcher Helen McFarland

ADVERTISING
Sales Director/Sponsorship Mark Phillips
International Sales Manager (North America) Rani Vavilis
International Sales Consultant Ross Canadé
International Sales Executive Charlie Sokol
Advertising Assistant Kate Staddon

MARKETING
Marketing Manager Yvonne Poon
Sales & Marketing Director, North America Lisa Levinson
Marketing Designer Anthony Huggins

PRODUCTION
Production Manager Brendan McKeown
Production Co-ordinator Caroline Bradford
Production Controller Susan Whittaker

CONTRIBUTORS
Written and researched by Deke Castleman, Dayvid Figler, Will Fulford-Jones, Phil Hagen, PJ Perez, James P Reza, Amy Schmidt, Kate Silver and David Surratt. Thanks also to all other contributors to *Time Out Las Vegas*.

PHOTOGRAPHY
Photography by Jonathan Perugia, except: pages 26, 91 Tomas Muscionico; pages 33, 121, 122, 164, 167 Heloise Bergman; page 106 Isaac Brekken; page 166 Will Fulford-Jones. The following images were provided by the featured establishments/artists: pages 12, 93, 143, 172.

Cover photograph: Fremont Street. Credit: Miles Ertman/Masterfile.

MAPS
JS Graphics (john @jsgraphics.co.uk).

About Time Out

Founded in 1968, Time Out has expanded from humble London beginnings into the leading resource for those wanting to know what's happening in the world's greatest cities. As well as our influential what's-on weeklies in London, New York and Chicago, we publish more than a dozen other listings magazines in cities as varied as Beijing and Mumbai. The magazines established Time Out's trademark style: sharp writing, informed reviewing and bang up-to-date inside knowledge of every scene.

Time Out made the natural leap into travel guides in the 1980s with the City Guide series, which now extends to over 50 destinations around the world. Written and researched by expert local writers and generously illustrated with original photography, the full-size guides cover a larger area than our Shortlist guides and include many more venue reviews, along with additional background features and a full set of maps.

Throughout this rapid growth, the company has remained proudly independent, still owned by Tony Elliott nearly four decades after he started Time Out London as a single fold-out sheet of A5 paper. This independence extends to the editorial content of all our publications, this Shortlist included. No establishment has been featured because it has advertised, and no payment has influenced any of our reviews. And, for our critics, there's definitely no such thing as a free lunch: all restaurants and bars are visited and reviewed anonymously, and Time Out always picks up the bill. For more about the company, see www.timeout.com.

Don't Miss

The Strip p112

WHAT'S BEST

Casinos & Resorts

Slowly but surely forming a fresh skyline for the city, new casino buildings are sprouting like mushrooms around Las Vegas. The grand, paradigm-shifting openings of the two enormous new resorts, Fontainebleau Las Vegas and CityCenter (see box p117), aren't expected until 2009. Still, even before they open their doors, there's plenty new under the sun in Sin City.

Perhaps the most eye-catching recent development is the Trump International (p177), the newest and shiniest development on Las Vegas Boulevard. But unless you're a guest or an owner of one of its condos, you can only gawp at the city's tallest building from outside it. There's no casino, no showroom and no restaurant, and the only ride is reserved for the occupants of the 64th-floor penthouse.

A stroll across the street will lead you to two more new developments at already established resorts, both of which are more than happy to welcome outsiders. Just north of Sands Avenue sits the buffed and bronzed Wynn Las Vegas; the brainchild of pioneering casino developer Steve Wynn, it's due to open its new Encore sister resort in 2008, complete with its own small casino, some inevitably upscale bars and restaurants, and a slew of high-end shops. However, the original Wynn will continue to house the campus's main attractions, from the city's highest-end dining to its most exclusive shops.

Just across Sands Avenue at Sheldon Adelson's Venetian, the late 2007 addition of the Palazzo casino has elevated the resort to the status of the world's largest hotel. A brand new Barneys department store anchors a new 80-retailer shopping, dining and entertainment complex prosaically named the Shops at Palazzo; it connects to the Grand Canal Shoppes (both p106), where the Venetian street theme includes waterways, bridges and gondola rides. Simultaneously, Adelson is quietly continuing to fuel the Broadway-to-Vegas fire: in addition to the already popular *Phantom*, he's bringing the Frankie Valli-inspired musical *Jersey Boys* to christen the Palazzo's showroom early in 2008.

Revamps and makeovers

Besides ambitious additions to existing properties, the other current theme in Las Vegas is 'retrofitting'. On the Strip, the rebranding of Treasure Island (p100) from kid-friendly resort to adult playground has been followed in recent years by a less dramatic but no less effective sprucing-up of the Mirage (p89), which has developed a new vibrancy after several fairly dreary years. And in 2006 and 2007, the Luxor (p50) began to shed much of its once-overbearing Egyptian theming, amid rumours that it's soon to be rebranded the Pyramid.

Most dramatically, the twice-bitten Aladdin has finally re-emerged as the far less shy Planet Hollywood (p96), a celebrity-led effort with a revamped interior (from Moroccan to retro chic), a remodelled and renamed mall (Desert Passage has become the Miracle Mile) and a redoubled magic spectacle. Next door to magician Steve Wyrick's new $35-million theatre is an even newer production called *The Beauty of Magic*, starring Hans Klok and a rotating special guest sexpot (the first was Pamela Anderson).

Even the Downtown casinos have been getting in on the act, albeit slowly. The revitalisation of the Golden Nugget (p148) has been

a great success: after buying the hotel a couple of years ago, Texas-based restaurateurs Landry's embarked on a dramatic sprucing-up of the property that's really laid down the gauntlet for its tired Fremont Street competitors. Most of them have been slow to respond, but changes are on the horizon.

That's entertainment

Old-fashioned Vegas shows are now few and far between: most have been revitalised or replaced by high-concept spectaculars, often produced by Cirque du Soleil, and imports from Broadway. (For more on this trend, see pp26-27.) It's a similar story in the city's kitchens, which continue to outdo each other in pomp, circumstance and – most crucially – food. For details on the hottest casino restaurants in town, see pp13-17. And for the casino's ever-expanding, ever-popular shopping malls, turn to pp18-21.

While Las Vegas's museums used to pretty much start and finish with Liberace (p127), the displays of art

and artefacts have at last flourished into a full day's worth of touring possibilities. The Bellagio Gallery of Fine Art (p75) and the Guggenheim-Hermitage Museum at the Venetian (p104) both rotate exhibits that range from Picasso to pop art. Indeed, it seems the appetite for art is growing in Vegas: several resorts, among them Thehotel at Mandalay Bay (p173), the Rio (p139) and Wynn Las Vegas (p113), are using their walls as exhibition spaces to draw the more discerning visitors.

Of course, not all exhibitions in Las Vegas revolve around high culture. Only a short walk from the Guggenheim-Hermitage Museum, the Venetian is also home to a recently revamped outpost of Madame Tussauds, the famous London museum of waxworks. And down at the Tropicana (p69) are semi-permanent exhibitions devoted to the *Titanic* (p70) and the inside of the human body (p69).

Vegas retains many of its older attractions, which continue to draw the crowds. The Mirage still has its famous dolphin and white-tiger habitats, and its erupting volcano, while the ever-popular dancing fountains still line up nearby at the grand Bellagio (p74). There's an indoor Shark Reef at Mandalay Bay (p53), a shark aquarium in the pool at the Golden Nugget (p148) and a Lion Habitat at the MGM Grand (p59). And on the really wild side, the silicone-enhanced Sirens of TI (p101) perform three cringeworthy shows every night at Treasure Island.

Elsewhere, Circus Circus is home to one of the last kid-friendly arcades in the post-family-era Strip: the pink Adventuredome (p110), which offers thrill rides and old-fashioned carnival activities. Daredevils can also find rollercoasters at the Sahara (p112), New York New York (p66) and atop the Stratosphere (p113), which have been joined by the less dramatic Dracula's Haunted Castle and Reboot rides at the Luxor (p50). And three new motion simulator rides have opened at Excalibur's Fantasy Faire Midway (p50), including a new Spongebob Squarepants 4D Special FX ride.

Adults only

However, these days, the true playgrounds are for adults. The Palms (p135) and Hard Rock (p121) still do it best when it comes to the all-round Vegas hipster experience, each one with trendy nightclub, pool and restaurant scenes. Treasure Island and Caesars Palace are hot on their heels, but just about every major resort comes with a nightclub as standard these days, the hottest of which are Tao at the Venetian (p107), Revolution at the Mirage (p92) and Risqué at Paris (p96).

And then, of course, there's the gambling: no longer Vegas's sole raison d'être, but still a crucial part of the city (and, of course, a massive moneymaker for the casinos). The big development in recent years has been the boom in the popularity of poker, with the Bellagio taking over from Binion's as the place to play in town. It seems as if almost every casino in the city is expanding its poker programme; you'll find it easy to get a game.

Rendering of CityCenter p117

Nove p136

Eating & Drinking

When people speak of the recent Vegas renaissance, they're referring in large part to the dramatic shift in the city's dining scene that has taken place over the past 15 years. It's a popular cliché to say that prior to the opening of Wolfgang Puck's venerable and still relevant Spago (p82), Vegas was awash in a sea of all-you-can-scoff buffets and not much else. It's not entirely correct, but the changes have nonetheless been sweeping.

Even so, chains dominate the landscape, with the same over-familiar signs to be found in nearly every casino food court. The trend for chains also goes upscale: for every Bradley Ogden (p81), where the namesake chef is frequently found in the kitchen, there are five

Puck-style outlets, where the star chef is rarely if ever seen. And while some ultra-heavy hitters have made their way here, at restaurants such as Bouchon (p104), Restaurant Guy Savoy (p81) and Daniel Boulud (p115), these are also chains of a sort, outposts of successful spots imported to capitalise on the tourist dollar in what has evolved into a pricey, food-themed playground.

Despite those caveats, 21st-century Las Vegas does hold its own when it comes to world-class dining. A chef such as Hubert Keller would never have bothered with Vegas ten years ago. Today, though, the Frenchman is a something of a local media hero, and his Fleur de Lys (p54) is widely acknowledged to be one of the city's best restaurants.

Spago p82

Home-grown goodness

Just as vitally, there is at last some movement towards nurturing the city's homegrown culinary talent, with the financial support of the big casinos. Perhaps the most renowned restaurant to emerge from this initiative is Alex (p114) at Wynn Las Vegas, where Alessandro Stratta presides over a Mediterranean menu served up in an OTT dining room with prices to match.

And then there's local French expat André Rochat, who continues to command great respect in culinary circles. André's (p152), his venerable Downtown institution, has given birth to a second location at the Monte Carlo, as well as the more flashy Alizé (p136) atop the Palms.

See and be scene

The N9ne Group, the Light Group and Pure Management were once known for their nightclubs and ultralounges. However, all three powerhouses have broadened their spheres of influence to create new,

Vegas-only 'scene eateries' with dining, dancing and cocktails, helping to make them the evening's final stop as well as the starting point for a big night. The N9ne steakhouse at the Palms now has on-property competition from Nove (both p136), while the Light Group's sister steakhouses Fix (at the Bellagio; p75) and the newer Stack (at the Mirage; p92) are linked to their nightclubs Light (p79) and Jet (p92). Upscale sushi star Social House (p102) is upstairs from Pure's Tangerine (p101) at Treasure Island. And in summer 2007, the Light Group opened Diablo's Cantina (p65), a two-storey tequila house fronting the Monte Carlo, with patio dining fronting the Strip.

Name dropping

At Joël Robuchon (p60), in the MGM Grand, diners have but two choices, either a six- or 16-course prix fixe menu. For a taste of the talk of the town at a fraction of the price, pomp and circumstance, snag a counter seat at the neighbouring L'Atelier de Joël Robuchon (p60), which overlooks the kitchen. Either way, he's arguably the biggest name in town.

Rick Moonen's RM (p54) seafood restaurant in Mandalay Bay has greatly benefited from the closing of the NYC location and the chef's relocation to Las Vegas. The less pricey, slightly more casual café downstairs gets you in if you carry gold rather than platinum. And David Burke (p104), a James Beard nominee who worked under Charlie Palmer, joined the big names in town when he opened an outpost in the Venetian in 2007, serving modern American cuisine.

Asia rising

The proliferation of Asian restaurants in Las Vegas may be due to the huge number of Asian visitors, or it could simply be that the cuisine has reached a high level of both quality and trendiness. Whatever the reason, sushi bars are popping up in all areas of the city, and 'Let's go for sushi' is an increasingly common metaphor for 'Let's eat light and drink heavily'.

It's hard to beat the 800-pound gorilla NYC import that is Tao (p107). Thanks to its unholy trinity of attractions (restaurant + nightclub + topless pool), the operation was recently named as the top-grossing independent restaurant in the US. However, Planet Hollywood's Asia (p96) is giving it a little competition. Opened in summer 2007 in the two-storey spot once occupied by Prana, the ill-fated outpost of Beverly Hills' Crustacean, the spot blends a restaurant, a lounge and a dancefloor, and is operated by Michael Bergos of Club New York and Vudu Lounge. Similarly upscale and trendy but less frenetic are the Mirage's Fin (Chinese seafood; p90) and Japonais

SHORTLIST

New & notable
- Café Martorano (p140)
- Diablo's Cantina (p65)
- Restaurant Guy Savoy (p81)

Best breakfast
- Bouchon (p104)
- Verandah Café (p56)

Best outdoor dining
- Café Ba Ba Reeba (p118)
- Mon Ami Gabi (p96)

Best vegetarian menu
- Gaylord's (p140)
- Origin India (p130)

Best views
- Alizé (p136)
- Mix (p54)
- Top of the World (p113)

OTT dinner
- Joël Robuchon (p60)
- Picasso (p78)

Bar scene
- Japonais (p92)
- N9ne (p136)
- Simon Kitchen & Bar (p124)

Chefs in the kitchen
- Alex (p114)
- Bradley Ogden (p81)

Cheap(er) eats
- Bay City Diner (p148)
- Esmerelda's (p154)
- Kabob Korner (p157)
- Mr Lucky's 24/7 (p124)

Pop the question
- Eiffel Tower (p95)
- Fleur de Lys (p54)

Kids & families
- Luv-It Frozen Custard (p157)
- Quark's Bar & Restaurant (p126)

Vintage Vegas
- Bay City Diner (p148)
- Hugo's Cellar (p156)
- Steak House (p110)

GET REAL

Real brands. Real selection. Real savings.

SAVE 25% TO 65% EVERY DAY AT MORE THAN 130 STORES FEATURING:

Adidas • Ashworth • Bose • Callaway Golf • Calvin Klein • Carter's
Dressbarn • Gymboree Outlet • Jones New York Country • Lane
Bryant Outlet • Liz Claiborne • Nike Factory Store • OshKosh B'Gosh
Perry Ellis • Quiksilver • Reebok • Samsonite
Skechers • Stride Rite Keds Sperry • Timberland
Tommy Hilfiger • Vans • Wet Seal • Wilsons
Leather Outlet • Zales Outlet and more

Las Vegas, NV • Las Vegas Blvd. South to Warm Springs Rd. or I-15
via Blue Diamond Interchange • (702) 896-5599 • Mon-Sat 10-9, Sun 10-8
www.lasvegasoutletcenter.com • Chelsea Property Group*

*A SIMON® Company

(p92), where the sushi lounge is usually better than the dining room for atmosphere and service.

Looking to escape the hectic Strip? Just east on Paradise Road you'll find Dragonfly, the sister restaurant to Spanish tapas bar Firefly (both p129), where Asian small plates feed hipster locals. Just south is Origin India (p130), an excellent Indian joint that's a far cry from a standard curry house. And out west, the Palms' ever-fashionable Little Buddha (p136) continues to pack in a crowd most nights of the week.

Steak out

In light of the new Asian dominance, the previous trend for nouveau steakhouses looks to be past its peak. Still, Downtown, the San Francisco-styled Triple George (p159) and its neighbouring Sidebar (p157) attract the lawyer lunch crowd. And for a real vintage Vegas atmosphere, it's hard to beat the venerable Bay City Diner (p148), though the Golden Nugget's new Vic & Anthony's (p150) apes the old-school style but does a better job in the kitchen.

Fresh finds

Well worth a stop is the rather obviously named Stripburger (next to Café Ba Ba Reeba; p118), which offers outdoor-only seating fronting the Strip in the Fashion Show Mall. Serving every variety of well-made burger you can imagine, it has two separate zones: an adults-only circular full-service bar, and a covered patio for families.

Downtown, leave the casinos for the Downtown Cocktail Room and the Griffin (both p154), two sharp new bars that are helping to revive Fremont Street east of the strip.

At the other end of the spectrum, coming late in 2007 is a new Wolfgang Puck concept at the Las Vegas Springs Preserve (p143). Puck's place will occupy a second-storey space with massive windows and a balcony looking toward Downtown. And in 2008, watch for the new project by chef and hospitality entrepreneur Charlie Palmer, who will open a boutique hotel and accompanying restaurant in Downtown's new Union Park, a non-gaming area where academics, arts and lifestyle converge.

Griffin p154

Chrome Hearts at Forum Shops p82

WHAT'S BEST
Shopping

Much like the family-friendly
themed hotels of the 1990s, the
hotel-casino mall has gone, in the
words of Martin Scorsese's Howard
Hughes, 'the way of the future'.
The old gimmicks that once defined
these malls (animatronic fountains,
opera-singing gondoliers) have been
replaced with new ones (marquee
labels, innovative design), as the
malls try to lure tourists and their
wallets into the shops.

It seems to be working. Recent
expansions and/or renovations by
the Forum Shops (p82) at Caesars
Palace, the Grand Canal Shoppes
(p106) at the Venetian and the
Miracle Mile Shops (p97) at Planet
Hollywood (formerly Desert
Passage) have put the malls firmly
on the visitors' checklist. But rather

than relying on floor shows, the
malls' store line-ups have come into
the spotlight as the main attraction.
Clearly, some shoppers find gazing
at pricey baubles inside glass cases
at Harry Winston as entertaining as
front-row seats at a Cirque show.

Along the Strip, you can buy a
pair of Jimmy Choos, an iPod nano,
Vosges chocolate, Zac Posen dresses,
Thomas Pink shirts, Louis Vuitton
sunglasses, a Birkin bag and even
a Ferrari. Speciality shops (Georg
Jensen, Swarovski) and big-name
designers (Gaultier, Prada) keep
things upscale. However, it's not
all hyper-expensive. Mixed in with
the designer labels are chains such
as Banana Republic, Lacoste, H&M,
Urban Outfitters and Zara, with
boutiques such as Intermix, Scoop,

Still and Kate Spade also drawing crowds. And the hits just keep on coming: Barneys and Barneys Co-Op will arrive in early 2008 as anchors for the new Shops at Palazzo, just across from the Fashion Show Mall.

The Strip heavyweights

When the Fashion Show Mall (p120) opened in the early 1980s, anchor Neiman Marcus held special events in an elaborate tent on a nearby empty lot. The only things empty these days are the wallets of the departing shoppers. The mall's new mega-extension houses the high-profile likes of Nordstrom and Bloomingdale's Home, along with an indoor runway featuring regular fashion shows, a Strip-front plaza and a plethora of new shops: Paul Frank, selling trendy clothes and accessories; Madewell, a new line from J Crew; Z Gallerie, dealing in home furnishings; Metropark, specialising in urban fashions; and Saltaire, an upscale men's label. However, the Fashion Show is also the best bet for everyday finds, especially within department stores such as Macy's and Dillard's.

As famous for its changing faux sky and elaborate fountains as for its stores, the Forum Shops (p82) at Caesars Palace was the first themed mall to open on the Strip, and proved to sceptical casino execs that devoting prime real estate to handbags rather than slots was an investment worth making. Since 1992, the Shops has expanded twice, attracting a huge list of marquee retailers eager to expose their brands to 50,000 people a day.

The popularity of the Forum Shops lies with its eclectic mix of designer labels (Robert Cavalli, Valentino, Burberry), name brands (Abercrombie & Fitch, Kenneth Cole, Niketown) and speciality shops (FAO Schwarz, Lalique, Montblanc). And there's always something new

DON'T MISS

SHORTLIST

Best new
- Barneys Co-Op (p106)
- Epic Shoos (p160)
- Las Vegas Paper Doll (p160)

Best boutiques
- Intermix (p84)
- Outfit (p116)
- Still (p120)
- Talulah G (p120)

Best designer
- Christian Lacroix (p82)
- Jean Paul Gaultier (p116)
- Kate Spade (p84)
- Oscar de La Renta (p116)

Best bargains
- Las Vegas Premium Outlets (p160)
- Off Fifth (p21)

Vintage condition
- Attic (p159)
- D'Loe's House of Style (p159)

Most-wanted accessories
- Bags, Belts & Baubles (p116)
- Chrome Hearts (p82)
- Lush Puppy (pets) (p56)
- Wynn LVNV (interiors) (p116)

Glitteratti
- Bulgari (p82)
- Chopard (p82)
- Harry Winston (p82)
- Tiffany & Co (p82)

Literary greats
- Gamblers Book Club (p160)
- Neverending Story (p21)
- Reading Room (p56)

Best possible taste
- 55° Wine + Design (p56)
- Teuscher (p98)

Most innovative
- Apple (p120)
- FAO Schwarz (p82)
- Penski Wynn Ferrari Maserati (p114)

Epic Shoos p160

to see: recent additions include Marciano (the heiress-inspired line from Guess), Miss Sixty (hip Italian fashion), Ron Herman (trendy designer labels), Judith Ripka (luxury gems) and the second Vegas locale of venerable jeweller Tiffany & Co.

The Venetian's Grand Canal Shoppes (p106) relies on gimmicks ('live' statues, carnival characters) to move shoppers along its cobbled 'streets'. There's a strong collection of middle-of-the-road shops here (Ann Taylor, Bebe, Brookstone) and a handful of stand-outs (Acca Kappa, Pal Zileri, Mikimoto), but the big news is the addition of the adjacent Shops at Palazzo (p106). The tight-lipped suits behind the $2-billion Palazzo expansion have let very little leak about the hotel's new 80-unit mall, aside from the biggest coup the shopping scene on the Strip has yet seen: the arrival of Barneys and Barneys Co-Op from New York. Eschewing the Venice theme, the Palazzo will reportedly have a Bel Air, Californian feel.

Already wowing Vegas visitors is the newly renovated Miracle Mile Shops (97) at Planet Hollywood, which has cast a line-up of fresh, hip, young retailers (H&M, Urban Outfitters, Ben Sherman et al) to complement its new image. Keep your eyes open for more changes, as the Miracle Mile trades in some C-list shops left over from its days as the Desert Passage mall and lures more up-and-coming A-listers.

Best of the rest

Steve Wynn ushered in the era of luxury shopping on the Strip with his Via Bellagio, but he's outdone himself with the Esplanade (p116) at Wynn Las Vegas. Label-conscious shoppers flock here for Chanel, Dior, Louis Vuitton, Gaultier and Manolo Blahnik, but can't believe their luck when they happen upon such shops as Outfit (hot-off-the-runway ready-to-wear), Shoe In (designer footwear) and Bags, Belts and Baubles (everything else). You can also drop untold dollars on European sports cars (Penske Wynn Ferrari Maserati), couture gowns (Oscar de la Renta) and some of the 'most fabulous jewels in the world' (Graff). Wynn LVNV sells the beds featured in Wynn's hotel suites, and table settings from its restaurants.

Via Bellagio (p78) may be old news but it's still worth a visit. The small mall is home to a collection of luxury boutiques: Hermès, Prada, Armani, Yves St Laurent and Fred Leighton have been joined lately by Fendi and Bottega Veneta.

There's similar variety at Mandalay Place (p56), which houses only stores otherwise absent from Vegas. Blankspace sells modern furniture and accessories; Lush Puppy carries pet accessories from high-end designers as well as its own line of collars, apparel and toys; and the Reading Room is one of the city's only independent bookstores.

Las Vegas Paper Doll p160

For unique gifts, don't miss the plethora of gift shops tied to big casino shows. Among the best are those devoted to Elton John's *Red Piano* at Caesars Palace and Cirque du Soleil's *Love* at the Mirage.

Urban renaissance

Las Vegas's much-derided 'Centennial Plan' calls for the revitalisation of long-neglected Downtown, promising to breathe new life into the city's urban core. The area retains its long-standing antique and vintage stores, among them Funk House (p160), Attic and D'Loe's House of Style (both p159). But the redevelopment plan is already taking hold, with a handful of innovative retail projects beginning to make a big impact.

Todd Burden's Epic Shoos (p160) is a gallery that focuses on the art of the sneaker and its impact on our urban landscape. Todd Von Bastiaan's Atomic Todd (1541 S Commerce Street, 386 8633) licenses original artworks for reproduction on T-shirts, hats and bags. And Durette Candito's Durette Studio (1007 S Main Street, at W Charleston Boulevard, 368 2601) specialises in unique hardware for the home.

Nearby, the Las Vegas Premium Outlets (p160) is hands-down the best outlet mall in the city. Look out for a planned expansion, which will add another 80 stores. Just across Charleston Boulevard is the Holsum Design Center (p161). This recently regenerated building is home to a number of independent shops such as Las Vegas Paper Doll (p160), a contemporary stationery shop that specialises in fine papers, cards and whimsical gifts.

In the 'burbs

You'll probably find everything you want on the Strip, but the suburban centres are worth a diversion if you're a diehard shopaholic. Fashion Village at Boca Park in Summerlin (8950 W Charleston Boulevard, at S Rampart Boulevard) has great boutiques, home design shops and speciality retailers, while Henderson's District at Green Valley Ranch (20 S Green Valley Parkway, between Paseo Verde Parkway & I-215 (564 8595/www.the districtatgvr.com), features Pottery Barn, William-Sonoma, Coach, Francesca's Collection, Chelsea Boutique and many more.

A handful of stores are even worth the cost of the cab ride in themselves. Among them are Off Fifth at the Las Vegas Outlet Center (7400 Las Vegas Boulevard South, at E Warm Springs Road, South of Strip, 896 5599/www. premiumoutlets.com); Fruition (4139 S Maryland Parkway, at E Flamingo Road, 796 4139), selling revivalist fashions from the 1980s and early '90s in the University District; and in the north-west, Neverending Story (9440 W Sahara Avenue, at S Fort Apache Road, 869 8943), a quaint children's bookshop with storytime every weekend.

Caesars Palace p79

Nightlife

Given the fact that, a decade ago, it offered little in the way of nightlife, Las Vegas's burgeoning clubbing scene is as unpredictable as it is undeniable. On and off the Strip, more than 40 spots call themselves nightclubs or ultralounges, competing to lure clubgoers to bustling dancefloors and highly priced booths.

Unlike the shiny-shirt and four-on-the-floor techno-beat days of the late 1990s, the new Sin City scene is diverse. The clubs and bars are distinguishing themselves aesthetically, musically and even geographically: the Downtown splinter scene has worked its way up from a dismissible anomaly to a viable force, highly influenced by a New York City vibe.

Landing Strip

In 2007, the headlines were made by the Luxor, which opened three new venues – exclusive ultralounge Noir Bar, ski lodge-themed eatery Aspen 702 and the LAX nightclub (p51) – to replace long-running club Ra. LAX is spread over two levels; its co-owner, mash-up maestro DJ AM, should be on hand to rock the house on a close-to-regular basis. The Noir Bar, touted as 'reservations only', offers a sharp contrast to the ultra-modern decor of most Vegas nightspots, featuring Old World furnishings, crystal and chandeliers. Along with the usual libations, desserts are served tableside on guerridon carts.

Beach beauties

Poolside partying in Sin City is nothing new (see box p175). However, a number of venues have upped the ante of late, most notably Tao Beach at the Venetian. An outdoor oasis adjacent to the ever-popular Tao nightclub (p107), Tao Beach offers optional topless bathing, gourmet food and VIP cabanas replete with plasma-screen TVs, Xboxes, iPod ports, fully stocked bars and DVD collections. On Sundays, a weekly house music party called Sunset Sessions takes over the place.

Other standout pool clubs include Venus at Caesars Palace (p80), Bare at the Mirage (p89) and Moorea at Mandalay Bay (p53), as well as the weekly Ditch Fridays at the Palms (p135) and Rehab at Hard Rock (p121), the granddaddy of them all. Most pool parties run from about mid April to mid October. Although Rehab and Ditch Fridays are daytime events, many of the venues, notably Tao Beach, offer partying well into the small hours.

Staying power

With a number of prominent Strip-side venues celebrating multi-year anniversaries, Las Vegas's top clubs have proven that their popularity can outlive their novelty value. At Caesars Palace, Pure (p85) continues to pull in the celebrities for birthdays, divorces, premières and the passing of just another night. And the abovementioned Tao has begun opening itself up to more than just DJs, dancing and drinking, hosting live music from the likes of the Rapture and Gym Glass Heroes.

For variety, Jet (p92) at the Mirage still offers one of the widest range of partying options under one roof. Its three rooms feature three different types of music, but the attractions in the main space

SHORTLIST

New and forthcoming
- LAX (p52)
- Lucky Strike Lanes (p140)
- Revolution (p92)

After-hours partying
- Drai's at Bill's Gamblin' Hall & Saloon (p174)
- Empire Ballroom (p71)

Celebrity sightings
- Body English (p125)
- LAX (p52)
- Pure (p85)
- Tao (p107)

Dives
- Champagne's Café (p128)
- Double Down Saloon (p129)

Live music
- Art Bar (p152)
- Bunkhouse Saloon (p162)
- Pearl (p139)

Lounging
- Artisan Lounge (p143)
- Downtown Cocktail Room (p154)

Great views
- Mix Lounge (p57)
- Foundation Room (Godspeed p57)

Most flesh per square foot
- Rehab (p121)
- Bare (p89)
- Venus (p80)

Swankiest of the swank
- Tryst (p118)
- Tabú (p64)

Thickest eyeliner
- Beauty Bar (p153)
- Red Room Saloon (p145)

DON'T MISS

itself can be just as varied, from live performances by the likes of Mickey Avalon to the eye-and-ear assault of Roonie G's A/V.

There's more variety up at Polly Esther's (p113), which opened at the Stratosphere in 2007. The Vegas outpost of this small chain leans towards the cheesy, with four themed rooms spanning the decades from the 1970s to today. But it's all good fun. And where else in town could you find such 'where are they now?' icons as Digital Underground, A Flock of Seagulls and LA Guns?

Live and direct

Speaking of live music, the Vegas scene got a shot in the arm in 2007 with the opening of Pearl (p60), a new venue at the Palms. Boasting great sightlines and immaculate sound, it's quickly taken its place at the top of the tree with a terrific roster of big-name acts.

Still, it's hardly the only venue in town. You can catch stadium-size acts at the MGM Grand Garden Arena (p63), and big-name performers at Mandalay Bay's House of Blues (p57) and the Hard Rock's Joint (p125). And there are even bands Downtown these days: check the Beauty Bar (p153) or the Bunkhouse Saloon (p162) for regular indie-level shows by fast-rising visitors and locals.

Of course, some acts like it so much here that they've moved into the casinos. (Well, that and the money.) The big arrival is Bette Midler (p84), who replaces Celine Dion at Caesars Palace in early 2008. When she's not around, Elton John (p84) plays 50 shows a year in the venue. Elsewhere, Toni Braxton (at the Flamingo; p85) and Barry Manilow (at the Las Vegas Hilton; p126) both have long-term deals, supplementing the various comedians who hold down casino residencies.

Beyond beer and nachos

Las Vegas's running theme of reinvention isn't limited to hotel rebuilds and nightclub openings. Take the seamless marriage of bowling and drinking at Lucky Strike (p140), which turns out to have been just what Vegas's nightlife needed: fun that doesn't involve queueing and crowds. With a nightclub atmosphere (low lighting, cocktail service, doormen) and a terrific menu of Californian comfort food, Lucky Strike is worth the short trip west of the Strip.

Going Downtown

Once merely a punchline for jokes about hookers and drug dealers, the eastern edge of Fremont Street is becoming a fully functioning bar crawl destination, offering a number of unique, gaming-free venues within a block of one other. The most prominent is the Beauty Bar (p153), a New York City import that expands on the original's proven formula of retro beauty salon fixtures and manicure-and-martini happy hours with DJs spinning indie rock and soul, weekly gigs by touring and local bands, and some of the cheapest drinks Downtown.

A few doors west, the Griffin (p154) opened in February 2007. On any night, its faux stone-and-brick interior is filled with musicians, artists and raconteurs leaning on the long bar or gathering around the two fireplaces. On the weekends, the rustic back room features a live DJ.

Just around the corner on Las Vegas Boulevard, the Downtown Cocktail Room (p154) has become a favourite in which Vegas socialites and industry folk can get away from their lives on the Strip. Obscured behind tinted glass and a steel door, DCR is dark, sexy and cinematic. It's an ultralounge for hipsters, with no bottle service required.

Tao p23

House of the rising sun

If a party that ends before sunrise doesn't float your boat, a number of after-parties don't even get started until other clubs are closing. One of the oldest is Drai's Afterhours, open from Thursday to Sunday in the basement of Bill's Gamblin' Hall (p174). This swanky spot draws well-heeled clubbers into its lush interior all night.

A more casual but no less enticing scene is to be found at the Empire Ballroom (p71), where a Late Night Empire promotion gets rolling from about 1am (Thursday to Sunday). Featuring three areas - (chandelier-adorned main room, VIP lounge and Strip-facing patio), Late Night Empire lasts well into the morning, and is one of the few clubs in town to specialise in house music.

For something off the beaten track, the Seamless strip club (4740 S Arville Street, at W Tropicana Avenue, 227 5200) operates as an after-hours party spot, complete with bottle service and top DJs,

every night from 4am. It's just one of a number of strip joints breaking barriers that exist between themselves and traditional clubs; Scores Las Vegas (3355 Procyon Street, at W Desert Inn Road, 367 4000) serves a similar purpose.

Money talks

Most clubs in Vegas operate from roughly 10pm until 3am or 4am. With the exception of the Downtown bars, almost all nightclubs charge an admission fee, ranging from $10 to $30. Reserving a table requires 'bottle service': effectively, buying a bottle of high-end liquor, plus mixer, for about $300. It's dear, but you'll appreciate having a seat after being on your feet for five hours.

Women get preferential treatment, and though dress codes are enforced, they have loosened to accommodate newer fashion trends. In other words, emo boys in black T-shirts, Chuck Taylors and heavy eyeliner are rampant.

Love at the Mirage p92

Arts & Leisure

For the first century or so of Las Vegas's existence, coming to town for its art scene made about as much sense as heading to Death Valley for the water sports. Today, the notion is a little less outlandish. Culturally speaking, Las Vegas may not be a patch on New York, Chicago or even Atlanta. However, with stacks of casino dollars being thrown at upgrading the town's attractions, and with an authentic local art scene having steadily blossomed over the last few years, the city has generated some semblance of cultural life to balance out the pervading blitz of neon.

Night lights

However, it's still spectacle that dominates, especially on the Strip. Although the grinning showgirls have gradually been pensioned off, put out to pasture in favour of dancers prepared to show off a little more than their feathers, the singers still remain in the casino showrooms, as do the magicians. But they're all overshadowed by the high-end, high-budget stage spectaculars, increasingly imported from Broadway and beyond.

Leading the pack is Cirque du Soleil, which now offers no fewer than five acrobatic extravaganzas in a quintet of different casinos along the length of the Strip. What's more, the all-conquering French-Canadian troupe has another two shows in the pipeline (see box p62), meaning that audiences will soon be faced with the daunting possibility of being able to see a different Cirque show every night of the week. Assuming, of course, that their wallets will stretch to the often immense ticket prices, something common to most major Las Vegas shows.

Outside of the Cirque du Soleil franchise, the city remains an impersonator rather than an innovator. The Broadway and West End shows that arrive here are tried, tested and trimmed to a bite-sized, interval-free 90 minutes: witness *The Producers* (p96) and Monty Python's *Spamalot* (p118), a pair of 2007 arrivals that are both shorter than their Broadway versions, and *Phantom* (p107), the Venetian's reworking of the Andrew Lloyd Webber show that even abbreviates the original title.

Curiously, many of Las Vegas's most successful new shows share a British connection. *Spamalot* (at Wynn Las Vegas) and the Venetian's *Phantom* both originated from British creators, while *Stomp Out Loud* (p98), which delivers a percussive din more or less nightly at Planet Hollywood, is a spin-off from the Brighton troupe that has been performing all over the world for more than a decade. And then there's *Love* (p92): Cirque's newest production – at least until the 2008 arrival of its show co-created with magician Criss Angel – is built entirely around the music of the Beatles.

On the fringe

Away from the Strip, a handful of small theatre companies are attempting to bring a little life to the local scene. Among them are Stagedoor Entertainment, the new kid on the block (www.stagedoorlv. com), and the well-established Las Vegas Little Theatre (www.lvlt. org), a community theatre company that performs in various small theatres across the city. The theatre

S H O R T L I S T

Local artists
- Arts Factory (p29)
- Contemporary Arts Collective (p29)

Musical shows on the Strip
- Love (p92)
- Stomp Out Loud (p98)

New theatre companies
- New American Theatre Project (p28)
- SEAT (p163)

Contemporary art from all over
- Dust (p162)
- G-C Arts (p163)

Great spectacles
- O (p79)
- Le Rêve (p118)

World-class art
- Bellagio Gallery of Fine Art (p75)
- Guggenheim-Hermitage Museum (p104)

Theatre venues
- Las Vegas Little Theatre (left)
- Super Summer Theatre (p28)

Broadway imports
- Mamma Mia (p58)
- The Producers (p96)

By or for kids
- Las Vegas Academy (p28)
- Rainbow Company Children's Theatre (p28)

Art/alcohol fusion
- Art Bar (p152)
- First Friday (p29)

Something to take home
- Funk House (p160)
- Trifecta Gallery (p163)
- S² Art Group (p163)

Celebrity impersonators
- An Evening at La Cage (p111)
- Danny Gans (p92)

scene has recently enjoyed a shot in the arm with the emergence of the New American Theatre Project (www.newamericantheatreproject. com), a talented, community-level company founded by performers from the big-ticket Strip shows.

There are two companies that stage kid-friendly productions. Shows by the students at the Las Vegas Academy (www. lvacademytheatre.org) are an unexpected treat, as are the low-key productions delivered by the Rainbow Company Children's Theatre (www.rainbowcompany. info). And if you travel out to Red Rock Canyon during the summer months (June to August; p168), you'll be rewarded by a performance under the stars at the Super Summer Theatre (www.supersummertheatre.com).

Culture vultures

Nearly a decade after it first opened, the Bellagio Gallery of Fine Art (p75) remains the jewel in the cultural crown of the Strip. Rather than housing a permanent collection, it displays temporary exhibitions for extended periods, with the focus on modernism and postmodernism. Recent shows have included a retrospective of photographer Ansel Adams, two exhibitions of paintings loaned from the Boston Museum of Fine Arts (one of impressionist pieces, the other a more general selection of works) and a display of priceless antiques from the collection of Chatsworth House in England. Running until early 2008, Picasso's Ceramics brings together a collection of works from the estate of the legendary Spanish heavyweight, who only turned to the medium at the age of 65.

Across the Strip, inside the Venetian complex, is the other big player on the Vegas fine art scene,

the Guggenheim-Hermitage Museum (p104). Designed by influential architect Rem Koolhaas, the sparse, modern structure is the result of a union between New York's Guggenheim Museum and the Hermitage Museum in St Petersburg. The rotating exhibitions, which generally run for nine months, are culled from the collections of its two parent museums. In residence until April 2008, Modern Masters from the Guggenheim Collection displays 37 paintings by, among others, Monet, Picasso and Cézanne.

Casino mogul Steve Wynn closed his Wynn Las Vegas Gallery, an exhibition space along the same lines as the Guggenheim-Hermitage and the Bellagio Gallery, in 2006 due to lacklustre ticket sales. However, signature pieces from his collection, by Gauguin, Manet, Matisse and others, still hang conspicuously throughout the resort. Thehotel at Mandalay Bay also offers an impressive collection of modern art in its public areas.

DON'T MISS

Trifecta Gallery p163

Down your street

Away from the Strip, the Downtown art scene has coalesced impressively over the last few years, with commercial galleries Dust (p162) and G-C Arts (p163) leading the way. Dust displays the works of edgier local artists, plus a few from Los Angeles and New York. Meanwhile, G-C Arts casts a wider net, with pieces by Warhol, Koons, Johns, Rauschenberg, Oldenburg and other darlings of the postmodern art world that are clearly aimed at sating the voracious appetites of the increasing number of serious art collectors coming to Vegas. But the gallery also welcomes casual art lovers.

Down the street, the S² Art Group (p163) caters to collectors with somewhat smaller budgets, cranking out fine art lithographs (think Toulouse-Lautrec and vintage film poster reproductions). Meanwhile, the eclectic Funk House (p160) antiques shop always keeps a few walls clear in order to show off the local talent. Also in Downtown is the Arts Factory, a complex housing design businesses and studios, along with the SEAT experimental theatre company (p163). There are also galleries, such as Trifecta Gallery (p163) and the non-profit, artist-run Contemporary Arts Collective, which shows a mix of travelling exhibitions and work by locals.

The best opportunity to see these places in full swing is at the First Friday event (www.firstfriday-lasvegas.org), when a party atmosphere pervades on the blocks just south of the junction of Charleston Boulevard and Main Street. The brainchild of Cindy Funkhouser, owner of the Funk House, it's held from 6pm to 10pm on the first Friday of every month and is essentially a massive block party with an artistic bent. Local galleries and shops stay open late as the roads fill with performers, psychics and ice-sculptors; bands and DJs play on temporary stages; and there's plenty of great street food – and drink – on offer. Lively after-parties kick off at Dino's and the Beauty Bar (both p153).

WHAT'S ON
Calendar

High Rollers Scooter Weekend

Las Vegas has a habit of attracting the kind of events that don't happen anywhere else. As the spiritual home of gambling, it's obvious that the city should host the **World Series of Poker**, while a town with the nickname Sin City is a natural location for the risqué **Black & White Party**. And then there are the innumerable events dominated by vintage cars, bikes and scooters.

For detailed information and listings, check the *Las Vegas Weekly* or *CityLife* (p189).

January

Mid Jan **An American Trilogy**
Cannery Casino & Hotel
www.cannerycasinos.com
This annual celebration of the King welcomes hosts of Elvis-lovers plus plenty of Elvis impersonators on the days around 16 Jan, his birthday.

February

Feb **African American History Month**
West Las Vegas Library
www.lvccld.org
A celebration of African American culture in the region, with spoken word, dance, theatre and music.

Mid Feb **High Rollers Scooter Weekend**
Various locations
www.lvscooterrally.com
A weekend of mod rock and showing off for sharp-looking multi-mirrored scooters and those who love them.

25 Feb **Chinese New Year Celebration & Asian Food Festival**
Las Vegas Chinatown Plaza
www.lvchinatown.com
Vegas's Chinese New Year celebrations are actually Pan-Asian Expect traditional lion- and dragon-dancing and a feast of eastern delicacies.

March

Early Mar NASCAR Nextel Cup
Las Vegas Motor Speedway
www.lvms.com
One of the biggest events in the
national auto racing calendar.

**Mid Mar Monster Jam
World Finals**
Sam Boyd Stadium
www.monsterjamonline.com
A feast of automotive carnage, featuring an array of giant trucks with enormous wheels.

17 Mar St Patrick's Day
Various locations

Late Mar Extreme Thing Festival
Desert Breeze Skate Park
www.extremething.com
Extreme sports, such as skateboarding,
BMX and wrestling championships.

Late Mar Pet-a-Palooza
Location varies
www.mix941.fm
Rock bands share the stage with animal
performers at this pet-friendly festival.

April

Easter weekend Viva Las Vegas
Gold Coast, p182
www.vivalasvegas.net
A chance to dance to rockabilly bands,
check out the burlesque competition and
shop for the perfect '50s cocktail dress.

Apr Las Vegas Grand Prix
Downtown
www.vegasgrandprix.com

Early Apr Mardi Gras Celebration
Fremont Street
www.vegasexperience.com

Mid Apr Pure Aloha Festival
Cannery Casino & Hotel
www.vizzun.com
This two-day festival celebrates
Polynesian food, music, art and dance.

**Mid Apr Clark County
Fair & Rodeo**
Clark County Fairgrounds
www.ccfair.com
All kinds of ropin', ridin', country music,
hoedown and carnival fun.

Credit cards

For nearly seven weeks every summer, the Rio's biggest ballroom is packed with dizzying rows of tables. This impressive sight is the **World Series of Poker** (WSOP), a contest that in 2006 saw more than 8,700 players competing for a staggering $12.5-million jackpot.

Despite its current grandeur, the WSOP was launched by Benny Binion in 1970 with just seven players. Poker legend Johnny Moss took the first title but, bizarrely, he didn't win: he was simply voted the winner by the other players. A year later, the game grew to 13 and Johnny Moss won again, this time in a freezeout tournament.

The introduction in 2002 of the televised World Poker Tour made poker exciting for viewers by revealing the players' hole cards and resulted in a rise in the number of WSOP participants. The subsequent explosion of poker websites fuelled the increase, with player numbers first exceeding 1,000 in 2003.

The following year, Binion's sold the WSOP to Harrah's, which moved the 2005 tournament to the Rio. Since then, the event has grown to almost unmanageable proportions. The vast number of players now renders the WSOP a chaotic affair, necessitating continuous adjustments in rules and schedules. It's daunting for players and can be hard for spectators to follow; the big poker-lifestyle trade show in the adjacent ballroom may prove more interesting and is certainly much less confusing.

Chinese New Year p30

Mid Apr **UNLVino**
Paris Las Vegas, p92
www.unlvino.com
More than 100 international wine-growers participate in this fundraiser for UNLV, with auctions of wine-themed art and vintage crates.

Late Apr-late May **Epicurean Affair**
Location varies
www.nvrestaurants.com
Local restaurants compete to outdo each other in this industry food festival.

May

Ongoing Epicurean Affair
(see April)

Weekend closest to 5 May
Cinco de Mayo
Lorenzi Park
The city's Mexican community comes together with all-day dancing, mariachi bands, fireworks and traditional cuisine.

Mid May **Dark Skies
Arts Festivals**
Near Primm
http://darkskies.vegasartists.com

This festival blazes for three days in the desert – expect legions of hippies, decorated cars and weird performance art.

Mid May **Helldorado Days**
Various locations
www.elkshelldorado.com
Celebrating Las Vegas's wild west beginnings with golf and poker contests, trail rides and a parade.

Late May/early June
Vegas Cruise
Fremont Street, at Las Vegas Boulevard South
www.vegasexperience.com
A three-day event for enthusiasts to show off their gleaming vintage cars.

June

June-July **World Series of Poker**
Rio, p139
www.harrahs.com
International poker fest. See box p31.

July

Ongoing World Series of Poker
(see June)

New Year's Eve p34

Weekend of 4 July
Red White & Boom
Desert Breeze Park
www.redwhitenboom.com
Fun for the whole family with fireworks,
a carnival and a passel of rock acts.

August

Mid Aug **Las Vegas
Harvest Festival**
Cashman Center
www.harvestfestival.com
Hundreds of artisans bring their hand-
blown glass, silver jewellery and jars
of chutney to this fair.

Mid Aug **Star Trek
Las Vegas Convention**
Las Vegas Hilton, p125
www.creationent.com

September

Sept **San Gennaro Feast**
Location varies
www.sangennarofeast.net
This Italian-American festival is mostly
about food, but it also includes carnival rides and a traditional procession.

Early Sept **Greek Food Festival**
St John the Baptist Greek
Orthodox Church
www.vegasgreekorthodox.com

Mid Sept **Black & White Party**
Palms, p135
http://afanlv.org
An AIDS fundraiser with black-and-
white costumes, good food and risqué
amusements such as a spanking booth.

Mid Sept **SuperRun**
Downtown Henderson
www.superrun.com
The area's largest classic car show.

Late Sept **Las Vegas BikeFest**
Fremont Street, at Las Vegas
Boulevard South
www.lasvegasbikefest.com

October

Early Oct **Grand Slam for Children**
MGM Grand, p58
www.agassifoundation.org
Andre Agassi's annual gala auction and
dinner to benefit his children's charity.
An A-list concert always follows.

Ride 'em, cowboy

For ten days in late November and early December, Las Vegas morphs into Texas as more than 40,000 rodeo riders and their fans flock to the city. There's plenty of fun to be had at the various hoedowns, concerts and beauty pageants. But the real action occurs at the Thomas & Mack Center (p134): wearing tight jeans, a manly scowl and, of course, a cowboy hat, the man who rides best and stays on longest will win the annual **National Finals Rodeo**.

Grab your chewin' tobacco and some jerky to snack on: you can expect to find bigger crowds and stronger-than-usual twangs at waterin' holes that appeal to a partic'lar demographic. Take the always-packed Toby Keith's **I Love this Bar & Grill** (p87), which supplements its usual Southern fare with fried bologna sandwiches during the merry mayhem of rodeo season.

Strip clubs, buffets and stalls selling beer-filled footballs all keep extra busy. There are even experts on hand to steam your stetson. And if that's not enough, the North Hall at the **Las Vegas Convention Center** (p187) becomes temporary home to the Original Cowboy Christmas, the NFR's only officially sanctioned western shopping experience. You'll find over 400 vendors, plus autograph signings and fashion shows. Or just enjoy the experience of steer wrestlers, bareback riders and bullfighters filling the city in a celebration of Wild West machismo.

Mid Oct **Age of Chivalry Renaissance Fair**
Sunset Park
www.lvrenfair.com
Chivalrous battles, costumed maidens and other historical displays.

Mid Oct **Professional Bull Riders Tour**
Thomas & Mack Center, p134
www.pbrnow.com
A chance to rub shoulders with the world's finest bull riders and their fans and see some of the action up close.

Mid Oct **Rockabilly Rod Reunion**
Las Vegas Motor Speedway
www.rockabillyrodreunion.com
A mixture of vintage dragsters, rockabilly bands, DJs and burlesque acts.

3rd weekend in Oct **Las Vegas Balloon Classic**
Silver Bowl Park
452 8066
Hot-air balloons fill the sky for this weekend of flying competitions.

31 Oct **Halloween**
Citywide

November

Early Nov **Vegas Valley Book Festival**
Various locations
www.vegasvalleybookfest.org

Late Nov **Motor Trend International Auto Show**
Las Vegas Convention Center
www.motortrendautoshows.com
A chance to see all the shiniest new models and industry prototypes.

December

Early Dec **National Finals Rodeo**
Thomas & Mack Center, p134
www.nfr-rodeo.com
Cowboys and girls set Vegas ablaze for nine days of rodeo related revelry.

Early Dec **New Las Vegas Marathon & Half-Marathon**
Citywide
www.lvmarathon.com

31 Dec **New Year's Eve**
Citywide

Itineraries

Place Your Bets

If you can't tell your chips from your craps, don't know whether to hit or stand, and think that baccarat was a popular disco act in the 1970s, then don't worry: you're not alone. Many visitors arrive in Vegas as gambling virgins with only a vague grasp of casino etiquette, unsure of how to play any of the major games.

The town's keen-eyed casino moguls have noticed that many visitors have little or no experience of casino gambling. And so in order to make their guests feel more at home, many casinos lay on free gambling lessons, priming novices for a weekend (or longer) spent gambling their hard-earned at tables around town. This itinerary, which takes a morning, shows you where to learn how to play three of the most popular games in town. However, please note that the times of gambling lessons are subject to change at short notice; it's always wise to phone ahead to confirm them before making a special trip.

Las Vegas is, and always has been, a city built on risk. Gambling paid for all those flashy hotel towers; indeed, gambling paid for the casinos themselves. But if you play your cards right, gambling may also pay you simply for playing. Those who love gambling are enthralled with the ephemeral nature of the game: that fleeting moment when the card turns, the ball falls or the reels freeze, and fate hangs in the balance before the verdict – win or lose, with rarely an in-between –

is revealed. Dedicated gamers insist that this transcendental buzz is the reason they play. Well, that and the money.

As any seasoned player will tell you, gambling is hard work, so you'll need to start by lining your stomach before the challenges of the morning ahead. Before you hit the tables, fill up with a hearty brunch buffet at **Bally's**, served from 7am to 4pm in the **Big Kitchen**. From here, it's a short walk to the day's first lesson.

At 10am, the casino floor at **Caesars Palace** is nice and quiet. All the pros have gone, leaving the room to the beginners who are keen to hone their skills at **blackjack (21)**. Arrive shortly before 10am and head over to the empty pit by the sports book, where a handful of people will be sitting at a gaming table awaiting an instructor. When he or she arrives, they'll take you through the rules, the playing procedures and the etiquette of this hugely popular game.

At the lesson table, you'll first put up a practice chip in your betting circle on the table layout; the instructor will direct you how to do this. Everyone at the table will then be dealt two cards. In a nutshell, each player competes against the dealer's hand, trying to get to a total of 21 without exceeding it ('busting'). Face cards count as ten and aces can count as one or 11.

First, check your cards and the dealer's 'up' card; only one of the dealer's cards is on show from the start, with the other (the 'hole' card) hidden from view. Then, signal to the dealer what you want to do next. There are four options: you can 'hit' (take another card), 'stand' (refuse another card, effectively passing the game to the next player), 'double down'

(doubling your bet on the turn of the next card) or 'split' (only if you have a pair); the instructor will walk you through all the options in turn.

After all the players stand or bust, the dealer reveals his or her 'hole' card and plays out the hand. He or she has to hit on 16 or less, but must stand with 17 or more. Once the dealer has stood or busted, players who beat the dealer are paid off at even money. A tie is called a push and no money changes hands. If a player is dealt an ace and a ten-value card, it's considered a natural blackjack; unless the dealer also has a natural, the player is paid at 3:2.

During your lesson, the instructor might tell you to play your cards according to a set of standard rules known as basic strategy: basically, what you should do with any possible combination of cards. We've

ITINERARIES

mapped this out, in a chart format, on the book's back page. However, it's best to memorise the strategies before playing; that way, there's no impediment to getting into the zone.

Having learned the blackjack basics, it's time to dash across the road in time for the 11am **craps** lesson at the **Bellagio**. A dice game played on a large table staffed by up to four employees, craps is perhaps the most exciting casino game, and certainly its noisiest.

The craps table layout is identical at either end; the central area is reserved for proposition bets (aka sucker bets). Players bet on the 'pass' or 'don't pass' lines before the instructor offers two dice to a shooter, who tosses the bones so they bounce off the table's far wall.

The shooter's initial throw is called a 'come-out roll'. If a total of seven or 11 is rolled, 'pass' bettors win even money and 'don't pass' bettors lose. If the shooter throws a total of two or three, 'don't pass' wins and 'pass' loses. If 12 is tossed, 'pass' bettors lose and 'don't pass' bettors push. If four, five, six, eight, nine or ten is thrown, that number becomes the 'point'.

Once the point is established, the shooter keeps rolling. If he rolls the point again, 'pass' wins and 'don't pass' loses. If he rolls a seven first, 'pass' loses, 'don't pass' wins and the shooter gives up the dice. Other numbers tossed during this passage of play don't count. Every time the point is hit, the next throw is a fresh 'come-out roll', although all side bets remain in play.

'Come' bets can be made to run concurrently with 'pass' bets. The two have exactly the same set of outcomes: an immediate win, lose or push, or the establishment of a point. But 'come' bets can only be made after the point is determined. If, for example, that the shooter rolls four to set the point, you can then make a 'come' or 'don't come' bet. If the next roll is nine, then nine becomes the 'come' point. If a nine is rolled before a seven, you win.

Sounds complicated? It's a lot easier when you're actually playing the game. At your lesson, the instructor will show you how to back up 'pass' and 'come' bets with odds, and will demonstrate how to make field, place, lay and all the proposition bets. But by sticking to 'pass', 'come' and odds bets, you'll get the best of an action-filled, boisterous and low-edge dice game.

If your brain isn't already overloaded with the two games you've learned so far, then there's just about time to run across the Strip to **Paris Las Vegas**, which operates **poker** lessons every day at noon. Thanks to the advent of internet gaming websites and the televisual success of the World Series of Poker (p32), poker has exploded in popularity over the past five years, and is now the fastest growing game in the city. It's one of the easiest games to learn, but it's also one of the toughest to master.

At your lesson, the instructor will deal two cards face down to each player; these are called the 'hole' cards. A round of betting ensues, where you can fold your hand or choose to play. Betting depends on the limits: in a '$5/$10' game, you can bet only $5 on this first round.

Next, the instructor turns over three community cards, known as the 'flop'. Again, you can fold or bet, choosing to gamble up to $10 in a $5/$10 game. Players can also then raise a bet by $10, at which point other players can either

match the raise or fold. In the next two rounds, a sixth community card (the 'turn') and then a seventh (the 'river') are dealt, interspersed with rounds of betting. After this point, the player who holds the highest five-card poker hand, drawn from the two 'hole' cards and the five community cards, wins the pot. However, you may find that in many cases, the game doesn't go this far: one player may be left standing alone after all the others fold, in which case he or she wins the pot without showing his or her cards.

During your lesson, the instructor will explain hand rankings, etiquette, pot odds, bad-beat jackpots and psychology, including bluffing, tells, and tight and loose play. After the lesson, many poker rooms sponsor a small-stakes game ($1/$2), where students can practise

in live conditions. However, always remember that if you're risking real money, it's best to read up, take lessons and play for the lowest stakes possible. This is especially true of poker. However, for any game, it's certainly worth taking advantage of the free lessons: it's about all that most casinos will give away for nothing.

At this point, it'll be the early afternoon and you've almost certainly worked up another hunger. There are plenty of upscale dining options in Paris Las Vegas, although you may need to reserve during busy periods. However, **Le Village Buffet** (p95) is always a good bet: not only does it offer a decent variety of provincial French dishes, but it should also leave you with enough cash for a night of real gambling, where you can practise all the skills learned during the morning. Good luck…

The Strip

Through the Night

New York City claims to be the city that never sleeps, but Las Vegas brings the concept to a whole new level. The action never stops here: all of the casinos, the majority of the bars and even a number of the restaurants are open 24-7, and party-loving visitors are never stuck for somewhere to go. So crack open a Red Bull and get ready for a long one: this itinerary is devoted to the after-hours highlights along the Strip.

Contrary to the popular opinion of other, sleepier cities, shopping and daylight don't need to go hand in hand. In Las Vegas, most of the shopping is done in indoor malls, environments free from the interference of sunlight and thus liberated from its restrictive conventions. The **Mandalay Place** (p56) mall, which bridges Mandalay Bay and the Luxor, is open until 11pm during the week

and until midnight on Fridays and Saturdays (as, for that matter, are the **Grand Canal Shoppes** at the Venetian and the **Forum Shops** at Caesars Palace). Late at night is the best time to shop: there are no crowds and it all feels devilishly indulgent, like being back in school after everyone's left. Grab yourself a sexy (or not!) little number and slip into it: the night has yet to begin…

From Mandalay Place, follow the signs and head into the Mandalay Bay casino. Take the escalators down and turn right towards Thehotel at Mandalay Bay, where you'll soon see some nice people waiting to collect a cover charge (usually $20-$25) in order for you to gain access to the 64th-floor **Mix Lounge** (p57). The huge windows give 360-degree views of Las Vegas and the hills beyond are so breathtaking that it may just make you forget the $300-plus

Peppermill's Fireside Lounge p42

you'll need to shell out for a bottle of vodka in order to secure a table, either on the open-air patio or the indoor leather sofas. If you don't think the vista is worth quite that much, just spend a penny: the bathroom also has floor-to-ceiling windows in the cubicles, with the same stunning scenery. And if you find a stool at the bar, it's yours for the price of a single drink. After 11pm, resident DJs spin a soundtrack perfectly in keeping with the swanky vibe.

If, at this point, you decide that you don't want to pay any more cover charges or wait in any more lines, settle down into your seat and enjoy the view, and then skip to the last three paragraphs. However, those with an appetite for partying should head out on to the Strip and hop on the double-decker Deuce bus that goes up and down Las Vegas Boulevard 24 hours a day. You can get a one-way ticket for $2 or a day pass for $5; both afford better people-watching than you'll find in many of the casinos.

Heading north, get off at the stop in front of the MGM Grand. Inside the casino, follow the signs to **Tabú** (p64), a prime example of what's known in Vegas as an ultralounge – it's PR-speak for a nightspot that's more intimate than a club but swankier than a bar. The servers double as models, as does much of the clientele. Just be careful how much you drink or you may be confused by the 'human locator' technology, an image and lighting system that responds to motion and projects different images on you and those around you.

Add in an animated mural, three resident DJs and interior design by Jeffrey Beers and Roger Parent (formerly of Cirque du Soleil), and you may be so taken with Tabú that you'll stop scoffing at the whole ultralounge concept. The cover charge varies from $20 to $25, depending on the night. Again, if you're heading towards bankruptcy and tired of waiting in lines, jump ahead to the last three paragraphs.

If it's before 2am on Monday to Thursday or before 3am on Friday to Sunday, you've still got the chance to experience the town's beleaguered monorail. It's pricey, but it beats walking in your glad rags, and it can be fun after a few drinks. The monorail entrance is located towards the end of the Studio Walk in the MGM Grand. Buy your ticket from the machine and hop on the train (all northbound, as the MGM is the southernmost stop on the line) for the two-minute ride to Bally's.

Once off the train, walk through Bally's and emerge on to Las Vegas Boulevard, then cross the pedestrian bridge that runs over Flamingo Road towards **Bill's Gambling Hall & Saloon** (p174). Here, you'll find **Drai's**: owned by Victor Drai of *Weekend at Bernie's* semi-fame, it remains one of Vegas's most popular after-hours spots. You can dance until well after dawn here, in a room that manages to feel like an elegantly hip gentleman's library. The club doesn't even open until midnight and things tend to hot up around 4am. On Wednesdays, Thursdays and Sundays, there's a $20 cover charge, which rises to $30 on Fridays and Saturdays.

At about this time you should be struggling with the eternal sunrise quandary: a nightcap or an omelette? Find both, mixed with old-Vegas swank, at **Peppermill's Fireside Lounge** (p120), about a mile further north up Las Vegas Boulevard (and easily accessible on the aforementioned Deuce bus).

Once you've reached this long-standing Strip landmark, you've got two choices. If hunger has kicked in, convalesce in the restaurant's curvy, comfy booths, complete with surreal fake cherry trees, and sample the 24-hour, alcohol-absorbing breakfast.

Alternatively, keep going along the road to oblivion and walk straight through to Peppermill's Fireside Lounge, a vintage Vegas classic that hasn't quite been spoiled by the installation of TV screens on almost every surface. Full of mirrors, fake greenery and a bubbling pool that doubles as a fire pit, this swanky, glowing salon is the best make-out spot you'll find on the Strip. The best thing? There's no cover charge, and the drinks are less expensive than at most all-hours nightclubs.

By now, the sun will be rising and the time has come to call a cab and head for the nearest bed. The pain of the harsh light of day is only going to get worse; indeed, it's best not to venture out again until after dark, when you can start all over again.

Fremont Street

Back to Basics

The last 20 years have seen all manner of changes on the Strip. The street is now more or less unrecognisable from the mid 1980s, much less its Rat Pack-dominated, Mob-run 1960s heyday. Downtown, on the other hand, has been slow to regenerate. The Fremont Street Experience, a five-block electronic canopy that offers eye-catching light shows every night, adds a dash of modernity to the area. However, much of Downtown remains wedded to its past, which makes a visit here a welcome change from the relentless throb and rumble of the Strip.

This is a tour of vintage Downtown (the area covered by the maps on p147 and p149), stopping off at many of Vegas's old-school sights, shops, diversions and attractions. As a walking tour, it's good in the evening: the shops will

be closed, but the neon lights really bring the area alive. Note that while most of the spots are accessible on foot, at least outside the stifling heat of summer, you'll need wheels to complete the rest: rent a car or scooter, or simply grab a cab.

Start where Vegas itself started: at the corner of Main and Fremont Streets. In May 1905, land-hungry settlers and speculators gathered here, on land now occupied by the **Plaza** hotel-casino (p180), to bid on roughly 1,000 lots that together constituted the infant city of Las Vegas. It's appropriate, then, that across from here sits the city's oldest hotel: the historic, 106-room **Golden Gate** (p178), founded as the Sal Sagev (try reading it backwards) in 1906. If you're driving, have a valet park your car here for the price of a tip: Fremont Street is a pedestrian-only zone.

Shrimp cocktail at the Golden Gate

Inside, the Golden Gate is every bit the vintage Vegas icon. Visitors still head here for the bustling snack bar: it's a throwback to a cheesier time, when Downtown's famous low prices were epitomised by the 99¢ shrimp cocktail. (Those of more discerning taste may opt for the $2.99 'big' version.) Evening visitors may be lucky enough to catch boogie-woogie piano man Bob Long; ask him to play 'Your Cheatin' Heart' for a real old-school treat. On a nearby wall are artefacts commemorating the site of the first telephone installed in Las Vegas, which inevitably came with the number '1'.

Exit the Golden Gate into the bright-light weirdness that is the **Fremont Street Experience**, replete with punters, performers and kiosks hawking trashy souvenirs. At **La Bayou** casino (15 E Fremont Street), the theme is loosely Mardi Gras, though it's more big cheesy than Big Easy. Inside this walk-in closet of gambling and grime is a daiquiri buffet at which drinks are served in glasses taller than most midgets.

Back out on Fremont Street, continue east to the newly refurbished **Golden Nugget** (p180), forever the gem of Downtown. The Nugget's extraordinary pool contains an integrated shark tank along with cascading waterfalls and outdoor blackjack. Although it's officially reserved for hotel guests only, a good bluff on a slow night should gain you access; it's open until 2am. Back in the casino, be sure to admire the world's largest golden nugget, weighing in at 61 pounds and 11 ounces (nearly 28 kilograms).

Just east of here is the **Four Queens** (p178), which offers cocktails served in football-shaped vessels, threadbare carpets of dizzying patterns and **Hugo's Cellar** (p156), an old-styled Vegas eaterie. Try the veal. And close at hand is **Fitzgeralds** hotel-casino, where the nightly lounge entertainment includes impressionists, comedians and Elvis acts. Only suckers pay the full ticket price; haggling over the entry fee is allowed. The Vue Bar offers a second-storey outdoor patio from which to view the electric canopy shows. For the luck of the Irish, rub the Blarney Stone direct from County Cork, located in the slot club registration area (8am-midnight daily).

Head out of the casino towards the giant pint of Guinness and past **Vegas Vic**, a vast neon cowboy installed here in the 1940s. Close by sit a whole host of hipster drinking dens, all of which have opened in the last couple of years as Downtown continues to drag

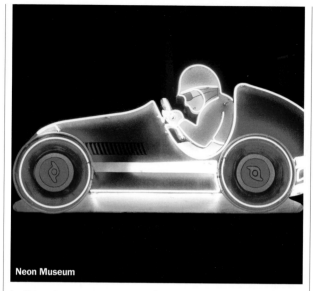

Neon Museum

itself into the 21st century. However, for the purposes of this tour, we're more interested in the outdoor **Neon Museum** (p152), a collection of vintage neon signs displayed along and just off this section of Fremont Street. Look out in particular for the old Flame sign (originally installed on Desert Inn Road in 1961, above a restaurant of the same name) and the classic Nevada Motel sign (c1950).

Heading back towards the Golden Gate, stop off to see the once-classic **Binion's** hotel-casino (p146): formerly known as the Horseshoe, this was where Vegas poker became famous thanks to Benny Binion's creation, in the 1970s, of the World Series of Poker. If you're feeling frisky, have a quick ride on the mechanical bull (7pm-2am Thur-Sun) before dusting yourself down and heading into **Mermaids** (32

E Fremont Street), a pokey little casino with the unexpected bonus of deep-fried Twinkies in the back.

If you're in the mood for more vintage Vegas sites, now's the time to collect your car from the Golden Gate and cruise south down Main Street. En route, look out for a host of curious shops dealing in vintage Vegasabilia. After browsing the oldies but goodies at **Main Street Antiques** (500 S Main Street), stop by the **Gamblers General Store** (p160), which supplements its stock of chips, books and dice with classic slot machines. Further down the road sit the **Attic** (p159) and **Opportunity Village Thrift Store** (921 S Main Street), both of which sell vintage clothes; prices at the latter are especially keen. If you're here at night, keep an eye out for the graceful animated neon sign outside the **Swim-In Pool Supply Co** (1314 S Main Street).

Further south down Main Street sit an array of funky art galleries and the modern **Art Bar** (p152) (look for the low-budget spire of multicoloured lights), but there are more remnants of old Vegas back on Las Vegas Boulevard. Turn left from Main Street on to Oakey Boulevard until you see the 24-hour **White Cross Drug Store** (1700 Las Vegas Boulevard South), where spangled hats co-exist with make-up and beauty products not seen since the 1970s. The food counter is another good bet; the trout and eggs are particularly tasty.

After a brief diversion to **Luv-It Frozen Custard** (p157), which has served the best desserts in Nevada from a tiny shack since 1973, return to Las Vegas Boulevard South and head north up what is a rather neglected stretch of road, lined with motels and wedding chapels. In business for more than 50 years, the **Little White Chapel** (1301 Las Vegas Boulevard South) found greater fame in recent years when it featured in both *Friends* and *Coronation Street*. If it's not busy, try to convince a member of staff to let you have a peek at its drive-thru wedding tunnel; the frescoed cherubs on the ceiling are pure Vegas. The sign informs passers-by that stars Joan Collins and Michael Jordan both got married here, but presumably not to each other.

Continue north past pawn shops and some adult-oriented businesses. Having passed over Fremont Street and under the freeway, turn right at E McWilliams Avenue, just before you reach the Cashman Field complex. Here you'll find the **Neon Boneyard**, where retired neon signs await destruction or restoration and possible replacement Downtown as part of the aforementioned Neon Museum. It's not open to the public for anything other than group tours, but it's possible to catch a glimpse of the incredible contents through the gates.

Back on Las Vegas Boulevard, this little pocket of town is also home to a handful of museums, but is perhaps most notable for the **Old Las Vegas Mormon Fort Historic Park** (p152). Built in 1855 by Mormon missionaries, it's the oldest Euro-American building in the state, and gives a sense of what life would have been like before the railroad arrived and changed Vegas forever. Only remnants of the original structure remain, but it's still very much worth a visit.

As a parting shot, a goodbye of sorts to Downtown, head south down Las Vegas Boulevard and turn left into the non-pedestrianised stretch of Fremont Street. The blocks of Fremont, nearest Las Vegas Boulevard, are currently being regenerated with newly fashionable hangouts such as the **Beauty Bar** (p153). But further along the road lie living (and dying) remnants of another era.

The huge collection of vintage neon motel signs along this eastern stretch of Fremont is unrivalled, from the **City Center Motel** (at Fremont and 7th Streets) all the way to the **Blue Angel** (at Fremont and 21st Streets). Sadly, the motels that lie behind them have all seen better days, as many of their down-on-their-luck residents. The further east you travel along Fremont, the sketchier it gets; remember to keep your car doors locked at all times. Even so, there's plenty to feed the eyes and mind as you travel out of Downtown and into the literal Vegas oblivion.

Las Vegas by Area

Luxor p50

South Strip

The small area around the intersection of Las Vegas Boulevard South and Tropicana Avenue contains more hotel rooms than the entire city of San Francisco. Dominated by properties owned by MGM Mirage (all in this chapter except the Tropicana), the South Strip is home to some of the city's most exotic theming, in evidence at the **Luxor**, **Excalibur**, **Tropicana** and **New York New York**.

Excalibur

3850 Las Vegas Boulevard South, at W Tropicana Avenue (reservations 1-877 750 5464/front desk & casino 597 7777/www.excalibur.com). Bus Deuce, 201. **Map** p49 B2.
The jury's still out on whether or not this caricature of a castle will become the next generation's Circus Circus. MGM Mirage has been too busy transforming

the pirate-themed Treasure Island and the Polynesian-tilted Mirage into hipper versions of their former selves, leaving Excalibur to fend for itself. However, there have been a few changes, in particular the addition of dining and entertainment options that eschew the family-friendly theme: a biker-themed bar, the silly Dick's Last Resort, and the 'edgy' comedy of everyone's favourite fat guy, Louie Anderson. Identity crisis, anyone?

Neon knights slay neon dragons in Excalibur's neon casino, one of the few in town where photography is allowed. Visitors are surrounded by images of playing-card kings and queens, but the table games are affordable for any commoner. Thousands of slots jam the joint; video poker is scarcer. When you're done throwing coins in machines, toss a few in the moat for good luck: they'll be donated to local charities.

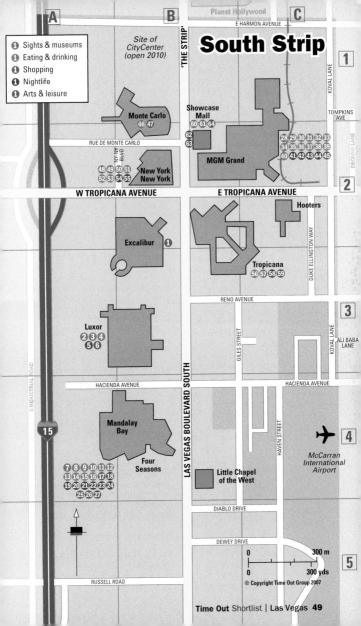

South Strip

Legend:
- ❶ Sights & museums
- ❶ Eating & drinking
- ❶ Shopping
- ❶ Nightlife
- ❶ Arts & leisure

Planet Hollywood

E HARMON AVENUE

'THE STRIP'

Site of CityCenter (open 2010)

Monte Carlo
46 47

RUE DE MONTE CARLO

New York New York
48 49 50 51
52 53 54 55

W TROPICANA AVENUE

Showcase Mall
60 61 64
62
63

MGM Grand
28 29 30 31 32 33
34 35 36 37 38 39
40 41 42 43 44 45

E TROPICANA AVENUE

Hooters

Excalibur ❶

Tropicana
56 57 58 59

RENO AVENUE

Luxor
❷ ❸ ❹
❺ ❻

HACIENDA AVENUE

Mandalay Bay

Four Seasons
❼ ❽ ❾ 10 11 12
13 14 15 16 17 18
19 20 21 22 23 24
25 26 27

Little Chapel of the West

McCarran International Airport

DIABLO DRIVE

DEWEY DRIVE

RUSSELL ROAD

KOVAL LANE

TOMPKINS AVE

DECKOW LANE

DUKE ELLINGTON WAY

GILES STREET

KOVAL LANE

ALI BABA LANE

HACIENDA AVENUE

HAVEN STREET

LAS VEGAS BOULEVARD SOUTH

S INDUSTRIAL ROAD

15

A   B   C

1

2

3

4

5

0   300 m
0   300 yds

© Copyright Time Out Group 2007

Sights & museums

The medieval (and still child-friendly) orientation extends into the night with the entertaining Tournament of Kings, which features jousting, pyrotechnics and a surprisingly decent game-hen dinner. The Fantasy Faire Midway keeps children busy with two Magic Motion Machine film rides, medieval-themed games and an arcade. Comic Louie Anderson and hilarious male revue Thunder from Down Under provide adult-oriented fare.

Eating & drinking

Tops among the restaurants is Sir Galahad's Pub & Prime Rib House, where you'll find generous portions of prime rib and Yorkshire pudding. The Steakhouse at Camelot serves decent cuts, while Regale dishes up pastas. At biker-themed Octane, flair bartenders serve up such cocktails as Blood, Sweat & Gears and Tailpipe Wind; also new is Dick's Last Resort, a playfully tacky watering hole that serves massive cocktails and finger foods by the bucket. There's also a children's menu at the 24-hour Sherwood Forest Café and an extensive Round Table Buffet.

Arts & leisure

Tournament of Kings
Shows 6pm, 8.30pm daily.
Map p49 B2 ❶
The phrase 'dinner and a show' takes on new meaning here. Kids and those with medieval fetishes will dig the jousting knights and galloping horses, as King Arthur and company recreate a bygone era with fine-tuned costumes, dialogue and mannerisms. The meal sans utensils is will please the children, but you may prefer one of the casino's buffets.

Luxor
3900 Las Vegas Boulevard South, at W Hacienda Avenue (reservations 1-888 777 0188/front desk & casino 262 4102/www.luxor.com). Bus Deuce, 104, 105. Map p49 B3.
Second only to New York New York in terms of the absurdity of its exterior, the Luxor impresses on scale long before you've set foot inside it. While some casinos limit theming to the interiors, leaving the buildings as smart but not altogether memorable towers, the 30-storey glass pyramid housing much of the Luxor makes one hell of a first impression. At night, a high-intensity light shoots skywards from the top; visible in space, it's also a beacon to a swarm of insects and bats during warmer months.

The homage to ancient Egypt continues inside, but to a far lesser extent than it did when the casino opened in 1993. The campiest elements of the theming evaporated a number of years ago, but even more Egyptiana was mummified during a still-ongoing renovation that began in 2006, lending credence to rumours that the casino may rebrand itself as the Pyramid. The theming of the two main shows on offer, zany comedian Carrot Top, and seductive adult-oriented extravaganza Fantasy, is mercifully non Egyptian. In addition, several of the hotel's Egyptian-slanted bars and restaurants have gone, replaced with shiny new dining and nightlife destinations.

The Luxor's massive casino, decorated with hieroglyphics and ancient artefacts, is filled with the latest high-tech slot and video poker machines. Expect $10 minimums at blackjack and craps, higher on weekends. For poker players, the card room offers weekend action so lively that Cleopatra herself would have been impressed. Take a few minutes to walk the perimeter of the circular casino and get your bearings; if you can't identify landmarks, you'll wind up going in circles.

Sights & museums

IMAX Ridefilm Motion Simulator Rides
Open 10am-11pm daily. Admission $9.99. Map p49 B3 ❷

Added to the classic ride In Search of the Obelisk, which takes the audience on a *Raiders of the Lost Ark*-style action adventure through the Luxor archaeological dig, come two new motion simulator experiences; Reboot the Ride and Dracula's Haunted Castle the Ride.

King Tut Museum

Open 10am-11pm daily. **Admission** $9.99. **Map** p49 B3 ❸

This full-size re-creation of king Tutankhamun's burial chamber and his golden throne and sarcophagus, apparently all hand-crafted by actual Egyptian artisans from historically correct materials, is extremely kitsch but undeniably good fun, if not particularly educational

Eating & drinking

Aside from Aspen 702, eating options at the Luxor are best described as reliable. The Luxor Steakhouse and the Pharaoh's Pheast buffet both have good reputations; the Backstage Deli apes New York Jewish food as only an Egyptian-themed casino in Nevada can; and Fusia offers upmarket Asian dishes. Burgers, pizzas and expensive coffees are available at the food court.

Aspen 702

NEW *www.purelv.com*. **Open** check online for details. **$$$**. **Steakhouse**. **Map** p49 B3 ❹

After slumbering for several years, the Luxor is making a concerted effort to revamp and regenerate itself in 2007. There's no better example of its new attitude than the presence of this hip-before-it-even-opened steakhouse: modelled after a Colorado ski lodge and with microcelebs Nick Lachey and Nicky Hilton among the owners, it's set to draw in the starry-eyed, moneyed crowd.

Shopping

Mandalay Place (p56) is a modest mall housing non-chain and boutique stores, located on a bridge that connects

Mandalay Bay to the Luxor, and easily accessible from either resort.

Nightlife

LAX

NEW *289 2002/www.laxthe nightclub.com*. **Open** call for details. **Map** p49 B3 ❺

Imported from LA, where it's immensely popular with celebs and the hangers-on who love them, LAX is the Luxor's attempt to revive its clubbing scene after years of relative dormancy. DJ AM, co-owner and resident disc-spinner at the Hollywood original, will play regularly for a crowd that seems likely to be among the most glamorous in town.

Arts & leisure

Luxor IMAX Theatre

Map p49 B3 ❻

Documentary-style and family-friendly features play all day at Luxor's towering seven-storey theatre, most of them

Tournament of Kings

Sit back, relax...

The second coming of the Las Vegas lounge.

Rouge

Back in their glory days, Las Vegas lounges were sleazy smoky rooms, but as Vegas entertainment got more glamorous and audiences' attention began to wander, the scenes evaporated, and the old-school lounges died out during the 1990s. Lately, though, they've been reinvented for the 21st century, the spotty bands and disinterested barmen replaced by hip DJs and skilful mixologists.

With the exception of the MGM's **Centrifuge** (p59), where bartenders and waitresses regularly dance on the bartops, many of today's most notable lounges sport tightly administered velvet ropes that stray wildly from the democratic policies of years gone by. Following the trend initiated by the Venetian's venerable **V Bar** (p105), these upscale spots carry a decidedly Vegas moniker – they're not lounges but 'ultralounges' – and they offer the decidedly Vegas affectation of pricey bottle service. Some, like the **Mix Lounge** (p57), also sell unbeatable views.

Discriminating doormen ensure that the expensive look of the ultralounges is upheld by the expensive look of their clientele. Boasting interiors styled by top designers (see AvroKo's eye-catching **Social House**; p102), ultralounges include luxuriously appointed booths and attractive staff, none more so than the revived bunnies at the **Playboy Club** at the Palms (p139). Most rely on DJs to work the crowd, but only to a point: they don't all have dancefloors, though that doesn't stop girls from dancing on the tables at **Tabú** (p64).

If all these ostentatious dress codes sound a bit too flashy, you might prefer MGM's casual but stylish **Rouge**, or the Beatles-themed **Revolution** (p92). Designed by the Cirque du Soleil team, it offers exclusivity but without the hefty cover charge (before 11pm). There's even enough room for the Cirque breakdancers to take to the floor, something you'd never see elsewhere. Vive la Revolution!

screened in 3D (wraparound goggles are provided). Tickets can only be purchased in person at least 15 minutes before showtime from the Pharaoh's Pavilion box office. There's another IMAX screen at the Brenden Las Vegas 14 (p139) at the Palms.

Mandalay Bay

3950 Las Vegas Boulevard South, at W Hacienda Avenue (reservations 1-877 632 7800/front desk & casino 632 7777/www.mandalaybay.com). Bus Deuce, 104, 105. **Map** p49 B4.

Not only do the suits at MGM Mirage know not to mess with a good thing, they also know how to make it better. There's no finer example of this skill than the South Seas island-themed Mandalay Bay, one of the Strip's most luxurious resorts. At its heart has always been an 11-acre water park with a sandy beach, a wave pool, a lazy river, two additional pools and a jogging track set in lush green foliage, plus the Moorea Beach Club, a limited-access South Beach-esque retreat that transforms into a sultry hotspot on warm-weather weekend nights. But a recent $30-million expansion added a three-storey, climate-controlled, glass-fronted casino on the sand, where guests can enjoy beachside gambling, casual dining or sun-worshipping. Book one of the decked-out Villas Soleil, where you and 15 pals can take advantage of your own bar, MP3 player, flat-screen TV and private third-level pool.

The interior is just as impressive. An understated oasis of water features, lush foliage, huge aquariums and island architecture, it encompasses a sensuous spa, a classy collection of restaurants, a pair of wedding chapels, several theatres and the kid-friendly Shark Reef aquarium. Mandalay Place, a nice sky-bridge mall that connects the hotel with the Luxor, contains a number of upscale boutiques and restaurants, a chic barber and even Ivan Kane's Forty Deuce (p57), a 'back-alley striptease lounge'. The convention facilities are among the city's best

as is the selection of restaurants. Alongside the highlights listed below is the very well executed Bay Side Buffet, which serves good quality, pocket-friendly food.

Mandalay Bay's 135,000sq ft (12,500 sq m) casino is airier than many, with 2,400 machines (including nickel video slots that take up to 45 or 90 coins), but you have to hunt for good video poker machines. Table games, 122 of them, include blackjack, roulette, craps, Let it Ride, Caribbean stud, pai gow poker and mini-baccarat. You'll also find a poker room where you can get your fix of seven-card stud and Texas or Omaha hold 'em. The race and sports book has 17 large screens, enough seating for some 300 sports fans, a bar and a good deli.

If all this doesn't work for you, there are two other hotels accessible via Mandalay Bay. A corridor off the lobby leads to the luxury Four Seasons (p171), which has its rooms on floors 35 to 39 but is run as a separate, but just as exclusive operation. Here you'll find the fashionable Verandah Café, (p56) a popular celebrity haunt which serves an exceptionally good brunch.

Meanwhile, Thehotel at Mandalay Bay (p173) is an all-suites, casino-free tower that eschews the island theme entirely, and comes complete with its own spa facilities (the Bathhouse), restaurants and nightlife (Mix).

Sights & museums

Shark Reef

Open 10am-11pm daily (last entry 10pm). **Admission** $15.95; $12.95 reductions; free under-4s.
Map p49 B4 **⑦**
A 'walk-through' aquarium, the AZA-accredited Shark Reef is filled with 100 species of underwater life, including rays, jellyfish, eels and, of course, 11 varieties of shark. A perfect complement to the exotic South Seas-themed Mandalay Bay, the Shark Reef is an unexpected gem in a city somewhat lacking in the educational entertainment department.

Eating & drinking

Aureole

632 7401. **Open** 6-10.30pm daily. **$$$.**
American. Map p49 B4 ⑧

Vegas is full of dramatic restaurants,
but where else can you dine within sight
of a four-storey, 4,500-bottle wine tower,
up and down which float harnessed
wine angels, fetching your choice on
demand? The food, orchestrated by
Charlie Palmer and overseen by
Vincent Pouessel, is also a delight, with
seasonal American dishes including
caramelised Sonoma duck and fennel
steamed Alaskan salmon. Megan
Romano's ethereal sweets make break-
ing your diet well worthwhile.

Border Grill

632 7403. **Open** 11.30am-10.30pm
daily. **$$. Mexican.** Map p49 B4 ⑨

Imported from Santa Monica, this
Angeleno take on Mexican food is not
especially authentic, but works a treat
regardless. Mary Sue Milliken and
Susan Feniger, frontwomen of popular
show *Too Hot Tamales*, have given
some classic dishes a twist (the quesadillas are a great call), but also look
to their home state for inspiration: witness the deep-fried snapper, served
over refried beans. Lively stuff.

Burger Bar

632 9364. **Open** 10.30am-11pm Mon-
Thur, Sun; 10am-3am Fri, Sat. **$$.**
American. Map p49 B4 ⑩

Cast images of McBurgers out of your
mind: the burgers at this chic yet
amenable spot are fresh, meaty and
deeply delicious, especially once you've
garnished them with your choice of
toppings. (Veggie options are avail-
able.) Ironically, it took a Frenchman to
reinvent this most American of meals:
it's the brainchild of Hubert Keller, the
chef behind Fleur de Lys.

Fleur de Lys

632 9400. **Open** 5.30-10pm Mon-Thur,
Sun; 5.30-10.30pm Fri, Sat. **$$$.**
French. Map p49 B4 ⑪

Fleur de Lys features 30ft walls of
cultured stone, a huge floral sculpture
containing more than 3,000 fresh-cut
roses, semi-private cabana tables and,
in the wine loft, a private dining area.
There are DJs in the lounge, but the
USP remains Hubert Keller's contemporary French cuisine. For the last
word in indulgence, the Fleurburger,
a Kobe burger served with truffles
and foie gras, and accompanied by a
bottle of 1990 Château Petrus, costs a
cool $5,000.

Mix

Thehotel at Mandalay Bay (632 9500).
Open 6-10.30pm daily. **$$$. French.**
Map p49 B4 ⑫

The food isn't cheap, but it appears that
culinary legend Alain Ducasse might
not be taking his Vegas eaterie as seri-
ously as his more expensive restaurants
in other cities. Both service and prepa-
ration seem rushed as the staff turn out
more meals than perhaps they can man-
age. It's hard to fault the view from the
43rd floor, but you'll get the same view,
and more bang for your buck, in the Mix
Lounge next door (p57).

Red Square

632 7407. **Open** 5pm-2am Mon-Thur,
Sun; 5pm-3am Fri, Sat. **$$$. Bar**. Map
p49 B4 ⑬

The vodkas here are so good they
made Lenin lose his head. Well, that's
the only rational explanation for the
enormous decapitated statue of the
father of the Soviet Union over the
entrance, though you can always ask
the barman what happened to Vlad's
missing body part (it's in the walk-in
'vodka locker' on ice). The food is fine
and the drinks are strong.

RM

632 9300. **Open** 5.30-10.30pm daily.
$$$. Seafood. Map p49 B4 ⑭

Rick Moonen moved to Vegas from
New York to ensure that everything at
his restaurant lives up to his initials. As
a result, the room is cosily contempo-
rary, the service is classic and the
seafood is out of this world. For about
half the price, you can sample Moonen's
cooking bistro-style downstairs at the
R Bar Café, which features a raw menu.

Aureole

Strip Steak

Strip Steak

NEW *632 7414*. **Open** 5.30-10.30pm daily. **$$$$**. **Steakhouse**. Map p49 B4 ⑮

Star chef Michael Mina's first steakhouse is also his first slight misstep. It's not that the food is bad, because it isn't. But at prices this extreme ($50 for a 10oz filet mignon, eight bucks for a side of baked potato), it really needs to be dazzling, and it's rarely quite that good. The slow-poached prime rib is the best bet, but do save room for the supreme desserts. The open-plan restaurant area can get loud when it's busy, which is reasonably often.

Verandah Café

Four Seasons (632 5121/www.four seasons.com). **Open** 6.30am-10pm Mon-Fri; 7am-10pm Sat, Sun. **$$**. **Buffet**. Map p49 B4 ⑯

Outfitted in everything from suits to tennis shorts, rock stars, real estate magnates and other riff-raff find this comfortable California country club-styled spot irresistible. The under promoted yet popular Sunday brunch is an all-you-can-savour taste treat, putting other buffets to shame at a price that says it should. A large poolside dining area (request to sit here when booking) spirits you away to Santa Barbara for bellinis and blintzes.

Shopping

Mandalay Place

632 9333. **Open** 10am-11pm daily. **Map** p49 B4 ⑰

What separates this smallish retail experience from other Strip malls is its vow to 'break the chains': it leases its stores only to companies otherwise absent from Vegas. It's a savvy move, and one that brought the city its first Urban Outfitters (which has since also opened in the Miracle Mile Shops); Lik Design, featuring beautiful palm wood furniture by Aussie designer Bruce Dowse; and the Reading Room, the city's best independent bookstore. The handful of great boutiques includes Nora Blue, Elton's Men Store and Max&Co; other highlights include the modern furniture and lighting at Blankspace; Lush Puppy, which carries fashion-conscious accessories for pets and distraction-packed toyshop Five Little Monkeys. For goodies to take home, 55° Wine + Design offers a comprehensive selection of fine wines and tasting bar, from the people behind the famous wine tower at Aureole. The mall is also accessible via the Luxor resort.

Nightlife

Godspeed
632 7777/www.hob.com. **Open** 11pm-5am Mon. **Map** p49 B4 ⑱
The House of Blues' exclusive Foundation Room atop Mandalay Bay opens its doors to non-members on Mondays. DJs provide a sexy house soundtrack, which, when combined with the lush Asian-inspired decor and breathtaking city views, creates an indulgent jet-set atmosphere.

House of Blues
632 7600/tickets 474 4000. **Tickets** $10-$70. **Map** p49 B4 ⑲
Though this is just one of several folk art-filled locations across the US, the House of Blues' exciting mix of up-and-coming and established artists makes it feel like a home-grown champion. The multi-level main floor is surrounded by three bars and tiered balcony seating. Kitschy cover bands play on weekend nights; it's Gospel Brunch on Sundays.

Ivan Kane's Forty Deuce
632 9442/www.fortydeuce.com. **Open** 10.30pm-4am (sometimes until 5am) Mon, Thur-Sun. **Map** p49 B4 ⑳
Burlesque-oriented clubs started re-emerging in Sin City a few years ago, but only Forty Deuce is founded entirely on the combination of stage-trained dancers and DJ-spun club sounds. Though smallish and lacking a sufficient dancefloor, this offshoot of an LA original is worth a visit. You can buy the dancers' costumes in the adjacent Champagne Suzy's boutique.

Mandalay Bay Beach
Information 632 7777/tickets 474 4000. **Map** p49 B4 ㉑
Las Vegas's clement weather makes Mandalay Bay's man-made beach ideal for outdoor gigs, and its summer concert series draws in a variety of crowd-pleasing favourites, including Billy Idol, the B-52s and the Go-Gos. If standing in the sand (or water), watching the action up-close isn't your thing, shell out a few bucks more and enjoy the concert from Moorea Beach Club, an open-air lounge outfitted with its own pool, cabanas, bar, loungers and video screens displaying the performance from a safe (and dry) distance.

Mandalay Bay Events Center
Information 632 7777/tickets 474 4000. **Map** p49 B4 ㉒
Though this massive arena isn't specifically a music venue per se (it also hosts expositions, boxing matches and awards ceremonies), it draws the biggest and the best international musical acts, from Aerosmith to Keith Urban via Luciano Pavarotti. Getting in and out of the Events Center becomes a logistical nightmare during big crowd-pullers, so plan accordingly.

Mix Lounge
Thehotel at Mandalay Bay (632 9500). **Open** 5pm-2am Mon-Thur, Sun; 5pm-3am Fri, Sat. **Map** p49 B4 ㉓
Surrounded by 30ft windows, the lounge at Alain Ducasse's dynamic restaurant (p54) atop Thehotel at Mandalay Bay attracts locals with its impressive panoramic views. Mix comes with the overly clubby feel that's attached to so many of the city's other towering venues. Its intimate vibe is enhanced by house and lounge sounds, though there's no proper dancefloor.

Rumjungle
632 7408. **Open** 11pm Mon, Wed, Fri, Sat; 11pm-2am Tue, Thur, Sun. **Map** p49 B4 ㉔
The exotic fire-and-water theme at Rumjungle perfectly complements the music, which varies from hip hop to Latin dance (especially during promotions such as Rumba on Wednesdays). It's popular with the college-age set, but its semi-strict dress code keeps out the rubes, and it's far less crowded since the once-legendary swank contingent dispersed to newer venues.

Verandah Café p56

Arts & leisure

ARCS: a Robert Cromeans Salon

632 6130/www.robertcromeans.com.
Open 9am-7pm Mon-Fri; 8am-8pm Sat; 10am-6pm Sun. **Map** p49 B4 ㉕
The prices at crazy coiffeur Cromean's trendy Paul Mitchell salon are about the same as his California salons: in other words, eye-watering.

Bathhouse

Thehotel at Mandalay Bay (1-877 632 9636/632 9636). **Open** 6am-8.30pm daily. **Map** p49 B4 ㉖
The first clue that the Bathhouse differs from other Vegas spas is revealed the moment you step into the long, suede-lined hallway and are greeted graciously by staff clad in slick, space-age uniforms before a backdrop of textured slate, frosted glass, cool running water and hints of shocking chartreuse. Indulge in an Asian tea bath (chai or green) capped off by the bamboo sugar scrub. Not a rubber ducky in sight.

Mamma Mia!

1-877 632 7400/474 4000. **Shows** 7.30pm Mon-Thur, Sun; 6pm, 10pm Sat. No under-5s. **Map** p49 B4 ㉗
While the story – a young woman trying to find her father on the eve of her wedding – plays a little too earnestly for the featherweight songs, fans of 1970s group Abba will have a heap of fun seeing how and where their favourite tunes – among them 'Take a Chance on Me' and 'Gimme! Gimme! Gimme!' – pop up in this West End smash hit. Hang in there: they'll get to 'Dancing Queen' eventually. The show is scheduled to close in mid 2008.

MGM Grand

3799 Las Vegas Boulevard South, at E Tropicana Avenue (reservations 1-877 880 0880/front desk & casino 891 7777/www.mgmgrand.com). Bus Deuce, 201. **Map** p49 B2.
There is a spa here, of course. Not to mention a pool, a convention centre and a kid-friendly animal attraction (the popular Lion Habitat). However,

LAS VEGAS BY AREA

Reading Room at Mandalay Place p56

the MGM Grand really comes alive after dark, when this immense resort is at its vibrant, buzzing best.

For a time, the largest hotel on earth (with, it should be said, one of the ugliest exteriors) aimed itself squarely at families. When Vegas fashion started to move back towards the adult market, the MGM was by no means quickest to react. However, it's since thrown itself into the grown-up market with commitment and smarts, building an unlikely but deserved reputation as one of the liveliest resorts on the Strip. Billing itself as 'Maximum Vegas' takes the point a bit far, but there's little doubt that the MGM balances the needs of cash-happy big spenders, easygoing middle Americans and youthful club kids as well as any resort in the city.

The MGM has four gaming areas (Entertainment, Hollywood, Monte Carlo and Sports) in which you'll find all the games, including Spanish 21. It's the largest casino in Las Vegas and boasts hundreds of tables. Table minimums can go down to $10 on weekdays, but most are higher; in the pit, you'll find $25 minimums and $15,000 maximums. There's also a large race and sports book with floor-to-ceiling screens, one of the best poker rooms in town, and 3,700 slots, from a nickel to $500.

Sights & museums

Lion Habitat
Open 11am-10pm daily. **Admission** free. **Map** p49 B2 ㉘
Not to be outdone by the Mirage's tigers, the MGM has its own pride of 'display' lions. The habitat is pretty small, but the glass walls mean you can get a close-up view of cubs and adult lions.

Eating & drinking

Centrifuge
NEW **Open** 4pm-2am daily. **$$$**. **Bar**. **Map** p49 B2 ㉙
Having dramatically remade its range of restaurants in recent years, the MGM is now turning its attention to its bars.

Along with Rouge, Centrifuge (opened in 2007) is one of the MGM's more eye-catching bars, with a circular layout, TV screens, dancing girls and excellent cocktails. It's more expensive than it should be, but worth a look nonetheless.

Craftsteak

891 7800/www.craftrestaurant.com.
Open 5.30-10pm Mon, Sun; 5-10pm Tue-Thur; 5-10.30pm Fri, Sat. **$$$**.
Steakhouse. Map p49 B2 ㉚
The selection of meats (grass-fed veal, lamb shank, filet mignon, braised short ribs) is impressive, but the sides and the quiet invention shown in the kitchen both elevate Tom Colicchio's Craftsteak from more run-of-the-mill casino steakhouses. Ingredients come from small family farms and other below-the-radar sources, and you can tell. It's all served in a cultured atmosphere, if a slightly noisy one.

Diego

NEW *891 7800.* **Open** 5.30-10pm Mon-Thur, Sun; 2-10pm Fri, Sat. **$$**.
Mexican. Map p49 B2 ㉛
The experience at MGM's lively *cocina* starts as soon as you see the bold colours and backlit tequila-bottle tower. Traditional Mexican recipes are exemplified and often modernised; Oaxacan *carne asada* (mesquite-grilled chilli-marinated beef), Yucatan-style braised pork, cactus and tequila salsa, and so on. A tasting menu offers some more unique bites, such as braised pit-style goat and table-made shrimp cocktail.

Fiamma

891 7800. **Open** 5.30-10.30pm Mon-Thur, Sun; 5.30-11pm Fri, Sat. **$$**.
Italian. Map p49 B2 ㉜
Stephen Hanson remodelled the once-proud Olio into this beautiful if over-sized trattoria, a sister to his Fiamma Osteria in New York's Soho. A favourite for its cosy, trendy bar scene, Fiamma also dishes up Italian faves, such as lobster gnocchi and short rib raviolini, as well as a few chophouse-style steak, seafood and poultry dishes. Save room for the crochette dessert, three ridiculously delicious fried doughnuts.

Joël Robuchon

NEW *693 7223.* **Open** 5.30-10pm Mon-Thur, Sun; 5.30-10.30pm Fri, Sat.
$$$$. French. Map p49 B2 ㉝
The only US fine dining restaurant by the so-called 'Chef of the Century' has a lot to live up to. But what goes on in the kitchen, from Robuchon's famous pommes purées to dishes such as la semoule de blé dur (confit of lamb with Mediterranean couscous), is even more spectacular than the five-room space, which feels like a 1930s Parisian mansion. It comes at a price, of course. But once you're here, you might as well splash out on the exquisite tasting menus.

L'Atelier de Joël Robuchon

NEW *693 7223.* **Open** 5-10.30pm Mon-Thur, Sun; 5-11pm Fri, Sat. **$$$**.
French. Map p49 B2 ㉞
This workshop-style dining room, right next door to Robuchon's signature restaurant, features a few tables and a counter at which you can sit and watch some of the world's best dishes (simpler and cheaper than at the other place) being prepared. Try a side order of the gorgeous pommes purées or push the boat out and go for the discovery tasting; it's worth the $150 price tag.

Nobhill

693 7223/www.michaelmina.net.
Open 5.30-10pm Mon-Thur, Sun; 5.30-10.30pm Fri, Sat. **$$$**. **American**.
Map p49 B2 ㉟
A classy San Franciscan treat on the Strip, Michael Mina's Nobhill serves such Bay Area classics as chicken tetrazzini, lobster pot pie and North Beach cioppino. Just as popular are his contemporary creations, particularly Niman Ranch rack of lamb. Cosy up in a bar booth made for two, throw back a few Cable Cars, slather sourdough bread in cheese fondue and polish off a tarte tatin for dessert.

Pearl

693 7223. **Open** 5.30-10pm daily.
$$$. Chinese. Map p49 B2 ㊱

Lion Habitat p59

Send in the clowns

Will Vegas ever get enough of Cirque du Soleil?

MYSTÈRE
CIRQUE DU SOLEIL

The very idea that there could be too much of anything in the city of excess is anathema to many, but Cirque du Soleil saturation point may be in sight. The forthcoming openings of two more acrobatic extravaganzas will bring the total number of Cirque shows on the Strip to seven.

Cirque's first show to open in Vegas was *Mystère* (p102), which made its debut at Treasure Island in 1993. After it took the city by storm, other hotels got in on the act, with the water-themed *O* (p79), the adult-oriented *Zumanity* (p68), the adventurous *Kà* (p64) and the Beatles-themed *Love* (p92). All opened to justifiably enthusiastic reviews and continue to play to big crowds.

The next Cirque production to reach Las Vegas, set to open at the Luxor in July 2008, will be a contemporary magic show by illusionist Criss Angel, who says that his goal is to 'redefine' magic as Cirque has redefined circus. And then, at the end of the following year, MGM Mirage's

CityCenter (p117) will open with a new permanent Cirque show devoted to Elvis Presley.

The popularity of the Cirque brand is well established, with its universal appeal rooted in the shows' skill in going from curtain-up to curtain-down without uttering a word. No doubt this strength will transfer nicely to its two new extravaganzas. Of course, Elvis shows and magic tricks have been filling Vegas auditoria for decades. However, when combined with the classic Cirque artistry, it's anyone's guess what will happen.

Perhaps that's why Guy Laliberté, Cirque's billionaire founder and former street performer, is taking some of his eggs out of the basket. In 2006, the Cirque team lent their talents to the nightlife scene by designing **Revolution** (p92) at the Mirage, which borrows the Beatles theme from *Love*. Since its successful opening, there's been talk of them doing more bar designs in town. It seems Vegas's appetite for the Cirque brand really is insatiable.

A quiet, time-honoured winner on the Strip's upscale restaurant scene, Pearl offers a fresh take on classic Chinese cuisine from Canton and Shanghai provinces with dishes that rotate to reflect the changing of the seasons. There are also plenty of memorable touches off the menu, including an exotic-tea cart and an elegant contemporary room designed by Tony Chi.

SeaBlue
891 7800/www.michaelmina.net.
Open 5.30-10pm Mon-Thur, Sun; 5.30-10.30pm Fri, Sat. **$$$**. **Seafood**. Map p49 B2 ③⑦
Following on from Nobhill at the MGM Grand (p60) and his eponymous seafooder at Bellagio (see left), Michael Mina's third Las Vegas venture is intimate and well designed, but aren't they all? Fish entrées grilled over wood and/or baked in clay are tasty, but what makes this place stand out is its big raw bar. Even the gimmicky lobster corndog appetiser is worth a bite.

Shibuya
NEW *891 7800*. **Open** 5.30-9.30pm Mon-Thur, Sun; 5.30-10pm Fri, Sat. **$$$**. **Japanese**. Map p49 B2 ③⑧
Shibuya is really three beautiful restaurants in one: a 50ft (15m) marble sushi bar; a collection of traditional *teppanyaki* (table cooking) grills under hot pink stainless steel canopies; and a pair of modern rooms where guests can indulge in chef Stephane Chevet's French spin on modern Japanese cuisine. Guests in any section are free to order from the various menus, and everything is easily shared.

'Wichcraft
891 3166/www.craftrestaurant.com.
Open 10am-6pm Mon-Thur, Sun; 10am-8pm Fri, Sat. **$**. **American**. Map p49 B2 ③⑨
Tom Colicchio's overexcited little sibling to Craftsteak (p60) peps up the previously dreary world of American sandwich culture; visitors used to Subway-standard sammiches will be dazzled. Generally speaking, the more appetising the description, the nicer the sandwich, so skip the so-so roast turkey in favour of the more exotic varieties. There's plenty for vegetarians, a novelty in such a meat-oriented town. Breakfast is served all day.

Wolfgang Puck Bar & Grill
891 3000/www.wolfgangpuck.com.
Open 11.30am-11pm Mon-Thur; 11.30am-11.30pm Fri; 10am-11.30pm Sat; 10am-11pm Sun. **$$**. **American**. Map p49 B2 ④⓪
Styled on a California beach bungalow, and a very modish one at that, this Puck outpost offers a contemporary take on Californian cuisine. Signature dishes include truffled potato chips with blue cheese, duck bratwurst and Puck pizzas; all of it is very edible indeed, and perfectly suited to a lazy lunch.

Nightlife

Crazy Horse Paris
Shows 8pm, 10.30pm Mon, Wed-Sun. No under-18s. **Map** p49 B2 ④①
Formerly known as La Femme but revamped in 2007, Crazy Horse Paris claims to 'reinvent the female form as art', a boast that somehow doesn't go unfounded. Lighting effects and film, ballet and cabaret, canvasses and zodiac signs: all add up to a show with lashings of international flair. Its dozen stars have performed with the original Crazy Horse dance troupe in Paris, a phenomenon dating back to 1951. Who says Vegas has no sense of history?

MGM Grand Garden Arena
Map p49 B2 ④②
From Britney Spears and U2 to Alan Jackson and the Police, this massive arena showcases the world's rock and pop royalty, as well as occasional special events such as the Billboard Music Awards. There are different vehicle drop-off points at the venue, so be prepared for a possible ten-minute hike through the casino if you enter via the Strip.

Studio 54

891 1111. **Open** 10pm-5am Tue-Sat.
Map p49 B2 ㊸

This 21st-century revamp of the legendary New York disco recently had a renovation, adding a high-ceilinged entry-way with lounge seating, more VIP areas on the upper levels and a private lounge for the DJ and his or her hangers-on. It remains a favourite with locals and visitors, thanks to top-notch sound and lighting, a cool, industrial feel and some of the most innovative promotions in Vegas.

Tabú

891 7183. **Open** 10pm-3am Mon, Wed-Sun. **Map** p49 B2 ㊹

Lots of spaces in Las Vegas call themselves ultralounges, but Tabú was the first and probably remains the best. Despite its lack of dancefloor and overabundance of seating, DJs manage to keep people on their feet all night in the upscale, modern space; especially during Super Slide Sundays, when B-boys and -girls tear up the floor as if *Breakin' 3* were being filmed right then and there.

Arts & leisure

Kà

1-877 880 0880/891 7777. **Shows** 7pm, 9.30pm Tue-Sat. No under-5s. **Map** p49 B2 ㊺

Having pushed the boat out for *O* (literally, in a couple of scenes), Cirque du Soleil had to work hard to top it in this multi-million-dollar extravaganza. *Kà* differs from other Vegas-based Cirque shows in that it has a plot (about twins struggling to reunite). The story gets a bit lost in an array of ever more breathtaking routines; yet for all the excess, the most touching moment in the piece is a section involving hand-shadows. It's undeniably very impressive, but *O* and *Love* are better.

Monte Carlo

3770 Las Vegas Boulevard South, between W Harmon & W Tropicana Avenues (reservations 1-888 529 4828/ front desk & casino 730 7777/ www.montecarlo.com). Bus Deuce, 201. **Map** p49 B1.

Modelled after the Place du Casino in (of course) Monte Carlo, this handsome but low-key resort will either be an appealing, mid-range option or, like the hotel's star magician Lance Burton, a master of deception, depending on your point of view. The many attractive features, not least of which is the impressive exterior architecture (twin archway entrances, a big streetside fountain), suggest this $344-million resort might be on the same page as, say, the $1.4-billion Bellagio. The truth is that the Monte Carlo successfully appeals to those after an approximation of high style at low prices.

Next to its neighbours, the Monte Carlo isn't an especially charismatic option, less energetic than New York New York and nothing like as fashionable as the MGM Grand. Still, its lack of flash and filigree is just what its admirers like about the hotel, which seems very popular with business travellers. The casino floor is about as mellow as they come, thanks to the bright lighting and high ceilings, and the rooms are simple and familiar. Attractions include not rollercoasters or animal shows but a waterfall-filled pool area and outdoor tennis courts. The front desk's picture windows look over the verdant water park, giving the best lobby view in town.

The casino at the Monte Carlo has plenty of $5 blackjack tables and many 5¢ opportunities among the 2,200 slots, and a bright, casual atmosphere. Players appreciate the details: stools with backs at every machine, wide walkways throughout the casino and even single-zero roulette. The Monte Carlo attracts brisk traffic from neighbouring casinos, but the tables never seem crowded. Players stand a better chance of landing a one-on-one blackjack game with the dealer than at most of the casinos in the Strip resorts.

Monte Carlo

Eating & drinking

The Monte Carlo's signature eaterie is a branch of André's (p152), the sole Strip location of André Rochat's venerable Downtown establishment.

Diablo's Cantina

NEW *www.diabloslv.com*. **Open** check online. **$$**. **Mexican**. **Map** p49 B1 **46**
Mexican restaurants in Vegas casinos tend towards one of two styles: unexpectedly sophisticated, like Isla (p101), or boisterous and fun, as at Pink Taco (p124). Due to open in 2007, Diablo's looks set to be in the latter category; its owners promising it will be like 'spring break year-round'. Expect spicy food, strong drinks and regular DJ sets.

Arts & leisure

Lance Burton

1-877 386 8224/730 7160/www.lance burton.com. **Shows** 7pm, 10pm Tue, Sat; 7pm Wed-Fri. **Map** p49 B1 **47**

Blessed with all the personal dynamism of a ventriloquist's dummy – his interaction with the audience is still mesmerically awkward, despite the fact that he's been performing professionally for upwards of two decades – Burton relies purely on his magic to keep the audience wrapped around his finger. And he just about manages it too, pulling doves from napkins, coins from ears and geese – geese! – from all over the place. One for all the family.

New York New York

3790 Las Vegas Boulevard South, at W Tropicana Avenue (reservations 1-866 815 4365/front desk & casino 740 6969/www.nynyhotelcasino.com). Bus Deuce, 201. **Map** p49 B2.

So good they named it twice? Well, yes, as it goes. The most audacious, preposterous example of hotel theming in Las Vegas – and, for that matter, perhaps even the world – remains a thrilling success more than a decade after it welcomed its first guests. Built at a cost of $460 million, it's been called the largest piece of pop art in the world.

A mini-New York Harbor, complete with tugboats, a scaled-down Brooklyn Bridge and a giant Statue of Liberty, looms over the Tropicana/Strip intersection. Above it, the resort's skyline includes a dozen of the Big Apple's most famous landmarks, among them the Empire State Building, the Chrysler Building and the New Yorker Hotel but not the World Trade Center; the hotel was themed after 1950s New York, long before the twin towers were built. Inside, along with representations of Times Square, Central Park, Greenwich Village and Wall Street, you'll find every New York cliché in the book: a Broadway subway station, graffitied mailboxes, steam rising from manhole covers… It sounds silly, but it's tremendous fun, and seems to inspire visitors to act as if they were out on the East Coast: it's got energy like no other casino floor in town.

The resort's greatest trick, one that New York City has yet to achieve, is to balance the needs of adult visitors with those of its younger guests. Grown-ups will enjoy the nightlife here, not to mention Cirque du Soleil's adult-oriented show *Zumanity*, but there's plenty for the young 'uns. The Coney Island Emporium is nirvana for kids and wanna-be-kids-again, a mix of old-fashioned midway games, high-tech interactive videos and virtual-reality rollercoasters. The hotel's real roller-coaster, the Manhattan Express, twists, turns and rolls around the property. The pool area and spa are, alas, real letdowns: a replica of the famousNew York City Vertical Club would have been fitting. Or, perhaps even, the Central Park Reservoir.

The capacious casino is modelled on Central Park, without the muggers but with twice the crowds. Minimums for blackjack (practically all six-deck shoes) and craps are $10; it's $5 for roulette. The range of slots is one of the best on the Strip. Dim sum hors-d'oeuvres are served in the Asian-styled Dragon Pit, with saké, plum wine, Asian beer and teas.

Sights & museums

Coney Island Emporium
740 6414. **Open** 9am-midnight Mon-Thur, Sun; 9am-1am Fri, Sat. **Admission** free. **Map** p49 B2 ④⑨
This arcade and family amusement centre attempts to recreate the atmosphere of the original Coney Island with more than 200 video and midway games, Bumper Cabs, a prize counter and lots of sticky candyfloss (but, sadly, no freak show).

Manhattan Express
740 6969. **Open** 11am-11pm Mon-Thur, Sun; 10am-midnight Fri, Sat. **Tickets** $12.50. Re-rides $6. All-day Scream Pass $25. **Map** p49 B2 ④⑨
Gotham never saw anything like it: a rollercoaster soaring around skyscrapers and old Lady Liberty. The Express twists, loops and dives at breakneck speeds, and features the first ever 'heartline roll', which creates the sensation a pilot feels when going through a barrel roll in an aeroplane. Try hard not to look too green and put on a smile in the last section: this is where the photographs are taken.

Eating & drinking

America
740 6451. **Open** 24hrs daily. **$$**. **Diner**. Map p49 B2 ⑤⓪
Like the casino in which it's housed, America is terrific fun. In both, a simple concept is executed with wonderfully playful enthusiasm. The all-purpose menu offers innumerable dishes from across the country, many of them inspired by a particular corner of the US: chicken quesadillas by way of Albuquerque, for example, or Philadelphia cheese steaks. It's not really about the authenticity, mind; this is just good, solid cooking served with an exclamation mark, a wide smile and a heartfelt 'have a nice day!'

New York New York p65

Centrifuge p59

Bar at Times Square

236 0374. **Open** 10am-2am Mon-Wed; 10am-3am Thur, Sun; 10am-4am Fri, Sat. **$$**. **Bar**. **Map** p49 B2 🟥

Bellowing voices pour from this packed bar, where duelling pianos provide the upbeat entertainment. Sure, there's beer behind the emotion, but there's also a lot of genuine fun being had. The musicians can and will play anything if you've got the money to tip 'em. The best of the city's piano bars.

Big Apple Bar

740 6969. **Open** 24hrs daily. **$$**. **Bar**. **Map** p49 B2 🟥

Reminiscent of a 1940s supper club, this art deco-esque lounge in New York New York features a heady drinks menu and suitably reminiscent live music nightly from 8pm to 3am. If you can make it here, you'll make it – bam! bam! – anywhere.

ESPN Zone

933 3776/www.espnzone.com/lasvegas. **Open** 11am-11pm Mon-Thur, Sun; 11am-midnight Fri, Sat. **$$**.
Bar/American. **Map** p49 B2 🟥

Each table at this restaurant/bar/funitorium has its own TV, and that's in addition to the two 16ft monitors, 12 flat screens and various headline

tickers letting drinkers know what they've missed. The smell of testosterone is almost overwhelming.

Nightlife

Coyote Ugly

740 6969/www.coyoteuglysaloon. com/vegas. **Open** 6pm-4am daily. **Map** p49 B2 🟥

Belly-baring servers stomp to choreographed dances in this saloon, based on the New York bar that was the subject of a ghastly movie. The schtick goes that the girls invite boozed-up revellers to join them up on the bar, while simultaneously hurling insults at the crowd below. To add injury to insults, there's nowhere to sit, and it takes a lot of expensive liquor to make you forget the $10 cover charge (after 9pm).

Zumanity

1-866 606 7111/740 6815/ www.zumanity.com. **Shows** 7.30pm, 10.30pm Wed-Sun. No under-18s.
Map p49 B2 🟥

The idea of asking Cirque du Soleil to compile its own adult revue was an unexpected one. In parts, it pulls it off, most notably the more comic stretches and the two-women-in-a-fishtank section towards the start of the show. A little too often it seems unsure whether it's better off trying to dazzle or arouse the audience, but those on the love seats (or, as the box office coyly calls them, 'duo sofas') seem to go upstairs happy enough.

Tropicana

3801 Las Vegas Boulevard South, at E Tropicana Avenue (reservations 1-888 826 8767/front desk & casino 739 2222/www.tropicanalv.com). Bus Deuce, 201. **Map** p49 B2.

The Tropicana was at the heart of the biggest bidding war in casino history when, in 2006, Columbia Sussex (owner of various Westin, Sheraton and Marriott hotels) paid $2.75 billion for the rights to redevelop the 50-year-old 'Tiffany of the Strip'. The Polynesian-themed hotel will soon undergo a multi-million-dollar, property-wide expansion, transforming it into the largest casino-resort in the city. Until then, the Trop is worth a look if you want a nice pool – between the hotel's two towers lie 5 acres of tropical landscaping with pools, lagoons, waterfalls and swim-up blackjack tables – without paying too much for it.

The swim-up blackjack bar is the Tropicana's one unique gaming pull. Otherwise, there's the usual variety of games in the casino, with a bit less video poker than other places and some of the slots showing their age. The casino is on the smallish side, and cramped, with a tiny, dingy sports book at the bottom of a stairway at the back, hidden as if the hotel were embarrassed by it. Which they should be.

Sights & museums

Bodies

NEW **Open** 10am-11pm daily (last entry 10pm). **Admission** $26. **Map** p49 B2 ●

In the unlikely event that you've ever fancied dropping the best part of $30 in order to peek underneath the skin

Do you?

Nevada started to become a popular wedding destination after California passed its infamous 'Gin Law' in 1912. The ruling required couples to wait for three days before receiving their licence to wed, in order to discourage intoxicated lovers from slurring 'I do' while under the influence. Nevada, naturally, had no problem with such behaviour. By the 1950s, the wedding industry had really taken off; these days, some 120,000 marriage licences are issued in Las Vegas each year.

A few vintage chapels remain in the city, among them the **Little Church of the West** at the south end of the Strip (4617 Las Vegas Boulevard South, 1-800 821 2452, www.littlechurchof thewest.com). Open since 1942 and designed to replicate an Old West mining church, it's one of the city's most famous 'quickie' venues and does the Vegas wedding factory job better than most, herding fiancés in and newly-weds out without making them feel in the least bit rushed.

Along with these stand-alone churches are the chapels and 'salons' inside the major Strip hotel-casinos. These swanky set-ups offer the elaborate wedding of your dreams, be it in a fairytale castle or the *Starship Enterprise* – but you'll pay handsomely for the privilege.

Take the 'Elegant Affair' package at **Wynn Las Vegas** (p113), which includes two nights in a luxury villa, dinner at Alex, tickets to *Le Rêve*, a 'couples massage', and much more, for a bargain $19,350.

of dead strangers, this is the show for you. Having donated their remains to medical science, around 20 altruistic souls have been dissected, preserved and put on display for the enlightenment and edification of visitors to the Trop. All things considered, the merchandise is in surprisingly good taste.

Titanic: the Exhibition

NEW **Open** 10am-11pm daily (last entry 10pm). **Admission** $22. **Map** p49 B2 ⑤⑦

More than 3,000 bits and pieces recovered from the mother of all seafaring disasters are now on permanent display at the Tropicana in this diverting but hauntingly insightful exhibition. Visitors are also given the chance to experience a life-like simulation of the kind of freezing weather conditions experienced by the poor unfortunates on the fateful night that the ship sank.

Eating & drinking

Mizuno's, a Japanese-style *teppan* room and steakhouse where staff cook the food (expect steaks, Gulf shrimp and Australian lobster among other delights from their meat- and fish-based menu) right infront of diners at their tables, is as fun as it sounds, and is one of the Tropicana's best eateries. The colossal shrimp cocktail and prime rib at Legends Steak & Seafood are a throwback to the classic Vegas steakhouse. Other choices include Tuscany for pizza and pasta, and the obligatory, all-you-can-eat Island Buffet.

Nightlife

Comedy Stop

1-800 829-9034/739 2714/www. comedystop.com. **Shows** 8pm, 10.30pm daily. **Map** p49 B2 ⑤⑧

This 300-capacity fixture on the Las Vegas comedy circuit features 'three comics and a mic' in two separate shows every night of the week. Performers tend to be in residence for a week at a time, and there's surprisingly little repetition of acts.

Arts & leisure

Folies Bergere

1-800 829 9034/739 2411. **Shows** 7.30pm, 10pm Mon, Wed, Thur, Sat; 8.30pm Tue, Fri. No under-16s for late show. **Map** p49 B2 ⑤⑨

This rather spartan feathers-and-sequins show, a by-the-decades homage to women's attitudes and fashions through the ages (including, of course, the obligatory can-can), opened in 1959 and is looking its age. But it's still packed with gorgeous showgirls – in bikinis for the early show from Monday to Thursday, topless for the late show and all weekend – and merits investigation simply for its status as one of the last remaining shows of its type in Vegas.

Other venues

Sights & museums

GameWorks

Showcase Mall, 3785 Las Vegas Boulevard South, between E Tropicana & E Harmon Avenues (432 4263/ www.gameworks.com). **Bus** Deuce, 201. **Open** 10am-midnight Mon-Thur, Sun; 10am-1am Fri, Sat. **Admission** free. **Map** p49 B2 ⑥⓪

If you'd rather shove your quarters into a video game than a slot machine, then this place is for you. This huge madhouse is a great place in which to try out the latest games on the market: you can save money if you pay by the hour, though none of it is cheap. There are more than 250 games, plus a billiards lounge, two restaurants, a coffee bar and a 75ft (23m) indoor climbing wall.

M&M's World

Showcase Mall, 3785 Las Vegas Boulevard South, between E Tropicana & E Harmon Avenues (736 7611/www. m-ms.com). **Bus** Deuce, 201. **Open** 9am-11pm Mon-Thur, Sun; 9am-midnight Fri, Sat. **Admission** free. **Map** p49 B2 ⑥①

This is a four-level chocolate-lover's paradise. Check out M&M Academy,

Empire Ballroom

an interactive entertainment attraction showing visitors how these chocolate candies earn their trademark. The attraction includes a 3D movie, and 'graduates' get a diploma. Yes, it's a bit overmarketed. But at least it's free.

Nightlife

Empire Ballroom

NEW *3785 Las Vegas Boulevard South, between E Tropicana & E Harmon Avenues (737 7376/www. empireballroom.com). Bus Deuce.* **Open** hrs vary. **Map** p49 B2 ⑥²
Formerly the home of pioneering dance den Club Utopia, this big space (with a great patio) remains the only independent nightclub on the Strip. The club's independent-spirited tradition continues with after-hours promotion Late Night Empire (from 3am, Thur-Sat nights), which delivers the kind of house music that's rarely heard in Vegas. It also serves as a part-time music venue, hosting acts as varied as local boys the Killers and Britain's Lady Sovereign.

Fashionistas

Empire Ballroom, 3785 Las Vegas Boulevard South, between E Tropicana & E Harmon Avenues (836 0833/ *www.fashionistastheshow.com). Bus Deuce.* **Shows** 9pm Mon, Tue, Thur-Sun. Over-21s only. **Map** p49 B2 ⑥³
Fashionistas is an adult revue for the artsy set. Under the supervision of adult-film magnate John 'Buttman' Stagliano, envelope-pushing costumes, visceral multimedia imagery and music by the likes of Tool meld even more than the show's own notions of gender identity in this story involving a love triangle, high fashion and a hearty helping of S&M.

Arts & leisure

UA Showcase 8

Showcase Mall, 3785 Las Vegas Boulevard South, at W Tropicana Avenue (221 2283/www.regmovies. com). Bus Deuce, 201. **Map** p49 B2 ⑥⁴
You won't find any art house or foreign language films here, but you can catch the latest blockbuster at the only movie theatre on the Strip. Just don't expect lots of locals, any great luxury or even cutting-edge cinema technology at this ageing cineplex just north of the MGM Grand. Parking in the Showcase garage is free with validation; if, that is, you can get past the parking lot that is Las Vegas Boulevard.

Bellagio Fountains p75

Mid Strip

LAS VEGAS BY AREA

The stretch of the Strip around the intersection of Flamingo Road and Las Vegas Boulevard South is the heart of 21st-century Las Vegas. The array of options for entertainment, dining, drinking and dancing range from the high-end **Bellagio** and **Venetian** resorts to some more basic (and considerably cheaper) hotels nearby. From retail therapy at Caesars' **Forum Shops** to the **Secret Garden & Dolphin Habitat** at the Mirage, you'll be spoiled for choice.

Bally's

3645 Las Vegas Boulevard South, at E Flamingo Road (reservations 1-877 603 4390/front desk & casino 967 4111/www.harrahs.com). Bus Deuce, 202. **Map** p73 B4.

A classic, Dan Tanna-esque *Vega$* experience can still be had at the grande dame of the Strip's Famous Four Corners. Though now owned by Harrah's, Bally's has stayed true to its Hollywood roots, albeit probably because management simply hasn't got around to renovating yet. The garish 8 miles of ostentatious looping neon, part of a multi-million-dollar 'grand entry' that delivers tourists to the hotel's elegant porte cochère, is pretty ugly, but Bally's retains its classic appeal inside. Amenities include an oversized heated pool with private cabanas; eight floodlit tennis courts next to a pro shop where you can sign up for lessons (it's one of the last hotels on the Strip with tennis courts); a full-service health club; and access to the Caesars-owned Cascata golf course. The Bally Avenue Shoppes house one-off boutiques.

The casino is a large, rectangular space, an inviting atmosphere of soft lighting and art deco accents with 65

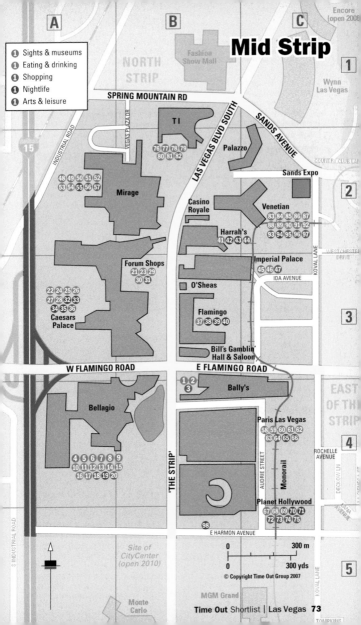

Mid Strip

A | B | C

Sights & museums
Eating & drinking
Shopping
Nightlife
Arts & leisure

Encore (open 2008)

1

NORTH STRIP

Fashion Show Mall

Wynn Las Vegas

SPRING MOUNTAIN RD

TI

76 77 78 79
80 81 82

Palazzo

SANDS AVENUE

COUNTRY CLUB LAN

VEGAS PLAZA DR

INDUSTRIAL ROAD

15

48 49 50 51 52
53 54 55 56 57

Mirage

Casino Royale

Sands Expo

2

LAS VEGAS BLVD SOUTH

Venetian

83 84 85 86 87
88 89 90 91 92
93 94 95 96 97

KOVAL LANE

WESTCHESTER DRIVE

Harrah's
41 42 43 44

Forum Shops
21 23 29
30 31

Imperial Palace
45 46 47

IDA AVENUE

22 24 25 26
27 28 32 33
34 35 36

Caesars Palace

O'Sheas

Flamingo
37 38 39 40

3

Bill's Gamblin'
Hall & Saloon

W FLAMINGO ROAD

E FLAMINGO ROAD

EAST OF THE STRIP

1 2
3

Bally's

Bellagio

'THE STRIP'

Paris Las Vegas
58 59 60 61 62
63 64 65 66

ROCHELLE AVENUE

AUDRIE STREET

Monorail

4

4 5 6 7 8 9
10 11 12 13 14 15
16 17 18 19 20

DESKUR LN

Planet Hollywood
67 68 69 70 71
72 73 74 75

98

E HARMON AVENUE

0   300 m
0   300 yds

© Copyright Time Out Group 2007

S INDUSTRIAL ROAD

Site of CityCenter (open 2010)

Monte Carlo

MGM GRAND

5

table games and 2,100 slot machines. Among them are 'champagne' $1,000 slots, with a top payout of a cool mil. Not surprisingly, you'll find all the latest creations from machine-maker Bally, including laserdisc versions of craps, roulette and blackjack; all are excellent practice tools before heading to the actual tables. The buy-ins at the tables start at $10 with an occasional $5 single-deck 6:5 21 game, though many players wager far more than the minimum. The video poker is fairly pitiful, but the sports book, on the lower level, is as classy and technically advanced as those at the Bellagio and the Hilton, and it's only crowded on big-game days.

Eating & drinking

Big Kitchen Buffet/ Sterling Brunch

Buffets *Big Kitchen Buffet* Brunch 7am-4pm daily. Dinner 4-10pm daily. *Sterling Brunch* 9.30am-2.30pm Sun. **$$/$$$ Buffet**. Map p73 B4 **❶**

The daily Big Kitchen Buffet at Bally's is one of the town's best. However, Sunday's swanky Sterling Brunch, which is held in a separate space, really takes the biscuit …and the caviar, the lobster, the beef tenderloin and the champagne cocktail. Skip church and indulge yourself.

Indigo Lounge

Open 3pm-3am Mon-Thur, Sun; 3pm-4am Fri, Sat. **$$. Lounge**. Map p73 B4 **❷**

Right next to the Bally's/Paris Las Vegas walkway, this casual, enjoyable lounge features a scattering of pop, dance, Motown and R&B acts.

Arts & leisure

Jubilee!

Shows 7.30pm, 10.30pm Mon-Thur, Sat, Sun. No under-18s. Map p73 B4 **❸**

Jubilee!'s staging of the sinking of the *Titanic* and Samson's destruction of the Philistines in the temple are beyond lame. But the production

numbers in this long-running spectacle, which feature endless parades of beauties wearing nothing more than outlandishly coloured feathers, headdresses and rhinestones, make it a one-of-a-kind show.

Bellagio

3600 Las Vegas Boulevard South, at W Flamingo Road (reservations 1-888 987 6667/front desk & casino 693 7111/www.bellagio.com). Bus Deuce, 202. Map p73 B4.

Since the Spa Tower opened at the Bellagio in 2005, the property seems to have paused for a breather. Sure, it's added the Adam Tihany-designed Club Prive, a high-limit gambling lounge that spotlights unbelievably rare spirits and world-class cigars. Granted, it's redone the poker room, and all the suites in the original tower will start getting a makeover by the end of 2007. And yes, there are more Picassos coming to the fine art gallery in 2008. Otherwise, though, why tamper with a winning formula?

The Bellagio continues to evoke a supersized, all-American Italian villa, complete with an 8-acre lake fronting the Strip, a lush garden conservatory that changes with the holidays and an elegant pool area that's been reimagined as a formal Italian garden. And it remains the archetypal playground for the well-heeled adult, with high-minded, grown-up entertainment in the form of posh restaurants, a tiny promenade of expensive boutiques, and Cirque du Soleil's most sophisticated show, *O*. The expanded spa in the Spa Tower features a salon, a fitness centre and even a one-chair barbershop; it's a lavish perk available only to guests, as is access to the renowned Shadow Creek golf course.

But by far the most eye-catching attraction at the Bellagio is the signature jumping fountain, which, in the afternoons and evenings, shoots water into the air to a variety of different soundtracks. The sidewalk on the Strip in front of the hotel offers superb views of the spectacle, as do the Bellagio's many lakefront dining and drinking options.

The Bellagio's casino draws in the big celebrity players such as Ben Affleck and Drew Barrymore, but at times its ostentatious luxury can feel like it's verging on vulgar: the upholstery, carpets, striped canopies and garish trimmings are a clash of colours and patterns. However, it's a great casino, though as you might expect, table limits are higher than at most Strip properties: minimums are often $25-$50 and it's difficult to find even $10 blackjack. The race and sports book is one of the most comfortable in town, and the poker room has replaced Binion's as the mecca for pros, sharks and big-time players.

Sights & museums

Bellagio Fountains

Shows 3pm-midnight Mon-Fri (every 30mins 3-8pm; every 15mins 8pm-midnight); noon-midnight Sat, Sun (every 30mins noon-8pm; every 15mins 8pm-midnight). **Admission** free. **Map** p73 B4 ❹

The Bellagio's lake throws up entrancing fountain displays choreographed to music from Pavarotti to Sinatra (and, less appealingly, Lee Greenwood). The 1,200 water cannons, arranged in lines and circles, shoot water that dances and sways to the music, reaching as high as 240ft (73m). The best seats are in the Bellagio restaurants, but you get a good view from the pavements out front, and from the top of the Eiffel Tower at Paris Las Vegas.

Bellagio Gallery of Fine Art

693 7871/www.bgfa.biz. **Open** 10am-6pm Mon-Thur, Sun; 10am-9pm Fri, Sat. **Admission** $15; $12 reductions. **Map** p73 B4 ❺

The longest-standing gallery on the Strip stages a strong selection of shows; they're here on a temporary basis, but in residence for a year apiece. Following a wildly popular and surprisingly meaty

Sensi p78

Monet exhibit leased directly from the Museum of Fine Arts, Boston, another Impressionism show and an exhibition of Ansel Adams photographs, the gallery launched a show devoted to Picasso's ceramics, due to run until early 2008.

Eating & drinking

Buffet at Bellagio

Buffets *Breakfast* 8-10.30am Mon-Fri. *Brunch* 8am-3.30pm Sat, Sun. *Lunch* 11am-3.30pm daily. *Dinner* 4-10pm Mon-Thur, Sun; 4-11pm Fri, Sat. **$$. Buffet**. Map p73 B4 ⑥

The Buffet at Bellagio is much like the rest of the hotel: smart yet approachable, stylish yet undemonstrative, expensive yet probably just about worth it. Usual buffet fare gets up graded with extras such as venison, steamed clams and crab legs.

Caramel

693 8300/www.caramelbar.com. **Open** 5pm-4am daily. **$$$. Lounge**. Map p73 B4 ⑦

With opaque marble tables, one-way windows on to the casino floor and a sophisticated, modern atmosphere, Caramel seems less like a lounge than a private club. And that, naturally, comes at a price: $15 speciality martinis are the norm. As the night wears on and the crowds thicken, the swanky couches are reserved for parties willing to pony up about $300 or more for bottle service.

Le Cirque

693 7223. **Open** 5.30-10pm daily. **$$$$. French**. Map p73 B4 ⑧

This Vegas version of the New York institution is overseen by Mario Maccioni, who grew up playing and working in his father Sirio's original. Chefs come and go at Le Cirque; some of the best in the world have passed through the kitchens of its various locations. But the unparalleled French cuisine and world-class service never change, and this incarnation has one attribute that none of the three New York locations could ever boast: views of the Bellagio's elegant Lake Como.

Fix

NEW *693 8400/www.fixlasvegas.com.* **Open** 5pm-midnight Mon-Thur, Sun; 5pm-2am Fri, Sat. **$$$. American/Bar**. Map p73 B4 ⑨

This upscale bar and restaurant is known for its tasty appetisers and tantalising beverages, striking a careful balance between sleekness and comfort in both decor and menu.

Fix aims to bring you the 'scene and the cuisine': rather than sequestering its cast of primped diners, it opens its classy, undulating interior design to the casino so everyone can smell the wood-fired surf 'n' turf. We suggest a lounge seat, a pomegranate martini, and salmon and caviar forks.

Fontana Bar

1-800 963 9634/693 7722. **Open** 5pm-1am Mon-Thur, Sun; 5pm-2am Fri, Sat. **$$. Lounge**. Map p73 B4 ⑩

The sophistication to which this lounge aspires is sometimes compromised by the function-band fluff who currently perform in it. Still, the views are great and the drinks are good; if the noise is too ghastly, adjourn to the balcony to watch the fountains.

Michael Mina

693 7223/www.michaelmina.net. **Open** 5.30-10pm daily. **$$$. Seafood**. Map p73 B4 ⑪

Michael Mina's flagship restaurant in Las Vegas may have changed its name (it was formerly called Aqua), but it still delivers what are, next to Mina's SeaBlue restaurant (p63), the best seafood dishes anywhere on the Strip. His caviar parfait is legendary, but the ever-changing menu also features such deep-sea delights as savoury black mussel soufflé and a miso-glazed Chilean sea bass.

Noodles

Open 11am-2am Mon-Thur; 11am-3am Fri-Sun. **$$$. Pan-Asian**. Map p73 B4 ⑫

Once a gem showcasing the subtle, modern elegance of Tony Chi's pan-Asian dishes, Noodles has somewhat declined in recent years. Still, you'll

Small is beautiful

Vegas welcomes a new wave of chic boutiques.

Fruition

If you're a label hound who worships at the altar of Gucci, Prada, Louis Vuitton et al, then you're in the right city. There's as high a concentration of designer emporia on the Strip as there is on Fifth Avenue or Bond Street. However, the city's shopping scene has recently begun to develop its own identity, with smaller boutiques that offer a more individual range of clothes.

Take, for example, **Scoop** and **Intermix**, both in the Forum Shops (p82). They've joined the burgeoning clique of runway-savvy, one-off boutiques, where the stock of unique pieces incorporates trends from both coasts to create a look that is pure Vegas.

The grande dame of the group, Meital Grantz's **Talulah G**, has a boutique inside the Fashion Show Mall (p120). From this popular store, Grantz sells an eclectic range of designer denim (Hudson, Ksubi), ready-to-wear clothing (Yigal Azrouel, Manoush) and playful sportswear (La Rok). Also

at the Fashion Show Mall is Todd Burden's **Still**, offering jetsetters (and aspiring jetsetters) a wide selection of trendy apparel perfect for the swanky Vegas clubbing scene. Lines here include Rich & Skinny and Hysteric Glamour.

Rather than compete with the big names in the city centre, some clever store-owners have chosen to set up shop closer to the locals. The nearest to the Strip is **Fruition** (near UNLV, at 4139 S Maryland Parkway, 796 4139), an urban boutique that specialises in revivalist fashions from the late 1980s and early '90s.

Other stores sit further out, but they're definitely worth the cab fare. At the District mall in Green Valley Ranch is **Chelsea Boutique** (120 S Green Valley Parkway, 270 7924), with selections of Milly dresses and Voom silk kimonos. And out west is Mariah Lewis's hippie-chic **Indra Grae** (6085 S Fort Apache Road, 636 9700), which stocks baubles from Brazil, and under-things from Barcelona.

enjoy the urban diner feel, the late hours, and the selection of dim sum (lunch), Hong Kong barbecue and, of course, the hot and chilled noodle dishes from across Asia. Reliable, at the very least.

Olives

693 8181/www.toddenglish.com.
Open 11am-2.30pm, 5-10.30pm Mon-Thur; 11am-10.30pm Fri-Sun. **$$.**
American. Map p73 B4 ⑬
A revamp by Jeffrey Beers has breathed new life into Todd English's 'casual' Las Vegas establishment overlooking the Bellagio's lake. Boston-based English (the original Olives is in Charlestown, MA) keeps his 'interpretive Mediterranean' cuisine alive and well with such appetising innovations as white clam pizza and butternut squash tortellini.

Pâtisserie Jean-Philippe

693 8788. **Open** 7am-11pm Mon-Thur, Sun; 7am-midnight Fri, Sat. **$$.** **Pâtisserie**. Map p73 B4 ⑭
The cascading chocolate fountain stops passers-by in their tracks, but it's pastry chef Jean-Philippe Maury's biscotti, truffles, macaroons, jellies and jams that lure them inside. This European-style pâtisserie sells an impressive range of sweet and savoury luxuries for people on the go (limited seating is available), plus exotic teas and coffees. Don't miss the Nutella brioche filled with caramelised hazelnuts.

Picasso

693 8105. **Open** 6-9.30pm Mon, Wed-Sun. **$$$.** **French**. Map p73 B4 ⑮
When your dining room is lined with $20 million worth of Picasso paintings, you have to work pretty hard to make an impression. No matter: Julian Serrano usually manages it. Unlike a lot of celebrity chefs with high-profile restaurants in Vegas, Serrano actually cooks at Picasso, building two crisp, daisy-fresh and wonderfully uncomplicated French-slanted menus nightly. Service is a treat and the wine list is stellar.

Prime

693 7223. **Open** 5-10pm daily. **$$$.**
Steakhouse. Map p73 B4 ⑯
Prime indeed. In fact, one could go further: first class, superior and pre-eminent pretty much sum up Jean-Georges Vongerichten's steakhouse, where the striking setting comes with a perfect view of the Bellagio's fountains. There's magic on the plate, too: steaks are the highlights, but don't overlook the free-range chicken, seared ahi tuna, wood-grilled veal chop and a selection of 11 sauces and seven mustards.

Sensi

693 7223. **Open** 11am-2.30pm, 5-10pm daily. **$$$.** **Fusion**. Map p73 B4 ⑰
Japanese firm Super Potato designed this culinary theatre to complement Martin Heierling's world cuisine, a combination of Italian and Asian influences, grilled dishes and seafood classics. Four glass-enclosed kitchens in the middle of the room provide an interactive stage: watch curries plunge into a red-hot tandoori oven on the Asian stage; focaccias with vacherin cheese and black truffles slipped into a wood-fire oven in the Italian corner; and blue point oysters shucked in the raw section.

Shopping

Via Bellagio

Open 10am-midnight daily.
Map p73 B4 ⑬
In line with its upmarket image, the Bellagio's small mall contains ten of the smartest designer names this side of Wynn Las Vegas. Long standing tenants such as Tiffany & Co, Prada, Gucci, Chanel, Dior, Giorgio Armani and Hermès have been joined of late by the likes of Fendi and Bottega Veneta. For high-minded shoppers, glass sculptor Dale Chihuly's unique artworks can be found in Chihuly Store. If your wallet can't cope, at least pop in to enjoy the location: the venue is a shrine to materialism, with daylight streaming through the vaulted glass ceilings on to opulent walkways and tidy storefronts. The food is a cut

Caesars Palace

above regular mall fodder too: try Olives (left), a Mediterranean bistro overlooking the lake.

Nightlife

Light

693 8303/www.lightlv.com.
Open 10.30pm-4am Thur-Sun.
Map p73 B4 ⑲

Light set the pace for the modern Las Vegas nightclub, introducing bottle service, exclusive door policies and a return to upscale dress codes. Though it has dumbed down a little in both its music (ubiquitous hip hop, bad rock remixes and so on) and its dress code, some things never change: groups of men larger than six are not allowed, VIP booths are scarce and the dancefloor is packed. But hey, it's all part of the experience.

Arts & leisure

O

1-888 488 7111/796 9999. **Shows**
7.30pm, 10.30pm Wed-Sun. No under-5s. **Map** p73 B4 ⑳

It's been surpassed in the extravagance stakes by *Kà* (p64), but this is still

the best Cirque du Soleil production in town, and maybe the best show on the Strip. *O* – a pun on *eau*, French for water – is a spectacle of Fellini-esque tableaux coupled with acrobatic feats performed by 70-plus swimmers, divers, aerialists, contortionists and clowns in, on, above and around a pool/stage containing 1.5 million gallons of water. None of which goes any way towards describing just how beautiful it all is.

Caesars Palace

3570 Las Vegas Boulevard South, at W Flamingo Road (reservations 1-866 277 5938/front desk & casino 731 7110/www.harrahs.com). Bus Deuce, 202. **Map** p73 B3.

When it was announced in 2005 that the powerful Harrah's group was set to take over Caesars Palace, many Vegas observers feared that the chain would denude the place of all its sass and turn it into Just Another Strip Resort. It hasn't happened yet. While the Bellagio is perhaps the epitome of new Vegas luxury, Caesars remains an icon of classic Sin City decadence,

LAS VEGAS BY AREA

Forum Shops p82

a meld of affluence, kitsch and glamour that continues to be a compelling sight more than four decades after its 1966 opening.

The resort remains a monument of sorts to ancient Greece and Rome, with miles of gold decor, marble columns, arches and colonnades, manicured gardens and copies of Greek and Roman statuary. These days, though, it's more about elegance than the kind of camp instilled in it by legendary founder Jay Sarno, at least in theory.

It's an enormous place, and it's about to get bigger. An additional tower is planned, bringing the total room count to almost 4,500. But the real key to Caesars' continuing allure is the 4.5-acre Garden of the Gods pool area, with its four mosaic pools, marble statuary, fountains and mini-throne lifeguard stands. A section of it, by the Venus pool, is set aside for topless sunbathing. While the pool draws crowds in summer, the ever-expanding Forum Shops pulls visitors year-round. Fashioned, in true Vegas style, after an ancient Roman streetscape, the mall contains an unmatched range of shops, many of them not found anywhere else in the city. Other selling points include the luxurious Qua Baths & Spa and the Venus salon; guests also get access to Cascata, the resort's golf course in Boulder City.

Few casinos offer the limits or the atmosphere of Caesars; when there's a big fight in town, limits on the main floor can go through the roof. The sports book is one of the liveliest spots to watch the action, and accepts some of the biggest bets. You get a good view of the baccarat pit, an intimate nook where huge wagers are common. And for the boldest of slot players, the $500 machine, with a $1-million jackpot, uses gold-plated tokens. (Caveat: it pays a winning spin of only two $500 coins; for every other payback, the machine locks and an attendant hand-pays, for tax paperwork purposes.) The high-limit slots are in the Palace

Casino near the main entrance; black-jack pits and slots in the Forum Casino offer slightly lower limits. There's also a Pussycat Dolls themed area.

Eating & drinking

Boa Steakhouse

NEW *Forum Shops (733 7373/ www.boasteak.com).* **Open** noon-10pm Mon-Thur; noon-11.30pm Fri, Sat; noon-10pm Sun. $$$. **Steakhouse**. Map p73 B3 ㉑

The austere, clinical design is is contemporary and a long way from the gentlemen's club standard fittings that decorate more traditional steakhouses, but then the menu at Boa (an LA import) goes beyond surf 'n' turf cliché. The classics are rendered well here, though there's plenty of fun to be had on a list of appetisers that might include such novelties as truffle nachos and goat's cheese baklava. Prices are high.

Bradley Ogden

1-877 346 4642. **Open** 5-11pm daily. $$$$. **American**. Map p73 B3 ㉒

Ogden has cultivated relationships with regional suppliers and boutique growers across the US, with everything from Utah salt to Oregon seafood purchased direct from specialist providers. The result is an American cuisine that doesn't come cheap, but if melt-in-the-mouth rack of Colorado lamb or slow-roasted Muscovy duck with purple artichokes and rhubarb ring your bell, consider this an essential stop. The best bit? Ogden sticks around to cook it.

Joe's Seafood, Prime Steak & Stone Crab

Forum Shops (792 9222/www.icon. com/joes). **Open** 11.30am-10pm Mon-Thur, Sun; 11.30am-11pm Fri, Sat. $$$. **American**. Map p73 B3 ㉓

When it opened a few years back, Joe's (affiliated with the legendary Miami restaurant) impressed many with its fresh-daily seafood, bone-in steaks and gracious service. Since then, more pricey seafood and steak joints of

higher pedigree have elevated local expectation. Still, Joe's represents rare value, and is one of the gems of the Forum Shops expansion.

Mesa Grill

NEW *1-877 346 4642/www.mesagrill. com.* **Open** 11am-3pm, 5-11pm Mon-Fri; 10.30am-3pm, 5-11pm Sat, Sun. $$$. **American**. Map p73 B3 ㉔

Rather like Bobby Flay, the celebrity chef behind this popular restaurant, the Mesa Grill is a little on the brash side. The room itself is dazzling in all the best ways, a flourish-packed riot of colour and energy. But the nuevo-American food, like Flay, could do with a little more subtlety. The likes of pork tenderloin with sweet potato tamale and crushed pecan butter are fine, but they read better than they sound and don't justify their high price tags.

Rao's

NEW *1-877 346 4642.* **Open** 11am-3pm, 5-11pm daily. $$$. **Italian**. Map p73 B3 ㉕

The original Rao's has been operating in New York for a century, and is known as one of the toughest reservations in the Big Apple. The Caesars spinoff is a lot easier to access, though you'll still need to book ahead. And the food is worth the wait, classic Italian recipes that have been fine-tuned by the same family over years. The house speciality is lemon chicken, but everything on the menu is sure to please.

Restaurant Guy Savoy

NEW *1-877 346 4642.* **Open** 5-11pm Wed-Sun. $$$$. **French**. Map p73 B3 ㉖

Managed by Guy's son Franck Savoy, with Adam Sobel presiding over the kitchen, this is among the most expensive dining rooms in Vegas. It's worth every penny, providing a level of culinary sophistication rarely glimpsed here. Highlights include artichoke and black truffle soup served with toasted mushroom brioche, and a guinea hen cooked inside a pig's bladder to preserve the moisture. If you have the cash, try the ten-course *menu prestige.*

Shadow Bar

731 7110. **Open** 4pm-2am Mon-Thur; 2pm-3am Fri, Sat; 2pm-2am Sun. $$$. **Lounge**. **Map** p73 B3 ㉗

Question: how do you get naked women to shake, writhe and strut their stuff without showing any flesh? Answer: shadow play. This saucy spot continues Las Vegas's hesitating shimmy towards bringing strip clubs to the Strip without having any stripping. The ladies concerned, silhouetted on screens, play up what comes naturally (or, possibly, surgically), while expensive drinks add a haughty note. The dress code is smart-casual.

Spago

Forum Shops (369 6300/ www.wolfgangpuck.com). **Open** *Café* 11am-11pm Mon-Thur, Sun; 11am-midnight Fri, Sat. *Restaurant* 5.30-10pm daily. $$$. **American**. **Map** p73 B3 ㉘

This is the eatery that reinvented the Vegas dining scene in 1992; Spago has managed to stay smart with the tourists and power-lunchers by regularly reinventing itself, most recently with the addition of art by Vegas success stories David Ryan and Tim Bavington. Options in the formal dining room include seasonal specialities (lobster, truffles) and organic vegetarian offerings; in the indoor patio café, there are signature salads, pizzas and sandwiches.

Sushi Roku

Forum Shops (733 7373/www.sushi roku.com). **Open** noon-10pm Mon-Thur, Sun; noon-11.30pm Fri, Sat. $$$. **Japanese**. **Map** p73 B3 ㉙

As if Las Vegas wasn't enough like LA, in slinks this Santa Monica/ Hollywood hotspot, all dressed up and ready for some celebrity action. Boasting similar prices to Nobu (p124) but with less of the cachet, Sushi Roku proves that getting fresh fish in the desert isn't cheap. Fanatics are split on whether the high price tag is justified, but anyone worth their $300 jeans knows that the Strip views and loungey bar scene are draws equal to the sensational sashimi.

Trevi

Forum Shops (735 4663/www.trevi-italian.com). **Open** 11am-11pm Mon-Thur, Sun; 11am-midnight Fri, Sat. $$$. **Italian**. **Map** p73 B3 ㉚

For the most part, Caesars and the adjacent Forum Shops wear their theming fairly lightly. One notable exception is this Italian eaterie, named for the fountain and located right by its Vegas reworking. It's a replacement for long-serving Bertolini's, and previous visitors may not notice a great deal of difference in its menu of Italian comfort food. But this is still a reliable option; and next to its competitors in the Forum Shops, it's pretty fairly priced.

Shopping

Forum Shops

1-877 427 7243/893 4800/www. caesars.com). **Open** 10am-11pm Mon-Thur, Sun; 10am-midnight Fri, Sat. **Map** p73 B3 ㉛

Sure, it might be trying too hard with the faux-Roman vibe (classical pillars, statues, huge fountains), but the Forum Shops rakes in a whopping $1,300 in sales per square foot each year, the nation's highest per-foot revenue. Far and away the best of the casino malls, the Forum Shops is a must for anyone with a shopping jones.

In the main mall, mid-range chains (Banana Republic, Gap, Abercrombie & Fitch, Diesel, Kenneth Cole and others) punctuate the serious designer line-up, which features the likes of Dolce & Gabbana, Christian Lacroix, Robert Cavalli and Valentino. Once you're dressed, accessorise your outfit at Chopard, David Yurman, Bulgari, De Beers, Harry Winston or Tiffany & Co. Chrome Hearts specialises in rock-inspired silver and leather jewellery; Oculus in designer eyewear (it also offers spectacle repair and a qualified optometrist); and FAO Schwarz in toys for kids and big kids alike. But the real jewels are the refined shops that front directly on to the Strip.

Take your pick

Variety is the spice of life at Vegas's upscale bars.

Tequilas at Isla

Once upon a time in Vegas, any drink that wasn't brown was considered a fancy cocktail. Today, though, quality counts more than ever. Bartenders here have been retitled 'mixologists', sourcing the freshest ingredients from across the globe. But the most impressive difference between the bars in the rest of the world and those on the Strip might be their collections of spirits.

For evidence, look no further than MGM Grand's restaurant row. The list of 109 sakés at **Shibuya** (p63) is one of the most coveted this side of the Pacific. Nearby, **Craftsteak** (p60) has one of the country's best collections of single-malt scotches: there are no fewer than 130 beauties lined up on shelves behind the bar. Equally impressive are Treasure Island's **Isla** (p101),

where the US-best 104-bottle collection of tequilas requires a full-time Tequila Goddess to serve and educate its customers, and Mandalay Bay's **Red Square** (p54), which keeps more than 200 varieties of vodka in a frosty, glass-enclosed locker that forms the centrepiece of the bar.

When it comes to wine, Vegas is also putting itself on the map. **Aureole** (p54) stocks a veritable anthology of wines, which, rather than being confined to a musty subterranean cellar are displayed in its legendary four-storey wine tower. Indeed, the tower is so tall that it requires harnessed 'wine angels' to retrieve the bottles (from a list of over 9,800).

But perhaps the most unusual drinks cabinet in Vegas belongs to André Rochat. The chef has almost single-handedly built up a unique collection of more than 120 brands of cognac and 47 bottles of Armagnac, which he keeps behind glass at his three restaurants: his two branches of **André's** – one Downtown (p152) and one at the Monte Carlo, and **Alizé** (p136) at the Palms.

A passionate cognac enthusiast, Rochat has tracked down bottles in basements of old distilleries and rural villages across his native France. The collection is remarkable, not just for the rarity of many of the bottles (some of the distillers have been out of existence for 80 years) but for the fact that all are available to drink right then and there. Even the Hardy Reserve, which dates from 1777 and comes with a price tag of $35,000.

Hot tickets

Any round-up of big shows scheduled to hit Vegas in the near future begins, inevitably, with Cirque du Soleil. Although they have five shows already in place on the Strip, in 2008 Cirque will launch an 'illusion-based show' at the Luxor starring magician Criss Angel. The Vegas resident (and star of the *Criss Angel Mindfreak* TV series) has walked on water and set himself on fire in the past, stunts that will no doubt challenge Lance Burton's more kid-friendly feats of fantasy.

The town's latest love affair with hit Broadway productions has already seen the arrival of shows as varied as *Spamalot* (p118) and *The Producers* (p96). And there are more imports from the Great White Way on the horizon. In 2008, a production of the Tony award-winning show **Jersey Boys**, a musical about Frankie Valli & the Four Seasons, will open in the new theatre at the Palazzo, the Venetian's new sister. There's no word on whether its creators will trim the two-and-a-half-hour production to the bite-size 90minutes that has become the standard for Vegas shows.

Trading one diva for another, **Bette Midler** (right) will take over the Colosseum at Caesars Palace when Celine Dion leaves at the end of 2007. The first time Midler played the Strip was in the early 1970s as an opening act for Johnny Carson. More than three decades later, she's been reported as saying that she wants her new show 'to be the funniest on the Strip'.

Spiral escalators and marble floors help create a swanky setting for tenants such as fashion powerhouses Kate Spade, Marc Jacobs, Pucci, Thomas Pink, John Varvatos and Carolina Herrera. Other highlights include exotic lingerie boutique Agent Provocateur, French sportswear Lacoste, British label Ted Baker and stores of the cosmetics brands Fresh and Kiehl's. Recent arrivals include Judith Ripka, Miss Sixty and Ron Herman. Several boutiques, including Scoop and Intermix, stock hand-picked selections of designer clothes and accessories. There are attractions at either end of the mall: statues come to life at one extremity, with Atlantis rising from the waves at the other.

Nightlife

Bette Midler
NEW *1-877 723 8836/866 1400.* **Shows** 7.30pm Mon-Wed, Fri, Sat. **Map** p73 B3 ⊕

Her show having grossed more than $500 million in its five-year run, Celine Dion will be leaving sizeable shoes to fill when her Caesars Palace slot finishes at the end of 2007. From February 2008, the divine Miss M will be attempting to match her. With Midler in place for 100 shows a year and Elton John playing a further 50, Caesars looks likely to enlist a third headliner to plug the gaps; check the website for details.

Elton John
1-888 435 8665/866 1400. **Shows** 7.30pm, days vary. **Map** p73 B3 ⊕

The Queen of England eschews his patchier recent material for a whirlwind of his greatest hits, opening a 100-minute show with 'Bennie and the Jets' and playing everything you could hope to find in an Elton John set list. David LaChapelle's outlandish films and increasingly ridiculous set decoration celebrate Elton's past; thankfully the veteran performer is sensible enough not to dwell on his less engaging present, making this popular blockbuster well worth a look if you happen to be in town for one of its 50 annual shows.

OPM

Forum Shops (369 4998/www. o-pmlv.com). **Open** 10pm-late Wed-Sun. **Map** p73 B3 ❸❹

It took a while for OPM, on the top floor of Wolfgang Puck's Chinois in the Forum Shops, to find its identity. However, it's now become the prime destination for the upscale, hip hop crowd in Las Vegas. DJs also spin reggae and R&B; the urban sounds and intimacy of the venue keep the blinging patrons grinding week after week.

Pure

731 7873/www.purethenight club.com. **Open** 10pm-4am Tue, Fri-Sun. **Map** p73 B3 ❸❺

Soon after opening in 2005, Pure became the hottest megaclub in Las Vegas, and remains so several years down the line. Its multiple levels, including a massive terrace overlooking the Strip, are always packed with patrons vying for a glimpse of the latest Hollywood celebs hosting parties in the labyrinthine venue. Attached is the Pussycat Dolls Lounge, in which its namesake burlesque troupe perform at regular intervals nightly.

Arts & leisure

Qua Baths & Spa

NEW *731 7776/www.quabathsand spa.com.* **Open** 6am-8pm daily. **Map** p73 B3 ❸❻

Caesars' luxurious spa is themed after Roman baths, but with all the modern touches one would expect in Vegas. Within tubs of mineral-rich waters, a Laconium sauna (inspired by ancient Roman steam baths) and an arctic ice room (heated floors and benches under falling snow), therapists practise ritualistic therapies. Take Qua's Mystic Journey and enjoy a bamboo body exfoliation, a lotus flower and water lily wrap and an essential oil facial and scalp massage. When in Rome…

Flamingo

3555 Las Vegas Boulevard South, at E Flamingo Road (reservations 1-888 902 9929/front desk & casino 733 3111/www.harrahs.com). Bus Deuce, 202. **Map** p73 B3.

The Flamingo is the Strip's sleeping giant, with the potential to be roused at any moment from its benign sleep. Its prime location at the heart of the action couldn't be better; and thanks to its beginnings under Bugsy Siegel, its name is virtually legendary. But while its competitors at Caesars Palace and the Bellagio across the street are raising their game in an attempt to draw new crowds, the Harrah's-owned Flamingo seems content to coast along in third gear, happy to milk a gradually ageing clientele who apparently aren't interested in what the competition might be able to offer them.

Behind the signature pink neon sign, the resort is huge, with six guestroom towers. Hidden between them is the resort's centrepiece: a lush 15-acre tropical pool area with waterslides, waterfalls and jungle-like foliage enveloping four distinct pools (including Bugsy's oval-shaped original). Also outdoors are four tennis courts and an assortment of wildlife, including (yes) flamingos. So far so good, then, but the interior of the Flamingo is markedly less impressive, wedged some time in the 1980s and unable or unwilling to escape. The new Go guestrooms are a sign that change may be on the horizon, but it's only the beginning of what's going to be a long and difficult job.

The Flamingo's casino area, though a bit claustrophobic and loud, offers you a real chance to survive: crap and blackjack minimums are a reasonable $5 outside prime time. It's tougher to come out ahead in the slot area: none of the 2,100 machines is considered loose (after all, the last renovation cost $130 million). You'll also find a lively card room, a keno parlour, and a race and sports book.

Eating & drinking

One gets the feeling that the gastronomic revolution that's enlivened Vegas over the last decade or so has yet to reach the Flamingo. Aside from a 24-hour coffeeshop and the inevitable buffet, visitors can choose from Italian (Ventuno), steaks and seafood (Steakhouse46) or sushi and teppanyaki (popular chain Hamada of Japan). None is a disgrace to their surroundings, but when your signature restaurant is Jimmy Buffet's Margaritaville (below), a tacky theme bar-restaurant decorated in colours loud enough to blind from 50 paces, perhaps a rethink is in order.

Jimmy Buffet's Margaritaville

733 3302/www.margaritaville.com.
Open 10.45am-2am Mon-Thur, Sun; 10.45am-3am Fri, Sat. **$$.**
Bar. Map p73 B3 ㊲
You've heard of Deadheads, right? Well, here you'll find their ornithological equivalent: Parrotheads, men dressed in khaki shorts and floral shirts with parrots perched on their heads, united in their devotion to the self-described 'gulf and western' music of Jimmy Buffet. The ambience is not for the faint of heart or the sophisticated of taste.

Nightlife

George Wallace

1-800 221 7299/733 3333. **Shows** 10pm Tue-Sat. No under-5s.
Map p73 B3 ㊳
George Wallace's evenly paced, conversational style of social criticism makes audiences think as well as laugh. Named one of Comedy Central's 100 greatest stand-ups of all time, Wallace veers between 'Yo' mama' jokes, comic bewilderment at the English language and crowd interaction; and you never know who (Jerry Seinfeld, Chris Tucker) might show up. Don't be surprised if you find Wallace mingling on the casino floor after the show.

Second City

1-800 221 7299/733 3333.
Shows 8pm Mon, Tue, Fri; 8pm, 10pm Thur, Sat, Sun. **Map** p73 B3 ㊴
The razor-witted Chicago troupe ditches the stand-up/headliner format in favour of comedy sketches and improv games that riff on topical events and other Vegas wackiness.

Toni Braxton Revealed

1-800 221 7299/733 3333.
Shows 7.30pm Tue-Sat. No under-5s. **Map** p73 B3 ㊵
With six Grammys and 40 million sales under her tiny belt, Braxton is the latest bona fide pop star to set up here. The former Broadway performer struts and sparkles (check out the million-dollar, diamond-studded microphone) her way through soulful R&B hits such as 'Unbreak My Heart', 'Breathe Again' and 'Love Shoulda Brought You Home'. Still, her financial and emotional histories make it a bit hard to swallow the on-top-of-the-world persona.

Harrah's

3475 Las Vegas Boulevard South, between Sands Avenue & E Flamingo Road (reservations 1-800 214 9110/ front desk & casino 369 5000/www. harrahs.com). Bus Deuce, 105, 203.
Map p73 B2.
This longstanding middle-of-the-road, middle-of-the-Strip resort might not have the same cachet as its neighbours, Caesars Palace and the Venetian among them, but its parent company is one of the most powerful in town. The acquisition in 2005 of the Imperial Palace, which sits between Harrah's and sibling property the Flamingo, might have been the catalyst for recent change. The 35-year-old resort still plays the tired Mardi Gras theme, but fresh entertainment options, new eateries and just-renovated guestrooms have injected the property with a little spirit.

Harrah's casino has a wide selection of table games, including Caribbean stud, Let it Ride and casino war. Most blackjack games are dealt from the shoe,

Mirage p89

but higher limits – at least $25 minimum – are dealt from hand-held decks. Beware the single decks, which have lower limits but pay a measly 6:5 for naturals. Occasionally, pit bosses will bring out the European single-zero roulette wheel for high rollers. For lively action, take a seat in the cosy poker room, while the race and sports book offers booths and table seating.

Eating & drinking

I Love this Bar & Grill

Open 11.30am-11pm Mon-Thur; 11.30am-midnight Fri; 10am-midnight Sat; 10am-11pm Sun. **$$. American. Map** p73 B2 ④

Boot-scoot your way on down here for a cold domestic and lots of Southern-fried fun. Named after his hit single 'I Love this Bar', Toby Keith's place is tinged with the country and western theme, especially during the National Finals Rodeo season (see box p34). But even those repelled by cowboys, spurs and line dancing might find it's their kind of place, since it doesn't smash you over the ten-gallon hat with its theme.

Nightlife

Improv

1-800 392 9002/369 5223. **Shows** 8.30pm, 10.30pm Tue-Sat. No under-21s. **Map** p73 B2 ④

After more than 40 years in the funny business, the jokes here at the Improv are still pretty fresh. The comedy isn't actually improv at all – it's straightforward stand-up, delivered by a weekly changing roster of three comics.

Rita Rudner

NEW *1-800 392 9002/369 5111*. **Shows** 8pm Mon-Thur, Sat; 9pm Fri. No under-7s. **Map** p73 B2 ④

In the mood for comedy that's not too blue-blooded, blue-collar or just plain blue? The former chorus girl's observational material is witty without being wanton, classy instead of crass. You'll be hard-pressed to find anyone with better lines on relationships, family and shopping, nor will you find a more earnest, likeable and amusing performer on the Strip. After a five-year run at New York New York, she's now been snapped up by Harrah's.

Arts & leisure

Mac King

1-800 392 9002/369 5111. **Shows** 1pm, 3pm Tue-Sat. No under-5s. **Map** p73 B2 ㊹

One of the real gems of Vegas's family entertainment roster is also one of its cheapest shows. Sure, there are no big bangs or grand illusions here: the budget extends to a pack of cards, some rope, a box of Fig Newtons and a silly suit. But King's warm manner, gentle humour and casually dazzling tricks keep the audience hooked, even now that King has moved to a bigger showroom. Look out for discount coupons in the local magazines, but even if you don't find them, this is well worth paying full price. An enjoyable afternoon.

Imperial Palace

3535 Las Vegas Boulevard South, between Sands Avenue & E Flamingo Road (reservations 1-800 634 6441/ front desk & casino 731 3311/www. imperialpalace.com). Bus Deuce, 105, 203. **Map** p73 B3.

You don't have to be royalty to stay at this oriental-themed hotel. In fact, with the Stardust's demise, there should be even more demand for an on-Strip property where rates often drop into double digits.

The monorail station on site helps you get around to the hipper places, but the resort does offer a few reasons to stay. The main attraction are the Auto Collections, which have more than 200 antique, classic and special-interest vehicles on display and for sale. You can even get your photo taken with an old car for free. Speaking of which, the IP's venerable *Legends in Concert* is still thriving. Indeed, it's spilling over into the remodelled casino, where, at the Dealertainers Pit, you might find Michael Jackson or Cher, primed to belt out a song from behind the blackjack table.

Thanks to its high-traffic location, the casino is always busy, though that doesn't necessarily mean it's especially favourable. Typical central-Strip blackjack rules and video poker paybacks gouge the first-time tourist; the rest of the games gouge the sucker, no matter

LAS VEGAS BY AREA

how experienced. 'Dealertainers' in the IP's party pit impersonate Madonna, the Blues Brothers, Elvis and other pop stars while pitching cards and rockin' out to the loud music. If you have to fade the bad odds, this is a fun place to do it.

Sights & museums

Imperial Palace Auto Collections

Open 9.30am-9.30pm daily. **Admission** $6.95; $3.50 reductions. **Map** p73 B3 ⑮

Tucked away in the parking garage are 200 rare and speciality cars (part of a rotating collection of 750, all for sale). Among them are Hitler's 1936 Mercedes, JFK's 1962 Lincoln, vehicles that once belonged to Al Capone, WC Fields and Howard Hughes, and a room full of Duesenbergs. This latter room was where former casino owner Ralph Engelstad held secretive 'Hitler birthday parties', before being fined by the Nevada Gaming Control Board for the activity.

Eating & drinking

There are restaurants to satisfy most basic cravings, from the Burger Palace to the Pizza Palace, plus a couple of decent buffets in between. Head to the fifth floor for fancier places: Embers (steak), the Cockeyed Clam (seafood), Fireside (barbecue) and Ming Terrace (pan-Asian). The Rockhouse has a mean daiquiri bar, rock music, and free shots poured 24-7 by the Rockhouse Dancers. The IP recently added the Madhouse Bar, a frathouse saloon by Jeff Beacher (of Beacher's Madhouse infamy) where scantily clad servers produce 'bottle service' of mini beer kegs.

Rockhouse

NEW 735 0977. **Open** 10am-4am daily. $$. **Bar**. **Map** p73 B3 ⑯

The new Rockhouse is like an adolescent searching for his identity before realising that it's easier to find large-breasted women. Other attractions

include a mechanical bull, go-go dancers, bottle service, multiple American flags, a stage, and a whole lot of people standing around, not quite sure what to do with themselves. If in doubt, ogle.

Arts & leisure

Legends in Concert

1-888 777 7664/794 3261. **Shows** 7.30pm, 10pm Mon-Sat. **Map** p73 B3 ⑰

Sorry you missed Elvis? Came here on a weekend when Tom Jones isn't performing at the MGM? Wish Barbra Streisand didn't charge $500 a ticket? Worry not: they're all here in this long-running tribute show. Unlike other shows of this type, these performers – backed by a fine band and surrounded by showgirls – actually sing, usually doing several numbers or a medley of top hits.

Mirage

3400 Las Vegas Boulevard South, between Spring Mountain & W Flamingo Roads (reservations 1-800 374 9000/front desk & casino 791 7111/www.mirage.com). Bus Deuce, 105, 202, 203. **Map** p73 B2.

With its Polynesian village decor, lush landscaping, lagoon-like pool and waterfalls, the $650-million Mirage set the standard for modern resorts when it was opened by Steve Wynn in 1989. But in much the same way that the likes of the Tropicana and the Flamingo were left standing at the gate when the Mirage welcomed its first guests, so the Mirage was in turn overtaken by its sassier competitors, who shrewdly realised that there was money to be made from a younger, more fashionable generation.

However, changes are afoot. Not in the guestrooms themselves, at least not yet. And not so much in the main public areas, which retain their long-standing island-paradise theme. But by vastly improving the hotel's dining options, introducing a few nightclubs and lounges aimed squarely at the under-thirties rather than the over-forties, and replacing the Christmas-camp Siegfried & Roy with a vibrant Beatles-based show, the owners have pepped things up no end. The Mirage might not look like a different resort, but it certainly feels like one.

For all that, many of the old favourites remain. The mocked-up volcano at the front is no more realistic than it ever was, but its hourly shows (evenings only) remain a draw. Also still here are the 90ft (27m) rainforest atrium filled with fresh and faux palm trees and orchids, the much-imitated 20,000-gallon aquarium behind the registration desk, and the charming Secret Garden & Dolphin Habitat. And do make time to stop by the gorgeous pool area, which comprises a series of blue lagoons, inlets and waterfalls, plus two islands exotically landscaped with various palm trees and tropical flowers.

The Mirage's casino has nearly 100 blackjack tables, most dealt from six-deck shoes. Minimums are high: $10 for 21, craps and roulette, $25 for mini-baccarat, $100 for baccarat. You can find a good game of poker at any hour; since many players are tourists, the action, both on the low- and high-limit tables, is plentiful. For a break, check out the high-limit slots: if you're polite, and it's not too busy, an attendant might offer you some freshly sliced fruit, normally reserved for players who insert $100 tokens five at a time. Their generosity truly knows no bounds. The Red, White & Blue slot offers a $1-million jackpot which you're not going to win.

Sights & museums

Secret Garden & Dolphin Habitat
791 7188/www.miragehabitat.com.
Open *Summer* 11am-7pm Mon-Fri; 10am-7pm Sat, Sun. *Autumn-spring* 11am-5.30pm Mon-Fri; 10am-5.30pm Sat, Sun. **Admission** $15; $10 reductions; free under-3s.
Map p73 B2 ㊽

Marine mammals in the desert? Nothing's impossible in fabulous Las Vegas. Here, bottle-nosed dolphins frolic in a special habitat behind the Mirage. Adjacent to their home is the Secret Garden, a small but attractive zoo with Asian-themed architecture and some big-ticket animals: white tigers, white lions, Bengal tigers, an Indian elephant, a panther and even a snow leopard.

Volcano
Shows Hourly on the hour. *Spring* 7pm-midnight daily. *Summer* 8pm-midnight daily. *Autumn-winter* 6pm-midnight daily. **Admission** free.
Map p73 B2 ㊾
When the Mirage opened as the Strip's first modern mega-resort in 1989, it's 54ft (16m) volcano started the trend for large-scale free spectacles. The revamped volcano is small, lacks a cinder dome and looks more like a granite wall than Mount Etna. However, the brief spectacle, spewing fire and a piña colada scent into the palm trees, waterfalls and lagoon, is worth a look.

Eating & drinking

Carnegie Deli
1-866 339 4566/www.carnegiedeli.com.
Open 7am-2am daily. **$$. Jewish.**
Map p73 B2 ㊿
Las Vegas has long delighted in bringing the world to its doorstep and reconstituting it for a theme-park crowd, a trend that reached its absolute apogee with the arrival of this Manhattan institution. Gone are the wisecracking staff and gigantic sandwiches; in their place are polite servers and surprisingly expensive (yet still sizeable) meals. It's not bad, but anyone who's been to the original may feel let down.

Fin
791 7337. **Open** 11am-2pm, 5-11pm daily. **$$$. Chinese. Map** p73 B2 51
The menu isn't anything out of the ordinary, but Chi Choi's renditions of Chinese classics, some slightly adapted for the modern world, are nonetheless very good, and the space

Love p92

in which they're served is sublime and cultured. There are plenty of options suitable for most wallets.

Japonais
NEW *792 7979.* **Open** 5-10.30pm Mon-Wed, Sun; 5-11pm Thur-Sat. **$$. Japanese. Map** p73 B2 52

Jun Ichikawa offers only the most traditional styles of sushi, shunning fusion cuisine and American-style rolls. Meanwhile, French-trained Gene Kato offers a large selection of entrées and hot appetisers. *Robata* (Japanese charcoal grill) is a speciality. The lounge is located under the Mirage's domed atrium, with a 110ft (34m) glowing red firewall alongside the main dining room.

Revolution
NEW *791 7111/www.thebeatles revolutionlounge.com.* **Open** 6pm-4am daily. **$$$. Lounge. Map** p73 B2 53

If you want to drink to the Beatles' music, arrive early, before the group are ditched in favour of a more contemporary soundtrack. That aside, the Fab Four theme is generally carried out well, with subtle and not-so-subtle nods to classic songs (crystals hanging from the ceiling, portholes behind the bar). Interactive tabletops, like giant Etch-a-Sketches, are a highlight.

Stack
NEW *792 7801.* **Open** 5-11pm Mon-Thur, Sun; 5pm-midnight Fri, Sat. **$$$. American. Map** p73 B2 54

The name refers to the design by the Graft Lab of Berlin, in which the mahogany walls have a canyon-like appearance. It will lure you in; the American-style cuisine (giant steaks, Kobe burgers, whipped potatoes and comfort desserts) will make you stay.

Nightlife

Jet
NEW *792 7900/www.lightgroup.com.* **Open** 10.30pm-4am Mon, Fri, Sat. **Map** p73 B2 55

As at sister club Light (see below), the main dancefloor at Jet is a sunken

rectangle surrounded by VIP seating and two bars. Hip hop and mash-ups keep the dancefloor packed, and clubbers drink superb cocktails served by gorgeous staff. But the real reasons to visit are the two side rooms, one with the very latest in house and the other pumping out rock and '80s dance music.

Arts & leisure

Danny Gans
1-800 963 9634/796 9999. **Shows** 8pm Tue, Wed, Fri, Sat. No under-5s. **Map** p73 B2 56

Any old impersonator can pull off a credible Elvis or Bill Clinton. But only actor/comedian/singer Danny Gans, who celebrated his 11th anniversary as a Strip headliner by extending his contract through to 2009, promises a vocal bank of more than 200 characters. Family-friendly and always packed, his show has something for everyone – including locals, who love his act as much as tourists.

Love
NEW *1-800 963 9634/796 9999.* **Shows** 7pm, 10pm Mon, Thur-Sun. No under-5s. **Map** p73 B2 57

This could have been horrific, a parade of paperback writers coming together in Sgt Pepper's yellow submarine to help Jude get back, or something. Sure, Cirque du Soleil's Beatles show is a little too literal with the lyrics in places, but from its spectacular opening until its cheesy climax, *Love* is mostly great fun, packed with Cirque's trademark acrobatics and punctuated with playful humour. Oh, and the music's never sounded better.

Paris Las Vegas

3655 Las Vegas Boulevard South, at E Flamingo Road (reservations 1-877 603 4386/front desk & casino 946 7000/www.harrahs.com). Bus Deuce, 202. **Map** p73 B4

What happens when the City of Lights collides with the City of Light?

The Producers p96

Planet Hollywood p96

Versions of Paris's greatest monuments cut down to size, all-you-can-eat crêpes at the buffet, reasonably polite waiters, ancient Rome across the street… and, of course, the lights never go out. If only the real Paris could be so accommodating. Even the French love Las Vegas.

To say that this huge resort in the heart of the Strip is one of the town's most eye-catching is to do its effervescent absurdity a rank injustice. Its reproductions of Parisian landmarks start with the 34-storey hotel tower modelled after the Hôtel de Ville, and also take in the Louvre, the Paris Opéra, the Arc de Triomphe and, of course, the half-scale replica of the Eiffel Tower, built using Gustav Eiffel's original plans, that plunges into the casino. The theming continues within, with French-themed restaurants, shops and even, though you'll need to look closely, the casino. It may seem rather sub-Disney at first glance, but it's by no means all haw-hee-haw cliché: you can also get a massage in a mock Balinese spa, sun yourself by the rooftop pool or take in one of Broadway's biggest recent hits.

Three of the Eiffel Tower's four legs plunge into the casino, which is smaller, noisier and rathe more energetically crowded than most. The 100 table games and 2,000-plus slot machines are not as budget-friendly as they used to be, though there are still plenty of 25¢ slots. The race and sports book has big TVs and 'pari-mutuel' betting on horse racing. Theming is rampant, from Monet-influenced carpets and Paris Métro-style wrought-iron canopies above the games to security guards in gendarme uniforms. Check out the LeRoy Neiman paintings in the high-limit pit.

Sights & museums

Eiffel Tower Experience
Open 9.30am-12.30am daily. **Tickets** $9-$12; $7-$10 reductions; free under-5s. **Map** p73 B4 ⑤⑧

OK, so it's only half the size of the original, but the Vegas Eiffel Tower gives visitors a great view of the Strip and the surrounding mountains, something you won't find in Paris. Take a lift to the 46th-floor observation deck; go at dusk to watch the Strip suddenly light up as if someone's flicked a switch.

Eating & drinking

Eiffel Tower Restaurant
948 6937/www.eiffeltowerrestaurant. com. **Open** 11am-3pm, 5-10pm Mon-Thur, Sun; 11am-3pm, 5-10.30pm Fri, Sat. $$$. **French. Map** p73 B4 ⑤⑨
The food – lamb, foie gras, steaks, which is to say high-class French dishes with subtle twists – doesn't live up to the location, but then how could it? Eleven floors above the Strip in the Eiffel Tower (with great views of the Bellagio's fountains) and designed with a beautifully modern sophistication, it's a stunner. The prices reflect this state of affairs, but then this is more about occasion than cuisine.

Le Cabaret
Open 2pm-3am daily. $$. **Lounge. Map** p73 B4 ⑥⓪
Le Cabaret has more character than most antiseptic casino lounges. With its faux shady trees and sparkling lights, you'll almost feel like you're doin' the 'Neutron Dance' in gay Paree. Or, at least, you will after the eighth drink of the evening.

Le Village Buffet
Buffets *Breakfast* 7-11am daily. *Brunch* 11am-3.30pm Sat, Sun. *Lunch* 11.30am-3.30pm Mon-Fri. *Dinner* 3.30-10pm daily. $$. **Buffet. Map** p73 B4 ⑥①
The one French-themed casino in town really should offer a good buffet, and so it goes. The 400-seat Le Village Buffet has stations representing five French provinces and dishes up a variety of surprisingly fine foods (it's especially good for meat-lovers). But go easy on starters and mains, so as to save room for the fabulous fresh pastries and desserts.

Mon Ami Gabi

944 4224/www.monamigabi.com.
Open 11.30am-11pm Mon-Thur,
Sun; 11.30am-midnight Fri, Sat.
$$. **French**. Map p73 B4 ⑫

Chicago-based Lettuce Entertain You
Enterprises (ouch!) is responsible
for, among others, the Eiffel Tower
Restaurant (see above) and this spot on
the ground floor. While the Eiffel is
decidedly upscale, Mon Ami Gabi
wears its French theming more casu-
ally. As such, it's enjoyable; and if the
food sometimes fails to live up to its
reputation, it's a people-watching par-
adise, especially from the alfresco bit.

Napoleon's

Open 4pm-2am Mon-Thur, Sun; 2pm-
3am Fri, Sat. **$$$**. **Bar**. Map p73 B4 ⑬
There are 100 varieties of champagne
from which to choose at this long-
standing hangout within the Paris
resort. They're a better choice than the
rather over-inventive cocktails, and
certainly more authentic than the
obligatory duelling pianists, who work
their way through Parisian classics
such as, er, 'Goodbye Yellow Brick
Road' and 'Living on a Prayer'.

Shopping

Le Boulevard

946 7000/www.parislasvegas.com.
Open 9am-11pm daily. Map p73 B4 ⑭
Just about every shop in this small
but divine mall (it's basically an
extended hallway) comes with a strong
but delightful French influence. La
Boutique offers a well-edited collection
of high-end accessories from such
French labels as Celine, Hermès and
Cartier; Les Enfants has Madeline,
Babar the Elephant and Eloise toys
and dolls; and Les Mémoires sells
sweet-smelling boudoir and bath gifts.
La Cave has cheeses, pâtés and wine,
while Lenôtre is known for its bread
and pastries. There's even a 24-hour
gift shop (Le Journal) where you
can purchase everything from a Paris
Las Vegas T-shirt to Diet Coke and
a pack of cigarettes.

Nightlife

Risqué

967 4589. **Open** 10pm-4am
Thur-Sun. Map p73 B4 ⑮
Though it bills itself as an ultralounge,
Risqué defies categorisation. It's less
spacious than most nightclubs but
more involving than a mere bar, with
modern Asian decor complementing a
space with private balconies overlooking the Strip, an intimate salon (with
its own events), a proper dancefloor
and occasional performances from
burlesque-style dancers.

Arts & leisure

The Producers

NEW *1-877 762 5746.* **Shows** 8pm
Mon, Tue, Thur, Fri, Sun; 2pm, 8pm
Sat. No under-6s. Map p73 B4 ⑯
The most honoured musical in
Broadway history heads from the
Great White Way to Eiffel Way. Mel
Brooks's tale about a scheming pro-
ducer and a starry-eyed accountant
hoping to make a mint from a surefire
flop called *Springtime for Hitler* boasts
the most outrageous plotlines, costumes and accents in town, not to mention the hottest tickets. But whittled
down to a tourist-friendly hour and a
half, it sacrifices the original's heart
and humour.

Planet Hollywood

NEW *3667 Las Vegas Boulevard
South, between E Harmon Avenue & E
Flamingo Road (reservations 1-877
333 9474/front desk & casino 785 55
55/www.planethollywoodresort.com).*
Bus Deuce, 202. Map p73 B4
The Aladdin rubbed its magic lamp for
the last time in spring 2007 and out
popped Planet Hollywood, a rather hipper casino version of the restaurant
chain. Amenities at the new arrival
include a new Spa by Mandara, to ready
guests for their 15 minutes of fame;
Asia, a swanky new restaurant and
nightspot; the adjacent Miracle Mile
Shops, a galleria of familiar brands

Miracle Mile

(Urban Outfitters, H&M) and eateries; and a modernised theatre. At the unveiling, owner Robert Earl was joined by Bruce Willis and Carmen Electra. But if the new Planet Hollywood plans to compete for the hipsters that flock to the Palms and the Hard Rock, it's going to have to appeal to Willis's kids' generation rather than Willis himself.

The years-long transition has reconfigured the casino endlessly, and further changes may be on the way. Well-heeled players frequent the high-limit pit on the second floor: the salon features 30 high-limit tables including blackjack, roulette and baccarat and 100 high-denomination slot machines.

Eating & drinking

Pampas

NEW *737 4748*. Open 11.30am-10pm daily. $$. **Brazilian**. Map p73 B4 ⑥⑦
This Brazilian *churrascaria rodizio* restaurant is a cheerful all-you-can-eat establishment where various barbecued meats are paraded from table to table on large skewers, and sliced right there and then for hungry diners. Not an ideal venue for vegetarians, perhaps, but carnivores will be licking their lips with delight at the very idea.

Pink's

NEW *785 5555/www.pinksholly wood.com*. Open 8am-5pm daily.
$. **American**. Map p73 B4 ⑥⑧
You're unlikely to catch the great and the good of Hollywood here, as you might if you spend enough time in the 70-year-old LA original. However, if you're in the mood for a diet-busting dog topped with all manner of greasy gloop, there's really nowhere else in town for such superior junk food.

Shopping

Miracle Mile Shops

NEW *1-888 800 8284/www.miracle mileshopslv.com)*. Open 10am-11pm

Mon-Thur, Sun; 10am-midnight Fri, Sat. **Map** p73 B4 ⑥

Formerly the Desert Passage, this 1.2-mile ring-mall recently underwent a multi-million-dollar makeover, transforming it from a Moroccan-style market into a contemporary urban centre. The Hollywood-style facelift added trendier, younger labels to attract the kind of hipsters usually found hanging at the Palms or the Hard Rock, among them Ben Sherman, H&M, Bettie Page Las Vegas, Metropark, Quiksilver, Marciano and Urban Outfitters. Peckish? Grab a Cheeseburger at the Oasis or head to Trader Vic's for mai tais and chicken curry. Other highlights include Teuscher luxury Swiss chocolates emporium, natural cosmetics brand Aveda and the endlessly charming Build-a-Bear Workshop, where you can create your own individual teddybear with the fur colour, eye colour, costume (the range is huge) and stuffing type of your choice.

Nightlife

Planet Hollywood Theatre for the Performing Arts

Information 736 0111/tickets 785 5000. **Map** p73 B4 ⑦

It was already one of the best sounding concert halls in Vegas before a $25-million makeover in 2000, which explains why this gem was left standing even as the original Aladdin was razed. With any luck, the eclectic programming – everything from Nine Inch Nails to Jamie Foxx – will continue.

Triq

NEW *785 5555.* **Open** midnight-8am Fri, Sat. **Map** p73 B4 ⑦

The trick here is that Triq is simply a lounge, albeit a well-appointed one, within the multipurpose space known as the Steve Wyrick Entertainment Complex. But the place comes to life late on Fridays and Saturdays, spreading across all levels of the facility: the stage of Wyrick's 500-seat theatre becomes a dancefloor, while pole dancing go-go girls entertain VIP guests in the lounge. Music is a Strip-standard mix of hip hop, 1980s rock and mash-ups.

Arts & leisure

Planet Hollywood Spa by Mandara

NEW *785 5772/www.mandaraspa.com.* **Open** 6am-7pm daily. **Map** p73 B4 ⑦

With its variety of resurfacing facials, miracle lip and eye therapies and scalp massages, the new Planet Hollywood spa will have you ready for your 15 minutes of fame. If you really want to be pampered like an A-lister, book the signature Mandara massage, a blend of Japanese shiatsu, Hawaiian Lomi Lomi, Swedish and Balinese massage techniques performed by two experienced therapists. Lights, camera, relax.

Steve Wyrick: Real Magic

NEW *Miracle Mile (777 7794/ www.miraclemileshopslv.com).* **Shows** 7pm, 9pm Mon-Thur, Sat, Sun. **Map** p73 B4 ⑦

For fast-paced, no-frills magic performed in an intimate setting, *Steve Wyrick: Real Magic* can't be beat; lock up your jets and motorcycles. When it comes to both magic and nightlife, Wyrick believes bigger is better: witness his new $34-million entertainment complex, comprising the Steve Wyrick Theater, the Magiq Shoppe retail store and a club/ultralounge punningly named Triq.

Stomp Out Loud

NEW *1-866 919 7472/785 5555.* **Shows** 8pm Mon, Tue, Thur-Sun. **Map** p73 B4 ⑦

At up to $110 a ticket, those must be some expensive trashcan lids, brooms and cigarette lighters that Stomp's cast spend 90 minutes tapping and bashing with such exuberance. The Stomp formula hasn't changed much since the troupe burst to attention in Edinburgh Fringe more than 15 years ago, but it has been refined for this often deafening show. They're one-trick ponies, but it's a good trick.

Renaissance cafés

Malted milk cake at the Coffee Shop

After several years missing in action, overwhelmed by high-end eateries and celebrity chefs, casual coffeeshop culture has at last returned to Las Vegas. The new-era coffeeshops are more ambitious than their predecessors, which is probably wise: this particular institution has been around on the Strip as long as cigarette girls and blackjack, and reinvention is definitely required.

For evidence, look no further than the long-standing staple of coffeeshop cuisine, the open-faced sandwich. After years of culinary neglect, this hitherto forgotten meal-in-one has once again started appearing on café menus at such esteemed resorts as Treasure Island and Wynn Las Vegas. However, the former makes it with prime Kobe beef and the latter uses free-range turkey, and the prices at both live up to the

expectations of today's wealthy diners ($19 and $13 respectively).

Treasure Island arguably kickstarted the revival when, during its semi-successful shift from family-oriented to adult-slanted entertainment, it opened a new coffeeshop named, um, the **Coffee Shop** (p101). Hot on its heels was Wynn Las Vegas, which opened a similar enterprise under the more memorable name of **Terrace Pointe** (p116). Both venues rise to the challenge of reinventing classic coffeeshop culture for the 21st century.

The menus at the Coffeeshop and Terrace Pointe, both available 24-7 and both, of course, supersized, include all the classic comfort foods you'd expect to find (French toast, Cobb salad, chicken noodle soup), alongside Vegas mainstays such as shrimp cocktail and prime rib. The Coffee Shop even offers value-packed blue-plate specials. But both venues add a twist or two, whether by marrying unlikely foods (Terrace Pointe serves a bacon-wrapped meatloaf) or bringing in unexpected dishes (the Coffee Shop serves fried chicken and waffle, a soul food staple).

Don't forget dessert. The Wynn's menu lists a 'warm chocolate chip cookie', and Treasure Island's diet-busting double chocolate icebox cake and warm, freshly baked cookie bag promise to put paid to even the most serious of sugar cravings. However, it's the Coffee Shop's famous malted milk cake, two treats in one, that offers the most convincing and delicious evidence of the coffeeshops' evolution into gastro-cafés.

Sirens of TI

V: the Ultimate Variety Show

892 7790/www.vtheshow.com. **Shows** 7.30pm, 9pm daily. **Map** p73 B4 **75**
V strives to feature the best of the best in variety acts: comedy, magic, music, juggling, acrobatics, daredevil stunts and the King Charles Troupe, which nearly treads Harlem Globetrotters territory through the little-known art of unicycle basketball. It's fast-paced and family-friendly, though the action can get a little schizoid at times.

Treasure Island

3300 Las Vegas Boulevard South, at Spring Mountain Road (reservations 1-800 288 7206/front desk & casino 894 7111/www.treasureisland.com). Bus Deuce, 105, 203. **Map** p73 B1.
An object lesson in what happens when you slavishly follow focus groups rather than your own commercial instincts. Treasure Island has struggled with an identity crisis in recent years – We're *Pirates of the Caribbean*! No, we're Robinson Crusoe! We're for families! No, adults! – and hasn't yet managed to make the transition from kid-friendly operation to more lucrative adult playground. Much of the campy pirate paraphernalia that lingered around the casino, leftovers from its original incarnation as a family resort, has been buried. But the general aesthetic doesn't quite match the fine assortment of adult-oriented shows, nightclubs and restaurants that the hotel has brought in to try and reposition itself in the market. It's not exactly helped by its signature event: the pyrotechnic pirate battle in the lagoon out front, which has dropped the kid-friendly content, employed some scantily clad women and rebranded itself Sirens of TI. It might be the most embarrassing and undignified spectacle in North America.

Still, though the hotel amounts to less than the sum of its parts, those parts are interesting and inviting enough to make Treasure Island an appealing option. The new line-up of restaurants is worlds better than what came before, as is the nightlife, which includes Tangerine, a rather tame burlesque club where exotic dancers shimmy down to their decorative undies at 9.30pm and 10.30pm (Thur-Sat only).

For those who think not of gimlets but of golf when they hear the word 'club', the hotel offers access to the exclusive Shadow Creek course, a perk reserved for guests of MGM Mirage resorts. The Wet Spa is disappointing, but the pool is a good one, surprisingly unheralded in the city. And though Treasure Island has little shopping to speak of on its own property, a pedestrian bridge provides easy access to the adjacent Fashion Show Mall (p120).

In Treasure Island's ever-crowded casino, you'll find all the usual games, as well as a race and sports book, but you're the one who's likely to be plundered. As at the Mirage, table limits are high and six-deck shoes are the rule, but you can still find a few video poker machines with pretty good payback percentages.

Sights & museums

Sirens of TI

Shows 7pm, 8.30pm, 10pm & 11.30pm nightly. **Admission** free. **Map** p73 B2 ⑦

With a replica of an 18th-century sea village set on a lagoon, surrounded by cliffs, palm trees and nautical artefacts, the setting for the *Sirens of TI* show is innocent enough. The two fully rigged ships add a touch of excitement, but anyone expecting the wholesome capers of the Captain Hook or Jack Sparrow variety is in for a disappointment. Formerly a family-friendly pantomime, the show received the same crass revamp that has tried to rebrand the TI as a more adult resort. Regardless, the saucy sirens clashing with a band of muscley renegade pirates fill the pavement to capacity, as onlookers stare at the blazing cannons, toppling masts, exploding powder kegs and – key to the whole spectacle – heaving bosoms.

Eating & drinking

Canter's Deli

894 6390. **Open** 10.30am-11pm daily. **$$. Jewish. Map** p73 B2 ⑦

New York-style cheesecake served in a famous LA restaurant? Welcome, of course, to Las Vegas. The original Canter's Deli is a glorious old shambles, its 75-year-old Naugahyde fittings lit by too-bright fluorescence and overseen by Jewish dears who've seen it all before. By comparison, the Vegas outpost lacks charm, but the sandwiches and soups hold their own.

Coffee Shop

Open 24hrs daily. **$$$.** **Café. Map** p73 B2 ⑦

The Coffee Shop touts itself as 'casual dining at its finest', and we're inclined to agree. Don't expect any big surprises though; it's simple all-America comfort food with the odd creative combo (see box p99) thown in for good measure.

Isla

894 7349. **Open** 4-10.45pm Mon, Thur, Sun; 4-9.15pm Tue; 4-11.45pm Wed, Fri, Sat. **$$. Mexican. Map** p73 B2 ⑦

Treasure Island's rebranding from family resort to adult pleasure palace hasn't been wholly successful, but the dining is certainly a vast improvement. The reinvention has been led by Richard Sandoval's Isla, which really adds a spark to some of the old Mexican favourites (burritos, chicken mole) while also bringing a slightly Californian angle to some less familiar dishes. Staff offer an enormous variety of different tequilas and will be happy to recommend the perfect cocktail to accompany your dinner or dessert choices.

Mist

894 7330/www.mistbar.com. **Open** 5pm-4am Mon-Fri; 10am-4pm Sat, Sun. **$$$. Bar. Map** p73 B2 ⑧

Treasure Island's attempt to evoke the Bellagio's Caramel, Mist is a handsomely appointed but slightly soulless bar done out with dark colours and sleek, minimalist decor. Try the

Social House

speciality Bugsy Siegel martini and then move right along; preferably before it hits 9pm, when you have to purchase a bottle of spirits to be allowed seating anywhere away from the bar.

Social House

NEW *894 7777/www.socialhouselv.com.* **Open** 5pm-2am Mon-Thur, Sun; 5pm-3.30am Fri, Sat. **$$$**. **Japanese**. **Map** p73 B2 ⑧①
Chef Joseph Elevado staked his claim as a major food force on the Strip when Social House opened in mid 2006. The food is great, with sushi a speciality, and the atmosphere is also a treat. Trendsetting New York design company AvroKO has created an elegant and intriguing multi-room, multi-level set-up, joined at the hip to burlesque club Tangerine. Living up to its name, Social House ingeniously converts itself into a stylish nightclub after dinner; the tables even lower themselves to coffee-table level – it's perfect for cocktails.

Arts & leisure

Mystère

1-800 392 1999/796 9999. **Shows** 7pm, 9.30pm Mon-Wed, Sat; 4.30pm, 7pm Sun. **Map** p73 B2 ⑧②
The first of five (soon to be seven; see box p62) Cirque du Soleil shows to reach Vegas, *Mystère* holds up very well next to the more spectacular and expensive siblings that have joined it. The reason? It doesn't take itself too seriously, and plays for slapsticky laughs (it's worth getting there 20 minutes early) as much as it does for astonishment (*taiko* drumming, *bunraku* puppetry, did-you-see-that gymnastic exhibitions). The design is showing its age just a little. But otherwise, this long-runner is in surprisingly rude health.

Venetian & Palazzo

3555 Las Vegas Boulevard South, between Sands Avenue & E Flamingo Road (reservations 1-877 883 6423/

Venetian

*front desk & casino 414 1000/www.
venetian.com). Bus Deuce, 105, 203.*
Map p73 B2

Sheldon Adelson's Venetian manages
the neat trick of recreating the city of
canals in the desert. To-scale replicas of
the Rialto Bridge, the Doge's Palace and
the Campanile are rendered with affec-
tion, and the singing gondoliers and
itinerant 'street' performers in St Mark's
Square perform with gusto and a wink.
It's not as tacky as you might expect.

Attractions here are, with the
arguable exceptions of Andrew Lloyd
Webber's The Phantom of the Opera
and the adjacent wax museum
Madame Tussaud's, pretty cultured.
Designed by Rem Koolhaas, the
Guggenheim-Hermitage Museum
offers an artistic selection of works
from home and abroad, while the
Grand Canal Shoppes is a meandering
mall with flowing canals and faux
façades that curve around to St Mark's
Square. Another key draw is the
Canyon Ranch SpaClub, which offers a
full range of spa services along with
wellness classes, a climbing wall and a
café. The resort connects to the Sands
Expo; indeed, the Venetian pulls in
much of its business from convention-
eers, especially midweek.

Not one to rest on his laurels,
Adelson will unveil the adjacent
$1.6-billion Palazzo in late 2007 or
early 2008. Aiming for an upper-crust
Beverly Hills feel, the resort will
feature a brand new mall, the Shops
at Palazzo, connected to the Venetian
via the Grand Canal Shoppes and
anchored by a Barneys department
store. Directly above it will be 300
new condo units that are expected
to sell for between $1,500 and $2,000
per sq ft, the Strip's most expensive
residential offerings.

In the casino, the 140 table games
include blackjack, craps, Caribbean
stud, Let it Ride and pai gow. The
casino's 2,600 slots are weighted
toward reel games, with a large mix
of $1 machines. For the player with

pull, there are high-denomination machines – $5, $25 and $100 – in the casino's high-limit salon, which also includes a baccarat pit and 12 table games (blackjack starting at $10,000 a hand).

Sights & museums

Gondola Rides
Open 10am-11pm Mon-Thur, Sun; 10am-midnight Fri, Sat. **Tickets** *Indoor ride* $15; $7.50 under-12s; $60 2-passenger gondola. *Outdoor ride* $12.50; $5 under-12s; $50 2-passenger gondola. **Map** p73 B2 ⓖ
Purchase your tickets at St Mark's Square, then take a ride along canals that weave through replica Venetian architecture. The wooden boats are authentic and the singing gondoliers are tuneful. However, despite the number of newly married couples that take the ride, the backdrop of gawking tourists will dampen any hopes of a romantic moment.

Guggenheim-Hermitage Museum
414 2440/www.guggenheimlas vegas.org. **Open** 8.30am-7.30pm daily. **Admission** $19.50; $9.50-$15 reductions; free under-6s. **Map** p73 B2 ⓤ
Designed by Rem Koolhaas, this is a joint project between the Guggenheim in New York and the Hermitage Museum of St Petersburg. Shows, which draw on both institutions' collections as well as that of Vienna's Kunsthistorisches Museum, have previously included 'The Pursuit of Pleasure': designed for Sin City, it featured paintings depicting celebration, flirtation and gaming.

Madame Tussaud's
367 1847/www.venetian.com. **Open** 10am-10pm daily. **Admission** $24; $14-$18 reductions; free under-6s. **Map** p73 B2 ⓥ
The first US incarnation of London's all-conquering attraction contains more than 100 wax celebs in various settings and rendered with various

degrees of accuracy (Johnny Depp good, Shaquille O'Neal less impressive). The comparatively small attraction tones down the British history in favour of celebrity and pop culture 'encounters': a photo opportunity to don a wedding dress and 'marry' George Clooney, for example, or a chance to sing in front of Simon Cowell. Hokey but fun.

Eating & drinking

Aquaknox
414 3772/www.aquaknox.net. **Open** 5-11pm Mon-Thur, Sun; 5-11.30pm Fri, Sat. **$$$. Seafood. Map** p73 B2 ⓦ
The prevalence of so many excellent seafood restaurants in this desert resort town remains baffling to outsiders, and understandably so, but Aquaknox stands as solid proof that with a little expense and a good deal of effort, it's possible to conjure up excellent fish out of next to nothing. Served in a sleek room that nods constantly to the cuisine's watery theme, Tom Moloney's food lets its fresh ingredients do the work; good idea.

Bouchon
414 6200/www.frenchlaundry.com. **Open** 7-10.30am, 5-11pm Mon-Fri; 8am-2pm, 5-11pm Sat, Sun. *Oyster bar* 3-11pm daily. **$$$. French. Map** p73 B2 ⓧ
Inside this bistro and oyster bar, much-garlanded Thomas Keller serves authentic French country fare modelled after the cuisine served in the original *bouchons* of Lyon. Indoors or on poolside seating in the gardens, indulge in Bouchon French toast for breakfast, served bread-pudding style with warm layers of brioche, custard and fresh fruit with maple syrup; or, for dinner, try the *truite aux amandes*, pan-roasted trout with almonds, brown butter and green beans.

David Burke Las Vegas
NEW *414 7111/www.davidburke.com.* **Open** *Restaurant* 5-10pm Mon-Thur, Sun; 5-11pm Fri, Sat. *Lounge* 3pm-late daily **$$$ American. Map** p73 B2 ⓨ

Having found fame in New York and consolidated it with a Chicago steakhouse, Burke has followed virtually every star US chef by opening a Vegas restaurant. The cooking will be familiar to anyone who's eaten at his other operations: food is playful but never silly, though it's all pretty expensive.

Pinot Brasserie

414 8888. **Open** 7-10am Mon-Fri; 11.30am-3pm, 5.30-10pm daily. **$$$. French**. Map p73 B2 ❻❾

Joachim Splichal gives his French cuisine a lighter touch, with pastas, seafood, steak and wild game. The homey decor is *très rustique*, with copper pots, leather club chairs and paintings depicting wildlife frolicking in the French countryside. The bistro also has a large rotisserie and oyster bar.

Postrio

796 1110/www.wolfgangpuck.com. **Open** 11.30am-10pm daily. **$$$. American**. Map p73 B2 ❾❿

The most intimate – and, some say, best – restaurant in Wolfgang Puck's Vegas collection, Postrio blends San Francisco and Venice to achieve a romantic atmosphere. Food fuses Mediterranean and Asian influences; seasonal specials include pan-roasted Vermont farm quail with sweet potato gnocchi, and Peking-style roasted duck with warm sesame crêpes. For dessert try the warm chocolate tart with crumbled toffee ice-cream and fresh raspberries.

V Bar

414 3200/www.venetian.com. **Open** 5pm-3am Mon-Wed, Sun; 5pm-4am Thur-Sat. **$$$. Bar**. Map p73 B2 ❾❶

Brought to you by the creators of the Big Apple's Lotus and LA's Sunset Room, V Bar is as basic, simple and understated as its name. The young and affluent clientele can be peeked upon by lesser mortals peeking through small slits in the frosted glass windows. Dress smart-casual unless you want to join them on the outside.

Tao p107

LAS VEGAS BY AREA

Gordie Brown

Valentino

*414 3000/www.valentinorestaurant
group.com.* **Open** 5.30-10.30pm daily.
$$$. **Italian**. Map p73 B2 ㉜
Piero Selvaggio's take on Italian cui-
sine, delivered by executive chef
Luciano Pellegrini, is authentic in
almost every regard but the prices,
which are a good deal higher than they
would be in Rome or Milan. Still, this
is the Venetian not Venice; and in any
case, the food here is pretty impressive,
delivered in a room that stays the right
side of a line separating handsome
from gauche.

Shopping

Grand Canal Shoppes & Shops at Palazzo

*414 4500/www.grandcanalshop
pes.com.* **Open** 10am-11pm Mon-
Thur, Sun; 10am-midnight Fri, Sat.
Map p73 B2 ㉝
The Grand Canal Shoppes felt like
a second-rate Forum Shops when it
first opened in 1999, and in places,
that's what it still resembles. The
walkways are narrow and cramped,
but the smaller space does at least give

a reasonable impression of an intimate
city streetscape. In fact, the designers
have done a good job of recreating the
cramped medieval streets of Venice –
just with more shops and mercifully
fewer pigeons and less dog mess than
in the original. Lladró, Movado, Jimmy
Choo, St John Sport and Burberry are
among the best of the generally high-
end retailers; there's pleasant 'patio'
dining at Postrio (p105) and a hyper-
fashionable dining and clubbing scene
at Tao (p107).

Those in search of beauty supplies
and perfumes will love cosmetics
emporium Sephora, or for a really
unusual gift head to Entertainment
Galleries. This amazing lithograph
shop specialises in limited editions of
Hollywood movie posters and classic
French posters, which it produces on
130-year-old printing presses in the
Downtown Arts District.

When the Palazzo, the luxury sister
complex currently being built beside
the Venetian, opens its doors to the
public in late 2007 or early 2008, it'll
bring with it the long awaited Shops
at Palazzo. The tight-lipped suits
behind the development have been

slow to release information about their new tenants. However, Barneys and Barneys Co-op will anchor the main wing of the Grand Canal Shoppes, which will also include 80 other stores and restaurants.

Nightlife
Tao
388 8588/www.taolasvegas.com.
Open 10pm-4am Thur, Fri; 9.30pm-4am Sat. **Map** p73 B2 ㉞
This ever-fashionable NYC import is a nightclub and restaurant in one, which serves good quality pan-Asian food. But it's best known these days for being an über-hip nightclub and lounge. It rivals Pure as the favourite party-spot of the beautiful people and celebrities visiting Las Vegas. And who can blame them? The Zen- and Buddhist-themed decor is intoxicating, and the multiple lounges and VIP areas lend an air of exclusivity to the venue. Among the other attractions are a cosy Strip-facing patio, a rooftop night time pool party (Tao Beach – in summer only), gorgeous bathing ladies (really) and some of the town's hottest house DJs, though the music is more mainstream at weekends.

Arts & leisure
Blue Man Group
NEW *1-800 258 3626/www.blueman. com.* **Shows** 8pm Mon, Wed, Thur, Sun; 7pm, 10pm Tue, Fri, Sat. No under-5s. **Map** p73 B2 ㉟
It's no surprise that Blue Man Group is such an international phenomenon: their witty, rhythmic and colourful appeal is universal, and has been very carefully pitched at all ages. In this industrial-themed theatre at the Venetian, the three blue-bodied baldies cull comedy from multimedia high jinks, a festival environment from audience reactions, and music from just about everything they can get their hands on. Few performers have ever expressed so much while saying so little.

Gordie Brown
NEW *1-800 258 3626/www.gordie brown.com.* **Shows** 8pm Mon, Wed, Thur, Sun; 7pm, 10pm Tue, Fri, Sat. No under-16s. **Map** p73 B2 ㊱
De Niro, Eastwood and Nicholson... Only a very few high-profile entertainers escape the attentions of this energetic singer/comic/actor/impressionist, a former political cartoonist from Canada who made his Vegas name up at the Golden Nugget before heading south in 2006. Some have accused Brown of trying too hard, of sacrificing himself to his characters, but it's a likeable enough show.

Phantom
NEW *1-800 258 3626/414 1000/www. venetian.com.* **Shows** 7pm Mon, Tue, Thur-Sat; 10pm Tue, Sat; 5pm, 8pm Sun. No under-6s. **Map** p73 B2 ㊲
One of the most beloved musicals of all time is now one of Vegas's most seductive shows. Housed in a theatre designed to evoke the show's own Paris Opera House, the abbreviated, snazzed-up Phantom claims to challenge the dramatic superiority of the original Lloyd Webber production. In truth, there's really nothing new to see here, but the production remains thrilling all the same.

Other venues
Nightlife
Krave
3663 Las Vegas Boulevard South, at E Harmon Avenue (836 0830/www. kravelasvegas.com). Bus Deuce, 201, 202. **Open** 11pm-late Tue-Sun. **Map** p73 B5 ㊳
Various enterprises have come and gone in this Strip space, but Krave has thrived as a true alternative club. Gay men constitute the venue's main clientele, though every demographic is made to feel welcome. There are Latin, hip hop, goth and lesbian promotions; Saturday's Everything You Desire is the most popular night in the club, if not the entire gay scene.

Adventuredome p110

North Strip

LAS VEGAS BY AREA

The stretch of Las Vegas Boulevard South between Sands Avenue and the Stratosphere is in flux. After the luxury of the **Wynn Las Vegas** hotel-casino resort and the hugely popular **Fashion Show Mall**, both sitting at the junction with Spring Mountain Road/Sands Avenue, the quality of businesses becomes patchier as you head north. Still, there's change on the way with the construction of three new resorts: **Encore**, the forthcoming suites-only addition to Wynn Las Vegas; **Fontainebleau Las Vegas**, between the Riviera and the Sahara (p117); and **Echelon Place**, on the site of the old Stardust (p117).

Circus Circus

2880 Las Vegas Boulevard South, between Desert Inn Road & W Sahara Avenue (reservations 1-877 434 9175/ front desk & casino 734 0410/ www.circuscircus.com). Bus Deuce. **Map** p109 B3.

After MGM Mirage purchased additional plots of land bordering Circus Circus, many in town muttered that it's simply a matter of time before Lucky the Laughing Clown is asked to fold up his Big Top and beat it. After all, he's been luring tourists into this garish casino for nearly 40 years, a lifetime by Vegas standards, and not much has changed. Sure, MGM Mirage could ask performers from Cirque du Soleil to perform on the stage above the casino, and the carnie-style midway could be transformed into a futuristic arcade. But then the place might well turn into the kind of joint that even Hunter S Thompson might struggle to enjoy, and who wants that?

Connected by walkways and a monorail, each of the three casinos offers the same gaming options. The race book is located near the back of the resort, in

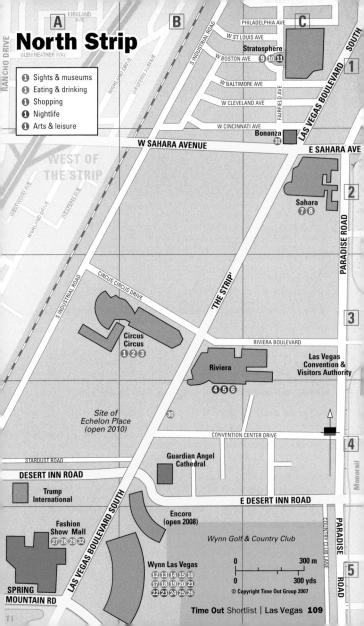

North Strip

A **B** **C**

KIRKLAND AVE
GLEN HEATHER WAY
RANCHO DRIVE
HIGHLAND DRIVE
WESTERN AVENUE
S INDUSTRIAL ROAD

PHILADELPHIA AVE
W ST LOUIS AVE
W BOSTON AVE
Stratosphere ⑨ ⑩ ⑪
W BALTIMORE AVE
W CLEVELAND AVE
FAIRFIELD AVE
W CINCINNATI AVE
Bonanza ㉛
LAS VEGAS BOULEVARD SOUTH

1

- ❶ Sights & museums
- ❶ Eating & drinking
- ❶ Shopping
- ❶ Nightlife
- ❶ Arts & leisure

WEST OF THE STRIP

WESTWOOD AVE
HIGHLAND DRIVE
WESTERN AVE

W SAHARA AVENUE **E SAHARA AVE**

Sahara ⑦ ⑧

2

PARADISE ROAD

CIRCUS CIRCUS DRIVE
S INDUSTRIAL ROAD

'THE STRIP'

3

Circus Circus ①②③

RIVIERA BOULEVARD

Riviera ④⑤⑥

Las Vegas Convention & Visitors Authority

Site of Echelon Place (open 2010)

㉚

4

CONVENTION CENTER DRIVE

STARDUST ROAD
DESERT INN ROAD

Guardian Angel Cathedral

Monorail

Trump International

E DESERT INN ROAD

Encore *(open 2008)*

Fashion Show Mall ㉗㉘㉙㉜

Wynn Golf & Country Club

COUNTRYCLUB LANE
PARADISE ROAD

5

SPRING MOUNTAIN RD

Wynn Las Vegas
⑫⑬⑭⑮⑯
⑰⑱⑲⑳㉑
㉒㉓㉔㉕㉖

0   300 m
0   300 yds

© Copyright Time Out Group 2007

Time Out Shortlist | Las Vegas **109**

the Skyways Tower area. A five-dollar bill is enough to get you started at most tables; it might take all day to find someone risking more than $10. You'll probably want to hide out in the casino; the rest of this place is a pre-pubescent madhouse.

Sights & museums

Adventuredome

794 3939/www.adventuredome.com. **Open** 10am-6pm Mon-Thur; 10am-midnight Fri, Sat; 10am-8pm Sun. **Admission** Unlimited rides $22.95. Individual rides $4-$7. **Map** p109 B3 ❶
This 5-acre park, climate-controlled under a pink plastic dome, is a scene Fred Flintstone would love: waterfalls, faux mountains and animated spitting dinosaurs stuck in fake tar pits. The rides here are good, though hardly white-knuckle; the best is the double-loop, double-corkscrew rollercoaster ($5), but it lasts a disappointingly brief 90 seconds. Tots will like the bumper cars, Ferris wheel and other small rides, as well as an obstacle course for creative crawling. In October, the park transforms into the pleasantly creepy FrightDome.

Eating & drinking

Horse-a-Round Bar

734 0410. **Open** 4.30pm-midnight Fri, Sat. **$$. Bar. Map** p109 B3 ❷
There are few more extraordinary places for a tipple in Las Vegas than this reopened merry-go-round bar, surrounded by screaming children, carousel horses, jugglers and deeply sinister clowns. Made famous by Hunter S Thompson in *Fear and Loathing in Las Vegas*, it remains an absolute must for seekers of the weird.

Steak House

794 3767. **Open** 5-10pm Mon-Fri, Sun; 5-11pm Sat. **$$. Steakhouse. Map** p109 B3 ❸
The casino in which it's housed neuters some of the sophistication, but this is still an excellent choice if you've a yen for a large lump of cow. The steaks here are aged for 21 days and then mesquite-grilled; even more so than usual, order rare or miss out on some of the flavour. What's more, the prices are well below those of other beef emporia along the Strip. A Vegas legend of sorts.

Riviera

2901 Las Vegas Boulevard South, between E Sahara Avenue & E Desert Inn Road (reservations 1-800 634 6753/ front desk & casino 734 5110/www. rivierahotel.com). Bus Deuce, 108, 204. **Map** p109 B3.
When the Riviera opened in 1955, Liberace headlined in its showroom. Though the original king of bling is long gone, the entertainment offerings at the Riv a half-century later are just as camp. The first high-rise hotel on the Strip continues to thumb its nose at family-style entertainment, staying true to its roots as an adult playground. Other throwbacks include two lighted tennis courts, an old-school pool (surrounded by hotel towers for too much shade) and guestrooms that haven't been dramatically upgraded for years. Still, there remains a market for this sort of hotel: unrepentantly old-fashioned, basic and – key to the entire operation's continued viability – cheap.

The gaming area is an L-shaped expanse of red and mock gold with an elevated lounge and bar in the centre (your best bet for a meeting place that everyone can find). Minimums at the tables are not as low as the surroundings would suggest: $5-$10 blackjack in a $2 setting. The lowest limits and nickel slots are found in a part of the casino dubbed Nickel Town, a plausible nickname for the whole resort.

Eating & drinking

As at most middlebrow resorts, there are a couple of smarter restaurants and a handful of casual, low-end ones. At the top, there's Ristorante Italiano and Kristofer's Steakhouse, though the specials at Kady's coffeeshop are better bargains. Elsewhere, Hound Doggies tilts at a 1950s diner vibe, the World's Fare Buffet offers a broad range of international dishes, and the food court contains such familiar staples as Pizza Hut amd KFC.

Nightlife

Crazy Girls

1-877 892 7469/794 9433. **Shows** 9.30pm Mon, Wed-Sun. No under-18s. **Map** p109 B3 ❹

'Girls! Girls! Crazy girls!' goes the infernally catchy theme song. Well, crazy they ain't, and, if local legend is to be believed, the butts displayed in bronze outside the Riviera by way of advertisement aren't all female. Regardless, this low-budget titfest, which celebrated its 20th birthday in 2007, is a giggle: about as arousing as a kick in the teeth, granted, but lovers of Vegas camp will be in heaven.

Riviera Comedy Club

794 9433. **Shows** 8.30pm, 10.30pm daily. **Map** p109 B3 ❺

The Riv's comedy club does pretty much what you might expect, booking three (or sometimes four) solid acts for two shows nightly in a fairly dreary room. As at the Trop, the line-ups change weekly.

Arts & leisure

An Evening at La Cage

1-877 892 7469/794 9433. **Shows** 7.30pm Mon, Wed-Sun. Ages 13-18 with adult. **Map** p109 B3 ❻

It may look from the stalls as though 95% of the ticket price has gone on the succession of increasingly preposterous frocks that Marlboro-voiced Vegas legend and host Frank Marino dons during the course of this drag revue. What remains has been used to enlist a number of dolled-up queens who are lip-synching to J-Lo, Madonna and (a scarily convincing) Celine Dion. It's entertaining enough, but it's nothing you won't find at FreeZone (p133).

Sahara

2535 Las Vegas Boulevard South, at E Sahara Avenue 1-866 382 8884/front desk & casino 737 2111/www.saharavegas.com). Bus Deuce, 108, 204. **Map** p109 C2.

When the Sahara first opened in 1952, its then-exotic African theme, from the famed camels perched outside to the Congo Showroom, seemed right at home on barren Las Vegas Boulevard. After a half-century of development, redevelopment and obliteration, the resort stands virtually alone at the north end of the Strip, an appropriate location for an operation that's far closer in spirit to the Stratosphere a few blocks north than it is to the Wynn Las Vegas just south.

No longer exciting, the Sahara in 2007 is a somewhat downtrodden property, ragged around the edges and soaked in a smoky fug. In some ways, though, its isolation can be seen to have worked in its favour: with the Strip's headline-grabbers just out of walking distance for most visitors, guests at the Sahara tend to stay on site, playing in the basic casino, dining in the NASCAR Café (the hotel is hugely popular among petrolheads, especially during NASCAR weekend at the Las Vegas Motor Speedway in March; p31) and sticking around for a show or two.

However, there is hope on the horizon. The Sahara was sold in March 2007 to the young LA developer Sam Nazarian, who was quick to state his desire to improve the property. Watch this space…

In the Sahara's casino, the days of $1 blackjack have sadly been lost in the sands of time. But you can still find single-deck, double-deck and shoe blackjack games with $5 minimums: among the Strip's lowest, though the single-decks pay 6:5 for naturals. Minimum crap bets are $5. Low-limit Texas hold 'em and seven-card stud games are spread daily in the card room. Lessons in poker, craps and blackjack are also available most days.

LAS VEGAS BY AREA

Sights & museums

Speedworld

Open 11am-9pm Mon-Thur, Sun; 11am-11pm Fri, Sat. **Admission** $10 1 ride; $18 2 rides. *All-day joint ticket with Speed: the Ride* $21.95. **Map** p109 C2 ❼

This high-tech virtual reality racing simulator teams effectively with the neighbouring NASCAR Café: you should see this place on race weekends. It's a fun schtick and frighteningly realistic; at these prices, so it should be.

Speed: the Ride

Open 11am-9pm Mon-Thur, Sun; 11am-11pm Fri, Sat. **Admission** $10 all-day pass. *All-day joint ticket with Las Vegas Cyber Speedway* $21.95. **Map** p109 C2 ❽

Although it may look like one, Speed is not, according to the strict definition, a rollercoaster: it doesn't have a lift hill, nor does it run by gravity. Instead, it's driven by the force of magnetic impellers that rush it from zero to soil-your-pants in three seconds. Riders shoot out from the Sahara into a tunnel drop, only to re-emerge directly into a vertical loop and up a 23-storey tower at 70mph. And then they do it all over again… backwards. Twice.

Eating & drinking

The reborn classic House of Lords steakhouse, which does what you might expect, is the Sahara's main eaterie, but there's also Mexican food at Paco's Hideaway, a 24-hour coffeeshop and a buffet. The car-themed NASCAR Café is proof of the resort's mid-America appeal.

Stratosphere

2000 Las Vegas Boulevard South, at W St Louis Avenue (reservations 1-800 998 6937/front desk & casino 380 7777/www.stratospherehotel.com). Bus Deuce, 108. **Map** p109 C1.

Speed: the Ride

The Stratosphere strives to be a desti-nation resort out of necessity: it's between the Strip and Fremont Street, essentially a no-man's land. Its lure starts at the summit, with a variety of rides atop the highest freestanding observation tower in the US (1,150ft/350m). There are indoor and outdoor observation decks, a revolving restau-rant, and thrill rides with names like Insanity. Down below are some 40 Tower Shops (not exactly the Fashion Show Mall), a remodelled casino and even a new nightclub.

The casino area is spacious and comfortable, if not particularly note-worthy. The layout approximates a series of circles, which looks good but seriously complicates any attempt to get directly from one end of the com-plex to the other. The emphasis is on liberal machines and table-game gimmicks that go some way to improving players' odds. The Stratosphere advertises a 98% return on more than 150 $1 dollar slots, a 100% return on some video poker machines and 10x odds on craps, as well as double-exposure blackjack and crapless craps (with cockamamie rules that aren't player-friendly).

Sights & museums

Big Shot, X Scream & Insanity: the Ride
Open 10am-1am Mon-Thur, Sun; 10am-2am Fri, Sat. **Tickets** $8 each. *All 3 rides* $24.95. *All-day pass* $29.95. **Map** p109 C1 ⑨
If you're afraid of heights, stay away from the 1,150ft (350m) Stratosphere Tower. And even if you don't suffer from vertigo, you might want to steer clear of the resort's thrill rides. The Big Shot will rocket you 160ft (49m) up the tower's spindle under a force of four Gs; at the top, you'll experience a moment of weightlessness before free-falling back to the launch pad. X Scream will propel you headfirst 27ft over the edge of the tower and then leave you there to dangle. And during Insanity, an arm will extend 64ft

(20m) over the edge of the tower and spin you around at a terrifying rate. Best save dinner for later.

Eating & drinking

Top of the World
380 7711/www.topoftheworldlv.com. **Open** 11am-3pm, 5.30-10.30pm Mon-Thur, Sun; 11am-3pm, 5.30-11pm Fri, Sat. $$$. **American**. **Map** p109 C1 ⑩
The views are the main selling point of this restaurant at the top of the Stratosphere, and with good reason: they're spectacular, especially on a clear night. However, the food is better than it needs to be, a cultured mix of American and French-influenced clas-sics. Prices are almost as high as the restaurant itself; just have a drink if your budget won't stretch to dinner.

Nightlife

Polly Esther's
NEW *889 1980/www.pollyestherslv.com.* **Open** 10pm-4am Wed-Sat. **Map** p109 C1 ⑪
Forget the complications of contempo-rary life: this national chain offers four themed rooms dedicated to the music and paraphernalia of the 1970s (most popular), '80s, '90s and 2000s. From the Brady Bunch shrine to the Back to the Future DeLorean car via the Partridge Family bus bar, it's all cheese. But sometimes, a break from reality (and good taste) makes you appreciate just how far we've come.

Wynn Las Vegas & Encore

3131 Las Vegas Boulevard South, between E Desert Inn Road & Sands Avenue (reservations 1-888 320 9966/front desk & casino 770 7000/www.wynnlasvegas.com). Bus Deuce, 203. **Map** p109 A5.
Before he'd even finished building his namesake hotel, Steve Wynn was, true to form, already planning an addition to it. However, Encore has since mor-phed into rather more than a mere

addendum: when it opens in 2009, the $2-billion project will be another full-scale resort, complete with new restaurants, bars and nightclubs. Wynn, after all, can't let himself be outdone by fellow mogul Sheldon Adelson and his neighbouring Palazzo (p103). But in the meantime, Wynn Las Vegas has more than enough diversions to keep visitors busy.

Known as the man who brought Vegas entertainment curbside, Wynn went against his own convention and designed this resort from the inside out. Luxury is everywhere, as you'd expect from a casino that cost somewhere in the region of $2.7 billion. On the far side of the faux mountain, the Lake of Dreams fuses light, water, horticulture and architecture into a multimedia experience. The garden-themed Spa at Wynn, houses 45 treatment rooms, a beauty salon and a fitness centre, while the 18-hole golf course (designed by Tom Fazio) is overlooked by 36 fairway villas.

The exclusivity extends to the Wynn Esplanade Mall, where you'll find the crème de la crème of high-end fashion designers, including Louis Vuitton, Christian Dior, Oscar de la Renta and Brioni. If you can't possibly fathom the thought of a hire car, there's also Penske Wynn Ferrari Maserati, Nevada's only factory-authorised Ferrari and Maserati dealership. The gallery, which featured paintings from Steve and Elaine Wynn's personal collection, is no longer open, but there are still several notable works of art hanging in the hotel's common areas.

As you might expect, the action at Wynn is both sophisticated and decidedly pricey. Blackjack minimums start at $15, with a few single-deck games that pay the reduced 6:5 for naturals; hotel guests can also play 21 poolside at the Cabana Bar. Crap minimums are similar to blackjack. A single-zero roulette wheel is usually open in the high-limit room, though the minimums are dear. The slots run the gamut from pennies to a $5,000

machine. Amazingly, Wynn has tried to attract local video poker players with full-pay machines at higher denominations (very rare), though the schedules change unexpectedly; check the *Las Vegas Advisor* for their comings and goings. The keno lounge is one of the most comfortable in town.

Eating & drinking

Alex

770 3463. **Open** 6-10pm Tue-Sun. **$$$$. French. Map** p109 A5 ⑫
While running oft-overlooked Renoir at the Mirage, Alessandro Stratta earned a reputation among many locals as the city's finest chef. At Alex, he's getting the chance to prove it to the world. With a sweeping staircase inspired by the film *Hello, Dolly!* this is the most elegant restaurant in the Strip's most elegant casino; there are even individual stools for ladies' purses, so they don't have to touch the floor. And Stratta's seasonal dishes, inspired by the flavours of the French Riviera, are as good as it gets.

Wynn Las Vegas p113

Bartolotta Ristorante di Mare

770 7000. **Open** 5.30-10.30pm daily. **$$$$. Seafood. Map** p109 A5 ⑬
If you're lucky, you'll land a table with a view of the water outside at this posh, but by no means flashy, eaterie within the Wynn Las Vegas resort, all the better to get you in the right frame of mind for Paul Bartolotta's cultured take on the Mediterranean seafood tradition. (That said, the menu also features pastas and a few meat options.) The expensive prices mean it's probably one best saved for those really special occasions.

Corsa Cucina

770 3463. **Open** 5-10.30pm Mon, Tue; 11.45am-2.30pm, 5-10.30pm Wed-Sun. **$$$. Italian. Map** p109 A5 ⑭
Chef Steven Kalt takes everyday Italian cuisine and infuses it with novel gourmet touches at this newly remodelled spot. The results will please both diners in the market for something traditional, and those who like thier food to be experimental. Try the cannelloni, made with sheep's milk ricotta, spinach and a sauce of butter, walnuts and aged pecorino romano. And the tomato, mozzarella and basil appetiser – a modern spin on the classic caprese salad with chopped tomato tartare, herbs and balsamic vinegar, which comes beautifully arranged in the shape of a rose – is not to be missed.

Daniel Boulud

770 3310/www.danielnyc.com.
Open 5.30-10.30pm daily. **$$$$.**
European. Map p109 A5 ⑮
New York superstar chef Daniel Boulud received a special exemption from Steve Wynn's edict that every head chef in his hotel must work on site full-time. But his absence isn't evident in this perfectly executed brasserie, which gives diners a chance to sample his less formal fare (burgers, raw bar selections, sweetbread schnitzel). The atmosphere in the casually cultured dining room, which has an incredible view of the hotel's man-made waterfall and surrealist light show, is warm and relaxed.

Parasol Up/Parasol Down

Open *Parasol Up* 24hrs daily. *Parasol Down* 9am-1am daily. **$$$. Lounge**. Map p109 A5 ⑯

Whether you're up or down, there's a Parasol cocktail for you. These two pricey, Euro-chi-chi hangouts overlooking the waterfall, itself projected with images and colours, have more charm than standard casino bars, and are full of the sort of well-groomed, wealthy people that like to hang out at Wynn.

Red 8

770 3463. Open 11am-11pm Mon-Thur, Sun; 11am-1am Fri, Sat. **$$. Thai. Map** p109 A5 ⑰

Many of the luxurious restaurants at Wynn Las Vegas set the sky as their limit when pricing their dishes, but this pleasingly simple Asian bistro keeps things so affordable that even the riff-raff can eat here. The food's all good; stick with the noodle dishes and you won't be disappointed.

Tableau

770 3463. Open 8am-10.15am, 11.30am-2.15pm, 5.30-10pm Mon-Fri; 8am-2.30pm, 5.30-10pm Sat, Sun. **$$$. American. Map** p109 A5 ⑱

Mark LoRusso cut his teeth working for increasingly visible chef Michael Mina of Nobhill and SeaBlue (both at MGM Grand; p59) fame; you can tell, and in a very, very good way. While Mina reigns more or less supreme towards the south of the Strip, LoRusso's cultured take on American cuisine is among the best restaurants at this end of the boulevard, his kitchen displaying a real lightness of touch when dealing with variations on classic themes such as rack of lamb. A real gem of a restaurant.

Terrace Pointe Café

Open 24hrs daily. **$$$. Café. Map** p109 A5 ⑲

A sunny, laid-back atmosphere pervades this casual café serving its own take on American classics and calorific comfort food. Ideal for a leisurely brunch or a cheeky midnight feast.

Wing Lei

770 3388. Open 5.30-10.30pm daily. **$$$. Chinese. Map** p109 A5 ⑳

As if naming your casino after yourself wasn't outlandish enough, Steve Wynn has also lent his identity to this super-smart restaurant: Wing translates as 'Wynn' in Chinese. Happily, the casino mogul's vanity doesn't extend to taking charge of the kitchen: chef Richard Chen looks after that side of the operation, dispensing beautifully presented modern Chinese food in a predictably luxurious, but cultured, environment.

Shopping

Wynn Esplanade

Open 10am-11pm Mon-Thur, Sun; 10am-midnight Fri, Sat. **Map** p109 A5 ㉑

Steve Wynn took Oscar de la Renta on a personal tour of a then under-construction Wynn Las Vegas, in an attempt to convince the couture tsar that it would be the finest resort in town. It worked. De la Renta located his signature shop inside the Wynn Esplanade, and an array of other designers and fashion houses – Jean-Paul Gaultier, Chanel, Manolo Blahnik (the second signature store in the US), Brioni, Dior and Louis Vuitton have all followed his lead. Adding to the requisite collection of designer fashion labels are Jo Malone (exclusive perfumers), Black Satin (luxury lingerie), Cartier and Graff Jewelers, to name but a few.

Peppered throughout the rest of the resort are other interesting spots, such as Shoe In (an assortment of designer shoes from Stuart Weitzman, Christian Louboutin and Giuseppe Zanotti) and Outfit (ready-to-wear clothes from Zac Posen, Narciso Rodriguez and Martin Margiela). Wynn LVNV sells home accessories that include the Wynn's dreamy beds, Murano chandeliers and exclusive confectionary by Frédéric Robert in Chocolat, while Bags, Belts and Baubles specialises in splendid leather goods.

Rising up

Vegas architects reach for the sky.

Construction of Encore p113

As the wave of Las Vegas resorts built in the 1990s and modelled after world monuments (the Great Pyramids, the Eiffel Tower, Venice) begins to fade, so the hotels of the future are aspiring to become monuments in their own right.

One example is Steve Wynn's new **Encore** (p113) set to open in 2009. But it was Glenn Schaeffer who helped launch the trend for statement architecture with **Thehotel at Mandalay Bay** (p173). And in his current tenure as the CEO of Fontainebleau Resorts, Schaeffer continues to contribute to the city's development as a destination for totemic buildings.

Another landmark resort is **CityCenter**, the $7.4-billion MGM Mirage project being built on the Strip between the Bellagio and the Monte Carlo. Top international architects have been employed to design its six unique high-rises, space-age people-mover and dramatic retail centre.

Just up the road from CityCenter, on the site of the now-demolished Stardust, will stand the five towers of **Echelon Place**. Like all projects of this generation, it is described using the buzz words 'sleek', 'urban' and 'contemporary'.

More projects are being announced all the time. **Pulse**, an $8-billion project featuring a trade centre and casinos, is due to go up at the corner of Main Street and Charleston Boulevard in Downtown. And a replica of New York City's landmark Plaza hotel is planned for the site of the old Frontier, across from the Fashion Show Mall.

But, it's the $2.8-billion, 4,000-room, 63-storey **Fontainebleau Las Vegas** that's really the one to watch, as it heads for its late 2009 opening where the classic El Rancho resort once stood (just north of the Riviera on Las Vegas Boulevard). The swanky project will be influenced by late architect Morris Lapidus, who designed the original Fontainebleau Hotel in Miami Beach and was known for his sweeping lines and kitsch details. According to Schaeffer, the design will be 'world-calibre' and (of course) 'contemporary'.

Nightlife

Lure

770 3350. **Open** 9pm-late
Tue-Sat. **Map** p109 A5 ㉒
Lure has never quite carved out a proper niche for itself, teetering between intimate, sexy cocktail lounge and low-key nightclub. Dimly lit in soothing blues and draped with delicate fabrics, it's a gorgeous space, often overlooked in the dizzying array of nightspot options in Sin City. A laid-back alternative to busier, more boisterous clubs elsewhere.

Tryst

770 3375. **Open** 10pm-4.30am
Thur-Sun. **Map** p109 A5 ㉓
Descend the stairs and follow a passage through a womb-like hallway into a dark, sensual space. The dancefloor extends outside to overlook a private lagoon and 94ft (29m) waterfall, with waterside bottle service and corset-wearing servers. The atmosphere is completed by the Library, a VIP area with bookshelf-lined walls and a stripper pole. A decadent nightlife experience for those who can afford it.

Arts & leisure

Le Rêve

1-888 320 7110/770 9966. **Shows**
7pm, 9.30pm Mon, Thur, Sun; 8.30pm
Fri; 8pm, 10.30pm Sat. **Map** p109 A5 ㉔
Named after mogul Steve Wynn's favourite Picasso painting ('the dream' in French), this big-budget spectacular features diving, acrobatics and amazing choreography, performed in an aqua-theatre with intimate, in-the-round seating. With out-of-the-box aesthetics and an independent vision (courtesy of several very public overhauls), it's pretty to watch, but it fades from memory as fast as a dream itself.

Spa at Wynn

770 3900. **Open** 9am-7pm daily.
Map p109 A5 ㉕
Reserve one of the 45 treatment rooms inside this Asian-inspired retreat and indulge in a bamboo lemongrass body scrub, a saké body treatment or a shiatsu massage. The Good Luck Ritual is based on feng shui, with a 50-minute heated Thai herb massage, a moisturising hand and foot massage, and a wild lime botanical scalp treatment. Hotel guests may use the lavish spa facilities without booking a salon session; non-guests can only use the spa by booking a salon treatment (Mon-Thur only).

Spamalot

NEW *1-888 320 7110/770 9966.*
Shows 8pm Mon, Wed, Sun; 7pm,
10pm Tue, Fri, Sat. **Map** p109 A5 ㉖
Boys meet Grail. Boys lose Grail. Boys are taunted by French knights, aided by a showboating Lady of the Lake and terrorised by one very perturbed rabbit in this stage adaptation of *Monty Python and the Holy Grail*. Crammed with nonsensical British humour, Vegas in-jokes and audience interaction, Spamalot delivers more laughs than any other show in town. Non-fans may scratch their heads, but Python devotees won't be able to bag their very own coconut halves, ingeniously 'imported' to the gift shop 'by African swallows', fast enough.

Other venues

Eating & drinking

Café Ba Ba Reeba

*Fashion Show Mall, 3200 Las
Vegas Boulevard South, at W Spring
Mountain Road (258 1211/www.cafe
babareeba.com). Bus Deuce, 105, 203.*
Open 11.30am-11pm Mon-Thur, Sun;
11.30am-midnight Fri, Sat. **$$**.
Mediterranean. **Map** p109 A5 ㉗
The spunky menu, featuring tapas and paella, suggests that this might not be the quietest spot on the Strip. So it proves. It's run by the people behind Mon Ami Gabi (p96) and the Spanish theming here is similarly inauthentic but just as enjoyable. Great Spanish restaurants are hard to find in the US. This isn't one, but it's good enough, and the sangria is excellent. The restaurant's north-side patio is home to the self-explanatory Stripburger.

Fashion Show Mall p120

Mariposa

Neiman Marcus, Fashion Show Mall, 3200 Las Vegas Boulevard South, at Spring Mountain Road (697 7330/ www.neimanmarcus.com). Bus Deuce, 105, 203. **Open** 11.30am-3pm Mon-Sat. **$$$. Mediterranean**. **Map** p109 A5 ㉓

Only a few stiletto steps from the temples to haute couture, David Glass's equally fashionable temple to haute cuisine mixes American classics with Asian, nouveau continental and Mediterranean flavours. Think truffle asiago mac and cheese, or miso-glazed ahi tuna burger. Request a seat by the floor-to-ceiling windows, and you'll enjoy unobstructed views of the Strip.

NM Café

Neiman Marcus, Fashion Show Mall, 3200 Las Vegas Boulevard South, at Spring Mountain Road (697 7340/ www.neimanmarcus.com). Bus Deuce, 105, 203. **Open** 11am-6pm Mon-Sat; noon-6pm Sun. **$$. American**. **Map** p109 A5 ㉙

Next door to Neiman Marcus's ultrachic Mariposa (above) sits its trendier sibling, more Juicy Couture than Chanel. Perch at the sleek bar nibbling on classic Middle Eastern fare from the meze sampler or sip cosmos on the shaded patio. Fashionistas flock here to see and be seen, but also to try exec chef Jason Horwitz's shrimp chermoula and greek salad.

Peppermill's Fireside Lounge

2985 Las Vegas Boulevard South, at Convention Center Drive (735 7635). Bus Deuce, 203. **Open** 24hrs daily. **$$. Bar. Map** p109 A5 ㉚

Known for the seats around the combination firepit-fountain and for the luxuriant dresses worn by the bosomy waitresses, this place is old Vegas at its best. Or, at least, it was, until they put flat-screen TVs on every available surface and made something of a mess of the original vintage feel. Still, the drinks are impressive; try a Scorpion, which will arrive in a glass that's bigger than your head.

Shopping

Bonanza Gifts

2460 Las Vegas Boulevard South, at W Sahara Avenue (385 7359/www. worldslargestgiftshop.com). Bus Deuce, 204. **Open** 8am-midnight daily. **Map** p109 C1 ㉛

Declaring itself to be the 'world's largest gift shop', Bonanza sells everything from postcards to place mats, Elvis shot glasses to dice clocks, playing cards to earrings. Harkening back to the halcyon days of Route 66 gift shops, there's also plenty of American Indian turquoise and silver jewellery.

Fashion Show Mall

3200 Las Vegas Boulevard South, at Spring Mountain Road (369 0704/ www.thefashionshow.com). Bus Deuce, 105, 203. **Open** 10am-9pm Mon-Sat; 11am-7pm Sun. **Map** p109 A5 ㉜

The recent $1-billion expansion of Fashion Show Mall included the addition of the Cloud, an amazing image projection screen/sunshade that hovers over the centre on the Strip. However, it's the line-up of stores that's the real draw at this hugely popular spot.

The mall has nearly doubled in size in recent years. Original tenants such as flagship Macy's, Neiman Marcus and Saks Fifth Avenue department stores, have been joined by anchors including Bloomingdale's Home and Nevada's only Nordstrom. Speciality shops include Apple and Swarovski, and fashion staples Gap, Banana Republic and Zara. Other arrivals include a cheaper, more casual version of J Crew called Madewell, and the stylishly metropolitan Ruehl, Abercrombie & Fitch's fresh take on clothing for young professionals.

Added to the mix are funky youthwear outlets such as Paul Frank and Quiksilver, plus several label-savvy designer boutiques, including Nylon Still, Talulah G and, for fashion-conscious kids, Janie & Jack. The range of restaurants is also very fine: Ra Sushi, Café Ba Ba Reeba (p118) and Capital Grille all merit a visit.

Star Trek: the Experience p126

East of the Strip

The area to the East of the Strip houses two important hotels, the old-school **Las Vegas Hilton** and the more modern **Hard Rock**, along with the perpetually busy **Las Vegas Convention Center** and the various buildings that make up **UNLV** (the University of Nevada, Las Vegas). Dotted between these are clusters of bars, restaurants and shops plus a couple of noteworthy sights, including the ridiculous **Liberace Museum**.

Hard Rock

4455 Paradise Road, at E Harmon Avenue (reservations 1-800 473 7625/front desk & casino 693 5000/ www.hardrockhotel.com). Bus 108. **Map** p123 A4.
The exact moment that rock 'n' roll sold its soul is a mystery, but you can bet the Hard Rock took a healthy cut.

The image of Sid Vicious adorns slot machines, Bob Dylan's lyrics line the elevators, and a notice reminds guests that smart dress is required, a rule that would bar more or less every one of the casino's icons. Still, despite its blazingly middle-American appropriation of rock imagery, the Hard Rock has been an unqualified success since opening in 1995. The golf-shooting, Dockers-wearing baby-boomer brigade is here in force midweek, but at the weekends, the hotel draws a crowd of boisterous funseekers, A-list glitterati and local hipsters.

The Palms may have stolen some of its thunder over the past few years, particularly on the nightlife front, but the Hard Rock remains a premier party destination. The casino design (circular, with a bar in the middle) is a gem, and means the place always feels buzzing even when it's half-empty. Out back, the pool scene's even hotter:

Hard Rock p121

sandy beaches, waterfalls and an unusual swim-up blackjack bar. Amenities include the RockSpa (hey, don't shoot the messenger), electric purple limos and SUVs for guests, some terrific restaurants and the coolest sundries boutique of any hotel in town: selling everything from liquor to lube, it embodies the concept of the convenience store.

After taking over the hotel from founder Peter Morton in early 2007, the Morgans Hotel Group (formerly owned by Ian Schrager) announced plans for an expansion of the property, which looks likely to add an additional 600 rooms, 400 VIP suites, a new convention centre and a mini-mall to the existing Hard Rock. Work is scheduled to be completed by the end of 2009.

A mid 1990s beast it may be, but the Hard Rock's casino is still a hip and popular gambling den. It remains small by Vegas standards: only 800 slots and video poker machines and 76 tables. The main floor is one big circle, with an outer hardwood walkway and an elevated bar in the centre. Dealers are encouraged to be friendly and enthusiastic; some will even give you a high-five if you hit a natural black-jack, a stunt that would give the pit boss a heart attack anywhere else.

Eating & drinking

AJ's Steakhouse
Open 6-11pm Tue-Sat. $$$.
American. Map p123 A4 ❶
The vibe outside AJ's upholstered door may be Hard Rock, but it's a Rat Pack state of mind within. Named after the father of Hard Rock founder Peter Morton, AJ's is a flashback to old Vegas. Powerful martinis at the bar, a pianist crooning standards and some of the finest cuts of meat in town are just a few reasons that so many stars make it a regular haunt.

Havana Cigar Bar
892 9555/www.havanasmoke.com.
Open 9am-2am Mon-Thur; 9am-1am Fri; 2pm-1am Sat; 2-10pm Sun. $$$.
Bar. Map p123 A4 ❷
Aficionados swear this cigar and wine bar is the best place in town to take time out, sit down and enjoy the pleasure of a fine cigar and a good glass of wine. Its range of accessories is as strong as that of its cigars.

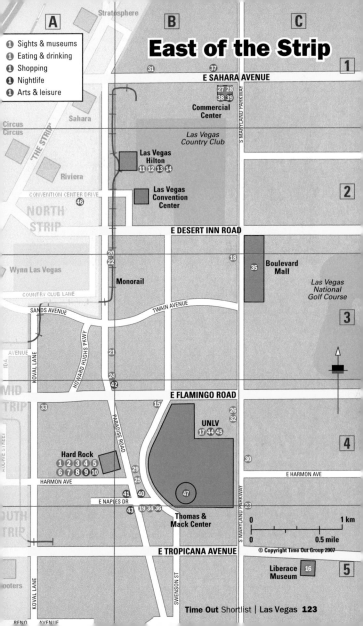

East of the Strip

- ❶ Sights & museums
- ❶ Eating & drinking
- ❶ Shopping
- ❶ Nightlife
- ❶ Arts & leisure

Stratosphere

A **B** **C**

1

E SAHARA AVENUE

31 37

27 28
38 39

Commercial
Center

Circus
Circus

Sahara

Las Vegas
Country Club

"THE STRIP"

Las Vegas
Hilton

11 12 13 14

Riviera

S MARYLAND PARKWAY

2

CONVENTION CENTER DRIVE

46

Las Vegas
Convention
Center

NORTH
STRIP

E DESERT INN ROAD

20
22

18

Wynn Las Vegas

35

Boulevard
Mall

Monorail

COUNTRY CLUB LANE

Las Vegas
National
Golf Course

SANDS AVENUE

TWAIN AVENUE

IDA

AVENUE

3

KOVAL LANE

HOWARD HUGHES PKWY

21

MID
TRIP

24
42

E FLAMINGO ROAD

33

15

26
32

UNLV

17 44 45

PARADISE ROAD

Hard Rock

1 2 3 4 5
6 7 8 9 10

30

E HARMON AVE

4

AUULINE STREET

HARMON AVE

29
25

0   1 km

41 40

E NAPLES DR

S MARYLAND PARKWAY

23

43 19 34 36

0   0.5 mile

47

© Copyright Time Out Group 2007

OUTH
STRIP

Thomas &
Mack Center

E TROPICANA AVENUE

SWENSON ST

KOVAL LANE

Liberace
Museum

16

5

ooters

RENO

AVENUE

Atomic Testing Museum p127

Mr Lucky's 24/7

693 5592. **Open** 24hrs daily.
$. American. Map p123 A4 **3**
The prices have gone up a little, the
servings seem to be smaller, and the
previously hush-hush steak-and-shrimp
special for the bargain price of $7.77 is
now advertised on a cue card placed on
every table. However, the Hard Rock's
mid '90s reinvention of the classic diner
otherwise rolls on unchanged, dishing
out various burgers, sandwiches and
breakfast classics (try the huevos
rancheros) to a disparate pre- and
post-party crowd. It's also a great spot
for people-watching.

Nobu

693 5090. **Open** 6-11pm daily.
$$$. Japanese. Map p123 A4 **4**
Plenty of imitators have emerged in
recent years, trying to replicate chef
Nobu Matsuhisa's Japanese fusion
cuisine and ultra-hip restaurant envi-
ronment. But Nobu remains the origi-
nal, one reason it will probably
never lose its credibility or its appeal.
Big prices and little slices follow the
leads of its New York and London
brethren. If you can, indulge in the
chef's Omakase tasting menu.

Pink Taco

Open 11am-10pm Mon-Thur,
Sun; 11am-midnight Fri, Sat. **$$.**
Mexican. Map p123 A4 **5**
Only the Hard Rock could get away
with giving a restaurant such a jaw-
droppingly euphemistic name. Happily,
though, this Mexican eaterie tran-
scends its rather smutty moniker, with
good, solid food. The menu doesn't
hold any surprises, at least not if you
stick to the favourites (burritos, enchi-
ladas). Join the buzzing bar scene
between 4pm and 7pm during the week
for two-for-one beers and margaritas,
plus half-price appetisers.

Simon Kitchen & Bar

693 4440. **Open** 6-10.30pm Mon-Fri;
6-11pm Sat, Sun. **$$$. American.**
Map p123 A4 **6**
With the sale of the Hard Rock, ru-
mours persist that Simon, arguably
the city's first scene eaterie, might be
short on life. But for now, it's very
much alive and kicking. When he's in
town, Kerry Simon acts the consum-
mate host, while groovy music pro-
vides the backdrop to the top-notch
retro comfort food (massive shrimp
cocktail, meatloaf, giant bowls of

Nightlife

Body English

693 4000/www.bodyenglish.com. **Open** 10.30pm-4am Fri-Sun. **Map** p123 A4 ⑨

Body English resembles something like a mod, Brit-rock star's bachelor pad on overdrive, various rich colours accented by crystal chandeliers. The most popular evening tends to be locals' night on Sunday, a good opportunity to avoid the tourist scene. If you grease a VIP host or make friends with the right person, you can check out the VIP parlour, an intimate, private space with its own DJ, booths and bar.

Joint

Information 693 5000/tickets 474 4000. **Map** p123 A4 ⑩

Though it's lost some of its pulling power to other similar-sized locations in recent years, the Joint remains one of the strongest mid-sized rock concert venues in Las Vegas, playing host to acts as diverse as Marilyn Manson, No Doubt and Air. The main floor is standing room only; there's reserved table seating available on the balcony.

cotton candy). Even if your album hasn't gone platinum, the friendly staff do a great job of making everyone feel like a superstar.

Viva Las Vegas Lounge

Open 24hrs daily. **$$.** **Lounge**. **Map** p123 A4 ⑦

Known as the 'side bar' owing to its location on the edge of the bustling Hard Rock casino floor, Viva Las Vegas is lively throughout the week but really jumps on Friday and Saturday nights, when young singles pack the place. The drinks are dear, but the quality of the people-watching make them worth it.

Shopping

Love Jones

693 5007/www.lovejones.com. **Open** 10am-11pm Mon-Thur, Sun; 10am-1am Fri, Sat. **Map** p123 A4 ⑧

Fur-lined handcuffs, paddles, silk stockings, garter belts and lingerie from the likes of Honey Dew and Christie's make this a mentionable unmentionables boutique. It also sells a few flavoured lotions, potions and toys (but nothing electric). Hotel guests have access to 24-hour room service.

Las Vegas Hilton

3000 Paradise Road, between E Sahara Avenue & E Desert Inn Road (reservations 1-888 732 7117/ front desk & casino 732 5111/www. lvhilton.com). Bus 108, 204, 213. **Map** p123 B2.

Given that it has the biggest stake in Vegas's convention business, it's no surprise that the Hilton is as self-sufficient as resorts come. There are 3,000 rooms, a smörgåsbord of fine restaurants and an endless list of amenities – a full-service spa, a rec deck with tennis courts, wedding facilities (at the only place where Elvis himself got married), a *Star Trek* theme park…

Aside from the kitschy Space Quest Casino, which has $5 tables and sci-fi slots that offer the singular experience of starting the game by passing your hand through a laser beam, this is a high-roller haven, where class divisions are more conspicuous than at most casinos and minimums go through the roof when there's a big convention in town. The baccarat pit and high-limit tables are detached from the main gaming area, and the Platinum Plus slot machines, $5 and up per pull, have their own space. High limits dominate the main floor: the $100 tables are jumping year-round. Managers will only bring out a single-zero roulette wheel if you agree to bet $25-plus per spin. Sports bettors still flock to the 400-seat Super Book, where explanations on how to bet on various sports are posted up to help novices.

Sights & museums

Star Trek: the Experience

www.startrekexp.com. **Open** *Attraction* noon-8pm daily. *Shops* 11am-10pm Mon-Thur, Sun; 10am-11pm Fri, Sat. **Admission** $42.99. **Map** p123 B2 ⓫

Promising to boldly go where no Vegas attraction has gone before, this perpetually popular piece of intergalactic hokum offers two different immersive 'experiences'. Although your trip includes a 'beaming' to the bridge of the Starship Enterprise and a ride in a virtual shuttle, most of your time is spent looking at costumes, props and weaponry from every Trek incarnation. Feringis and Klingons roam the site, happy to pose for photos and chat you up about their last trip through the Gamma Quadrant. There's also the Space Quest Casino, which uses dozens of monitors disguised as portholes to create the illusion that you're orbiting Earth. If you're not keen on throwing cash into 24th-century slot machines, at least step into Quark's Bar & Restaurant (right). You may not be surprised to learn that the management found room to squeeze in a couple of souvenir shops.

Eating & drinking

Teppanyaki chain Benihana has an impressive 'Japanese village' setting, though the food is costly. Three other Asian spots (Garden of the Dragon, Teru Sushi, 888 Noodle Bar) join Andiamo (Italian) and the obligatory Hilton Steakhouse.

Quark's Bar & Restaurant

697 8725/www.startrekexp.com. **Open** 11.30am-11pm daily. **$$ Bar**. **$$ American**. **Map** p123 B2 ⓬

We won't speak for the quality of the food at this establishment, which is named after the alien-run watering hole of *Deep Space Nine*. However, you can accompany your Harry Mudd martini or rum-based, dry-iced Warp Core Breach with Glop on a Stick (that's a corn dog to you) or the Holy Rings of Betazed (onion rings), while Feringis and Klingons walk around in character and poke fun at the humans.

Nightlife

Barry Manilow: Music & Passion

NEW *1-800 222 5361/702 5111.* **Shows** 8pm Wed-Sat. **Map** p123 B2 ⓭

The Hilton is so convinced that *Music & Passion* will always be in fashion that, in 2007, it immortalised Manilow on a gigantic building wrap, the largest of its kind in town. What's not to love? With classy back-up singers, a descending catwalk and a set list of favourites that takes in 'Mandy', 'Can't Smile Without You' and 'Copacabana', the man who writes the songs that make the whole world sing also gets the audience on its feet.

Arts & leisure

Menopause: the Musical

NEW *1-800 222 5361/702 5111.* **Shows** 7pm Mon-Fri; 4pm Sat, Sun. No under-14s. **Map** p123 B2 ⓮

The *Menopause* juggernaut finds a home in a city known for its own frequent hot flushes. With the unlikely setting of Bloomingdale's lingerie department, *Menopause* unites not only its four stars but women everywhere tackling 'the change' head-on, through dialogue and two dozen pop parodies. This will appeal to a particular demographic; women under 40 and men of all ages are best advised to stay as far away as possible.

Other venues

Sights & museums

Atomic Testing Museum

NEW *755 E Flamingo Road, between Swenson Street & Paradise Road (794 5151/www.atomictestingmuseum. org). Bus 202.* **Open** 9am-5pm Mon-Sat; 1-5pm Sun. **Admission** $12; $9 reductions; free under-6s. **Map** p123 B4 ⑮

From the city that once trotted out atomic pin-up girls in mushroom-cloud swimsuits for cheesy publicity stills comes a one-of-a-kind insight into the Nevada Test Site, the US's principal on-continent nuclear weapons testing facility from 1951 to 1992. The story it tells is fascinating: how nuclear power came to represent the future in the USA, how it came to be something approaching a tourist attraction in this most carefully blasé of states, and – most crucially, and in layman's terms – how it actually works.

The headline exhibit is the motion-simulator that endeavours to give visitors a taste of what it must have been like to sit in on one of the several hundred tests carried out at the site. But the real keys to the museum's success are the clarity with which it tells its tale (chronologically, through a succession of themed rooms), and the eye-popping quality of the exhibits (some kitsch, some terrifying). The last two or three rooms essentially comprise a bizarre advertorial for nuclear power, which doesn't sit well after what's gone before. Despite this, the Atomic Testing Museum is still comfortably the most interesting and enlightening museum in the city.

Liberace Museum

Liberace Plaza, 1775 E Tropicana Avenue, at Spencer Street (798 5595/ www.liberace.org). Bus 201. **Open**

Freakin' Frog p129

LAS VEGAS BY AREA

Origin India p130

10am-5pm Tue-Sat; noon-4pm Sun. **Admission** $12.50; $8.50 reductions; free under-10s. **Map** p123 C5

Unless you have a pathological aversion to camp, don't miss this place, a testament to Las Vegas's indefatigable dedication to the ersatz. On display are Mr Showmanship's rhinestones, stage jewellery (including a piano-shaped ring set with 260 diamonds), sequinned jackets, hot pants and a genuine mirrored Rolls-Royce. There are also a dozen of his finest antique pianos; on selected afternoons, Wes Winter's extraordinary tribute offers a taste of the deeply sinister pianist and entertainer. As Las Vegas rediscovers what it once meant to be 'Vegas, baby!', this shrine to bad taste anchors the city's bling heritage.

UNLV Barrick Museum

4505 S Maryland Parkway, at E Tropicana Avenue (895 3381/www. unlv.edu). Bus 109, 201. **Open** 8am-4.45pm Mon-Fri; 10am-2pm Sat. **Admission** free. No credit cards. **Map** p123 B4 ⑰

Technically UNLV's natural history museum, the Barrick has fine permanent displays on ancient and modern Vegas, including a wonderful collection of folk-art masks. It's also one of the city's finest exhibition spaces: a number of excellent shows have graced its front rooms, including work from UNLV's art faculty. It's a must for any gallery crawl; call for details of current shows.

Eating & drinking

Champagnes Café

3557 S Maryland Parkway, between E Desert Inn Road & E Twain Avenue (737 1699/www.champagnescafe.net). Bus 109, 213. **Open** 24hrs daily. **$**. No credit cards. **Bar**. **Map** p123 B3 ⑱

With velvety flock wallpaper, Frank and Dino on the jukebox, and a shrine (a martini, a coffee cup and a cigarette) dedicated to former manager Marty, this vintage bar is a Dom Perignon '53 among Vegas saloons. Hipsters and discerning locals head here at all hours for cheap drinks, many unwilling to leave.

Double Down Saloon

Paradise Plaza, 4640 Paradise Road, between E Harmon & E Tropicana Avenues (791 5775/www.doubledown saloon.com). Bus 108. **Open** 24hrs daily. **$$.** No credit cards. **Bar.** Map p123 B5 ⑲

No head for drink? Then hand over $20 for puke insurance: if you barf, staff'll clean up. Otherwise, you're on your own at this darkly chaotic bar; 'The Happiest Place on Earth', they bill it, and with good reason. The music is loud, whether from the impeccably punkish jukebox or the regular bands, and the vibe is welcoming. Specialities include Ass Juice ($3 each, three for $11) and bacon martinis (no one's ever had two). Beers are a better bet.

Dragonfly

NEW *3900 Paradise Road, between E Flamingo Road & Sands Avenue (699 9633/www.dragonflylv.com). Bus 108.* **Open** 11.30am-2am Mon-Sun. **$$. Pan-Asian.** Map p123 A3 ⑳

Dragonfly is the new baby sister of tapas bar Firefly (below), serving up small plates, sushi and saké to a trendy but unpretentious crowd, in a stylish, modern environment.

Envy

Renaissance, 3400 Paradise Road, between E Desert Inn Road & E Twain Avenue (784 5716/www.envysteak house.com). Bus 108, 213. **Open** 6.30am-2pm, 5-10.30pm daily. **$$$. American.** Map p123 A2 ㉑

Plenty of big deals are hammered out at this modern steakhouse during convention season. House specialities include American Kobe (or more properly, Wagyu) beef, and a bone-in filet served with foie gras and preserved cherry sauce; lobster arrives with a decadent vanilla-infused butter. Wash everything down with one of the 1,500 bottles of wine housed in a candlelit, walk-in cellar and wine wall.

Firefly

3900 Paradise Road, between E Flamingo Road & Sands Avenue (369 3971/www.fireflylv.com). Bus 108.

Open 11.30am-2am Mon-Thur; 11.30am-3am Fri; 5pm-3am Sat; 5pm-2am Sun. **$$. Tapas.** Map p123 A3 ㉒

This popular tapas bar is populated by a parade of pretty locals almost every night of the week. Music (downtempo to Latin house) competes with sangria-fuelled chatter, as small plates – scrumptious bacon-wrapped dates, mushroom tarts, shrimp ceviche – emerge from the busy kitchen. The loungey scene and reasonable prices conspire to let you spend as little or as much as you like.

Freakin' Frog

4700 S Maryland Parkway, at E Tropicana Avenue (597 9702/www.freakinfrog.com). Bus 109, 201. **Open** 11am-3am daily. **$$. Bar.** Map p123 C5 ㉓

Despite its irritatin' name, the Frog is a locals' favourite, and not just because of the 400-strong selection of beers. Located across the road from UNLV, this is about as close as Vegas gets to a college bar. Order some fried macaroni and cheese triangles or a corn dog to accompany your discussion of Peruvian beer versus, say, Colt 45 (impressively, Freakin' Frog stocks both). There's a whiskey bar upstairs.

Gandhi

4080 Paradise Road, at E Flamingo Road (734 0094/www.gandhicuisine. com). Bus 108, 202. **Open** 11am-2.30pm, 5-10.30pm daily. **$. Indian.** Map 336 A3 ㉔

Good Northern Indian and Southern Indian cuisines, including a fine selection of vegetarian dishes, are combined at this longtime local favourite. The all-you-can-eat lunch buffet is nice and spicy, and stars such dishes as keema naan (stuffed bread with minced lamb) chicken pakora and chicken tikka masala for next to nothing.

Hofbrauhaus

4510 Paradise Road, at E Harmon Avenue (853 2337/www.hofbrauhaus lasvegas.com). Bus 108. **Open** 11am-11pm Mon-Thur, Sun; 11am-midnight Fri, Sat. **$$. German.** Map p123 B4 ㉕

Planting this near-identical replica of the famous Munich beerhall across the road from the Hard Rock was a great idea, but the results are hot and cold. To wit: pretzel girls, hot; the rest of the menu, not. Still, while the authentic German grub is mostly bland, the beer makes up for it. Unlike the Munich original, the *biergarten* (beer garden) has a roof, making it feel like little more than a glorified cafeteria.

Hookah Lounge

Paymon's Mediterranean Café & Market, 4147 S Maryland Parkway, at E Flamingo Road (731 6030/www. hookahlounge.com). Bus 109, 202. **Open** 5pm-1am Mon-Thur; 5pm-3am Fri, Sat. **$$**. **Bar**. Map p123 B4 26

In this dark and ornate haven, a stark contrast to the adjoining Mediterranean Café (p132), you'll be served at low tables by a hookah jockey, who dispenses cocktails and water pipe. Flavours range from the flowery to fruity, but we recommend something traditional, like Turkish pistachio. Take a couple of puffs and then pass it on. There's food and herbal smoke before 9pm; afterwards, the kitchen closes and the real tobaccco is brought out.

Komol

Commercial Center, 953 E Sahara Avenue, between S 6th Street & S Maryland Parkway (731 6542/www. komolrestaurant.com). Bus 109, 204. **Open** 11am-10pm Mon-Sat; noon-10pm Sun. **$$**. **Thai**. Map p123 B1 27

Despite its location in the run-down Commercial Center, where it competes with the nationally renowned Lotus of Siam and a pair of nationally infamous sex clubs, Komol remains hugely popular for its authentic rendering of Thai cuisine, a vast vegetarian menu, plus 1950s Americana such as egg foo yung, all at bargain prices. Specify the degree of heat you'd like, and the kitchen will try to comply.

Lotus of Siam

Commercial Center, 953 E Sahara Avenue, between S 6th Street & S Maryland Parkway (735 3033/
www.lotusofsiamlv.com). Bus 109, 204. **Open** 11.30am-2pm Mon-Fri; 5.30-9pm daily. **$$**. **Thai**. Map p123 B1 28

The knowledgeable folks at *Gourmet* magazine have rated this the best Thai restaurant in the US. We might not go quite that far, but Lotus of Siam is certainly a rare and unexpected treat in an unprepossessing strip mall otherwise dominated by gay bars and swingers' clubs. Saipin Chutima puts her specialities on the easy-to-read menu, and isn't afraid to make her food spicy. However, many diners opt for the excellent and supercheap lunch buffet.

Origin India

NEW *4480 Paradise Road, at E Harmon Avenue (734 6342/www. originindiarestaurant.com). Bus 108.* **Open** 11.30am-11.30pm daily. **$$**. **Indian**. Map p123 B4 29

Having reigned unchallenged for years, Gandhi (p129) now has some genuine competition for the title of Vegas's best Indian restaurant, and it's less than half a mile down the street. The lowlit swanky interior of Origin India differentiates it from its competition, but the pleasingly authentic spicy food is also a class apart, with classics such as *saag gosht* (lamb with spinach) and a creamy chicken *makhani* rendered in exotic technicolour brilliance.

Otto's Malt Shop

NEW *4440 S Maryland Parkway, at E Harmon Avenue (796 6886/www. ottosmaltshop.com). Bus 109.* **Open** 11am-8pm Mon-Fri; noon-5pm Sat. **$**. **American**. Map p123 C4 30

Housed in one of Maryland Parkway's scruffiest strip malls, this jaunty little hangout is done with a rather curious mix of sci-fi memorabilia and bargain-basement diner furniture. However, the main reason to come here is for the food: alongside the eponymous, unmissable malts, Otto Miller and Ruthie Colgrove together dish up the best burgers in the city, serving their crowd of collegiate regulars with a smile.

Otto's Malt Shop

Pamplemousse

400 E Sahara Avenue, at Paradise Road (733 2066/www.pamplemousse restaurant.com). Bus 108, 204. **Open** 5.30-10.30pm Tue-Sun. **$$$. French**. Map p123 B1 ③①

Along with André's (p152), Georges La Forge's restaurant is one of a very few non-casino old Vegas classic eateries, having served country-style French fare to such regulars as Wayne Newton and Robin Leach for years. The menu-less tradition continues today: the staff recite the choices, so be sure to pay attention. Dishes include fettuccini a la Georges, reportedly invented when Frank Sinatra asked La Forge to create him a dish he'd never forget.

Paymon's Mediterranean Café & Market

4147 S Maryland Parkway, at E Flamingo Road (731 6030/ www.paymons.com). Bus 108, 202. **Open** *Café* 11am-1am Mon-Thur; 11am-3am Fri, Sat; 11am-5pm Sun. *Market* 9am-8pm Mon-Fri; 10am-5pm Sat. **$. Café. Map** p123 B4 ③②

Paymon Raouf was serving the kind of ethnic food so adored by the college crowd long before anyone else. Even now, when so many Middle Eastern restaurants have opened up in Vegas,

the Med – decent for dinner but best for lunch – still wins out, simply because its kebabs and salads are better than anyone else's. Next door's Hookah Lounge (p130) makes a fitting companion.

Platinum Restaurant

NEW *Platinum, 211 E Flamingo Road, at Koval Lane (365 2525/ www.platinumhotel.com). Bus 202.* **Open** 6am-3pm, 5-10pm daily. **$$$. American.** Map p123 A4 ③③

Chef Brenton Hammer is Las Vegas's foremost devotee of the new molecular gastronomy school, whereby chefs rely on cutting-edge technology to create novel dishes. His specialities include lamb served with a glass of aromatic 'rosemary air', and sorbet coated with Pop Rocks. But don't be intimidated. The food may sound weird and look silly, but Hammer relies on the finest ingredients. Breakfast and lunch are more traditional, but still on the playful side.

Suede Restaurant & Lounge

4640 S Paradise Road, between E Harmon & E Tropicana Avenues (791 3463/www.suedelasvegas.com). Bus 108, 201. **Open** 5pm-2am Wed-Sun. **$$. American.** Map p123 4B ③④

Get Booked

Formerly Sasha's, Suede is the only gay dining establishment in Vegas. The menu is frequently updated, as are the entertainers. Drag shows (except Sun), karaoke, trivia contests, dance music and drink specials round out the experience.

Shopping

Boulevard Mall
3528 S Maryland Parkway, at W Desert Inn Road (732 8949/ www.boulevardmall.com). Bus 109, 213. **Open** 10am-9pm Mon-Sat; 11am-6pm Sun. **Map** p123 C3 ❸
A bastion of the Las Vegas shopping scene and the first mall of its type to open in the city: centrally located, reasonably priced and loaded with familiar favourites such as Sears, Macy's and JC Penney, along with American classics Gap and Victoria's Secret, . When you're weighed down with bags and nearing collapse, head to the Panorama Café's food court for cheap but decent international cuisine.

Get Booked
Paradise Plaza, 4640 Paradise Road, between E Harmon & E Tropicana Avenues (737 7780/www.getbooked. com). Bus 108. **Open** 10am-midnight Mon-Thur, Sun; 10am-2am Fri, Sat. **Map** p123 B4 ❸
This is the last remaining general gay retail shop in Las Vegas. It is located in the Fruit Loop and divides its offerings between all the usual gift shop merchandise (T-shirts, books, greeting cards, CDs, gifts) and the naughty stuff (videos, DVDs, underwear, lubricants, adult magazines).

Rainbow's End Natural Foods
1100 E Sahara Avenue, at S Maryland Parkway (737 1338/www.rainbowsend lasvegas.com). Bus 109, 204. **Open** 9am-8pm Mon-Fri; 10am-8pm Sat; 11am-5pm Sun. **Map** p123 B1 ❸
The closest place to the Strip to buy good quality fresh fruit and groceries also offers a broad range of herbs, teas, vitamins and bodycare items.

Serge's Showgirl Wigs
Commercial Center, 953 E Sahara Avenue, between S 6th Street & S Maryland Parkway (732 1015/ www.showgirlwigs.com). Bus 109, 204. **Open** 10am-5.30pm Mon-Sat. **Map** p123 B1 ❸
In Las Vegas, wigs never went out of fashion. Serge's is the world's largest wig retailer, offering thousands of natural and synthetic hairpieces in hundreds of styles and colours.

Nightlife

Badlands Saloon
Commercial Center, 953 E Sahara Avenue, between S 6th Street & S Maryland Parkway (792 9262). Bus 109, 204. **Open** 24hrs daily. No credit cards. **Map** p123 B1 ❸
The smaller of the city's two western gay bars, Badlands is an intimate space patronised in the main by men over 30. A game of pool will set you back a mere quarter, making it the cheapest in Vegas (if not the state).

FreeZone
610 E Naples Drive, at Paradise Road (794 2300/www.freezonelasvegas.com). Bus 108, 213. **Open** 24hrs daily. Food served 6pm-2am Mon-Wed; 6pm-3am Thur-Sat. No credit cards. **Map** p123 B4 ❹
If the line at Piranha (p134) is too long or the drinks at Gipsy (below) are too pricey, FreeZone is the next best Fruit Loop option. Thursday's boys-night party remains a draw; weekends are reserved for the Queens of Las Vegas, the city's longest-running drag show. Lick Her Bust on Tuesdays is a ladies' affair, but you'll find the lesbian community well represented on any night.

Gipsy
4605 Paradise Road, between E Harmon & E Tropicana Avenues (731 1919/www.gipsylv.net). Bus 108, 201. **Open** from 10pm daily. No credit cards. **Map** p123 B4 ❹
Until the arrival of Krave (p107) and Piranha (p134), Gipsy had long reigned supreme as the most popular gay

nightspot in town. It still pulls in the punters with its diva house soundtracks, female impersonator shows and no-cover weekends, but the crowds are smaller than they once were.

New York Café

4080 Paradise Road, at E Flamingo Road (796 0589). Bus 108, 202. **Open** 24hrs daily. No credit cards. **Map** p123 A4 **42**

Just a few blocks north of the Hard Rock (and completely unrelated to the New York New York hotel-casino), this dive bar hosts punk and hard rock bands in its lobby on a regular basis. It's a great place to see a free show, throw back some cold beers and chow down on a pizza.

Piranha & 8½

NEW *4633 Paradise Road, between E Harmon & E Tropicana Avenues (791 0100/www.piranhasvegas.com). Bus 108, 213.* **Open** from 9pm daily. No credit cards. **Map** p123 B4 **43**

Done out with velvet curtains, a marble-topped bar and gigantic piranha aquariums, the $5-million Piranha dance hall and connecting 8½ lounge is gay Vegas's most beautiful nightlife palace. Go-go boys and girls are on display in Piranha, while guests take over the stage in 8½; the Skybox VIP rooms give welcome respite from the usual crowds. Cocktails can be expensive and low on booze, but it's easy to see why this complex has been a hit right out of the gate.

Arts & leisure

Donna Beam Fine Art Gallery

Alta Ham Fine Arts Building, UNLV, 4505 S Maryland Parkway, between E Flamingo Road & E Tropicana Avenue (895 3893/http://finearts.unlv.edu/galleries). Bus 109, 201. **Open** 9am-5pm Mon-Fri; 10am-2pm Sat. **Map** p123 B4 **44**

A bit tricky to find, this gallery is best visited on a weekday, when you're sure to run into an art student who can point you in the right direction. During the

academic year (Sept-May), it hosts work by students and faculty of UNLV's fine art programme, along with the occasional travelling exhibit.

Las Vegas Philharmonic

Artemus Ham Concert Hall, 4505 S Maryland Parkway, between E Flamingo Road & E Tropicana Avenue (895 2787/www.lvphil.com). Bus 109, 201. **Map** p123 B4 **45**

After emerging in 1998, Las Vegas's resident orchestra gradually gained recognition under recently retired music director Harold Weller; today, new director David Itkin and associate conductor Richard McGee continue the effort. Repertoire has remained largely highbrow, with occasional works commissioned from contemporary composers. Aside from the concerts at Ham Hall, the Phil also performs pop classics to family audiences in annual recitals at Christmas and for Independence Day.

Tribute to Frank, Sammy, Joey & Dean

Greek Isles, 305 Convention Center Drive, between Las Vegas Boulevard South & Paradise Road (1-800 634 6787/737 5540/www.greekislesvegas. com). Bus Deuce, 112. **Shows** 8.15pm Mon-Thur, Sat, Sun. **Map** p123 A2 **46**

The set-up's a bit artificial, to say the least: God (Buddy Hackett in a marvellous voiceover cameo) sends back the fantastic four (with a 'Happy Birthday'-singing Marilyn tagging along) for one night in Vegas. But complete with a nine-piece band, and all the off-colour jokes and locker-room razzing you remember, the show's a humdinger.

Thomas & Mack Center

4505 S Maryland Parkway, at E Tropicana Avenue (895 2787/www. thomasandmack.com). Bus 201, 202, 213. **Map** p123 B4 **47**

The Thomas & Mack Center hosts sporting events throughout the year, including the annual National Finals Rodeo (p34), FIBA championships and wrestling. The popular UNLV basketball team, the Runnin' Rebels, play here between November and March.

Playboy Club p139

West of the Strip

Aside from the principal hotel-casinos, there's little to write home about west of the Strip. Around the glitzy **Palms** and the gamblers' paradise that is the **Rio** are scattered a handful of decent independent bars and restaurants. Further north sits the newly opened and very eco-conscious **Las Vegas Springs Preserve**.

Palms

4321 W Flamingo Road, at S Valley View Boulevard (reservations 1-866 942 7770/front desk & casino 942 7777/www.palms.com). Bus 201. **Map** p137 A4.

Since MTV's *Real World* took over a floor at the Palms, owner George Maloof has shown a Midas touch for keeping up with everybody from twentysomething hipsters to blue-rinse daytime gamblers. At night, the Palms attracts a *Who's Who* of Hollywood players and sports stars with nightclubs, a new concert hall, chic restaurants, a tattoo parlour, 'bachelor suites' replete with dancer poles and some rooms with giant beds (Maloof and his brother own the Sacramento Kings basketball team). But the magic also works on locals, with a cinema, a food court, a slots-driven casino and, most of all, quality service. And still the expansion goes on: Palms Place, a condominium hotel and spa (the 'final' installment in the hotel's $650-million expansion), will connect to the hotel and its amenities via a moving walkway called the SkyTube.

Underpinned by a classy hardwood floor, the Palms casino includes 2,400 slots, 55 table games (many with $10 minimums), and a race and sports book. A survey conducted after the casino opened found the slots to be the loosest in Las Vegas; judging from the video poker, this relative generosity remains.

Eating & drinking

Alizé

951 7000/www.alizelv.com. **Open**
5.30-10pm daily. **$$$**. **French**.
Map p137 A4 ❶
Up on the 56th floor, venerated local
André Rochat (of greatly beloved
Downtown restaurant André's; p152)
has hired chef Mark Purdy to maintain
his classics and deliver some fresh
takes on French cuisine. Many of the
seasonal dishes – pan-seared Muscovy
duck with peach and foie gras tarte
tatin – taste as great as they sound. It
comes at a price, but Rochat, who's
been cooking foie gras in Vegas since
Dan Tana was around, is the business.

Ghostbar

*942 6832/http://ghostbar-las-vegas.
n9negroup.com.* **Open** 8pm-4am
daily. **Cover** $10 Mon-Thur; $25
Fri-Sun. **$$$**. **Bar**. **Map** p137 A4 ❷
Suspended 51 floors above the city
(check the see-through patio looking all
the way to the ground), decked out in
blues and space-age silvers, Ghostbar
is a dramatic spot. Enter via the private
elevator (and prepare to pay the private
cover charge of $10-$20), and try to get
here before the glamorous masses: it
starts to get busy from 11pm.

Little Buddha

*942 7778/www.littlebuddhalasvegas.
com.* **Open** 5.30-11pm Mon-Thur, Sun;
5.30pm-midnight Fri, Sat. **$$$ Bar**.
$$$. Pan-Asian. Map p137 A4 ❸
This restaurant and bar, a smaller ver-
sion of Paris's famed Buddha Bar (it's
operated by the same people), has a
low-key and sophisticated air, as
smooth and relaxing as the popular
ambient DJ compilations created in its
name. The bar area is small and busy,
but it's still worth a look for the Asian
decor and sophisticated drinks.
   The restaurant serves decent fusion
food; for want of space, the now-larger
sushi bar is in the back room, but you
can still belly up to the main room bar
to bark your sashimi order over the
soundtrack. Come here for the lively
scene and the sushi, and be sure to look

as fabulous as possible, but leave the
Asian cooking to the restaurants a mile
north at Chinatown Plaza, where similar fare can be had for a lot less money.

N9ne

933 9900/www.n9nesteaks.com.
Open 5.30-10pm Mon-Thur, Sun;
5.30-11pm Fri, Sat. **$$$**. **American**.
Map p137 A4 ❹
Superb steak and seafood? Absolutely.
A quiet spot for a date? Absolutely not.
A busy bar scene, a DJ, busy lighting
and acoustics seemingly designed to
force diners to yell, make N9ne feel like
a nightclub – and it's all intentional. The
appetisers and sides are well-executed
complements to the mains, and the flam-
ing S'mores dessert is a show unto itself.
A Saturday booking requires an A-list
name or months of planning.

Nove

NEW *942 6800/www.n9negroup.com.*
Open 5-11pm daily. **$$$**. **Italian**.
Map p137 A4 ❺
This expensive sister to N9ne (above)
sits atop the Palms' new super-luxury
Fantasy Tower and boasts one of the
best views in town, along with beautiful modern decor. The steaks are
mediocre and the service is steeped
with attitude. But for all that, the only
complaint you'll hear about the Nove
spaghetti, prepared with lobster,
shrimp, crab, scallops, calamari and
basil, will relate to its $42 price tag.

Shopping

Hart & Huntington Tattoo Company

*942 7777/http://hartandhuntington
tattoo.com.* **Open** 11am-2am Mon-Fri;
10am-2am Sat, Sun. **Map** p137 A4 ❻
Motocross legend Carey Hart and club
promoter John Huntington (the man
behind the original Pimp 'n' Ho Costume
Ball) set up this hip tattoo parlour inside
the Palms, and promptly landed their
own TV show, *Inked*. Huntington has
since sold the shop to Hart, but the
patrons hardly seem to care. Guests can
book a slot at the same time as they
make their hotel reservations.

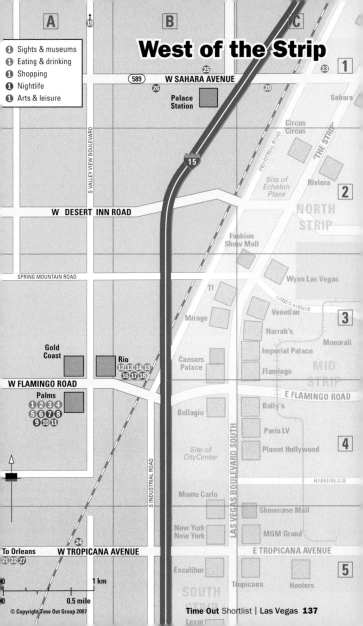

West of the Strip

Legend:
- Sights & museums
- Eating & drinking
- Shopping
- Nightlife
- Arts & leisure

© Copyright Time Out Group 2007

Nightlife

Moon & Playboy Club

NEW *942 6832/http://moon-las-vegas. n9egroup.com.* **Open** 8pm-4am daily. **Map** p137 A4 ❼

In space, no one can hear you scream. However, they sure can see you dance, at least if they happen to be looking through Moon's retractable roof. The club's space-age design has a retro feel, but its location 53 floors up the Palms' Fantasy Tower offers incredible views from its two balconies and its bead-curtained, floor-to-ceiling windows. The music can be a bit schizophrenic, ranging from top 40 remixes to hip hop/rock mash-ups and occasional house nights. Most evenings, admission includes access to the swanky Playboy Club (on the 51st floor) via a direct escalator.

Palms Lounge

474 4000. **Shows** 8pm, 10.30pm last Sat of mth. No under-21s. **Map** p137 A4 ❽

This normally dark lounge lights up on one Saturday every month with Playboy Comedy, studded with relatively well-known comics you may recognise from Comedy Central, HBO or other TV shows.

Pearl

NEW *944 3200/www.palmspearl.com.* **Map** p137 A4 ❾

Since opening, the Palms has appeared very keen to steal the Hard Rock's thunder: first with its boutique accommodation, then with its numerous rooftop clubs, and now with this rock music venue, which staged shows by Gwen Stefani, Tool and Fall Out Boy soon after opening. With a capacity ranging from 1,100 (seated) to 2,500 (standing), all within 120 unobstructed feet (35m) of the stage, the Pearl comes with an intimacy rarely found in a venue of this size.

Rain

942 6832/www.rainatthepalms. com. **Open** 11pm-4am Fri, Sat. **Map** p137 A4 ❿

One of the last Vegas nightclubs built in an oversized, industrial style, Rain now looks a bit dated. However, it's still the best at what it does, with the non-stop dance music and eyebrow-searing pyrotechnics perhaps best heard and viewed from one of the private cabanas that overlook all the action from upstairs.

Arts & leisure

Brenden Las Vegas 14

507 4849/www.brendentheatres.com. **Map** p137 A4 ⓫

This cinema and IMAX complex has won countless consumer awards, and regular high-profile premières pay tribute to its central role in the Vegas moviegoing experience. With the exception of June's CineVegas Film Festival (www.cinevegas.com), blockbusters dominate, with one major feature usually configured for the sole IMAX screen.

Rio

3700 W Flamingo Road, at S Valley View Boulevard (reservations 1-866 746 7671/front desk & casino 777 7777/www.harrahs.com). Bus 201. **Map** p137 A3.

The Rio is another identity crisis in progress. In a bid to appeal to a younger audience, the all-suites Rio hired Prince to play here in 2006 and 2007, while Pure Management Group brought in hipster bowling lounge Lucky Strike Lanes. But some things remain unchanged: Masquerade Show in the Sky, a free parade with musicians and dancers, is still staged seven times daily. It's part of the hyperactive Masquerade Village, which features two storeys of dining, a variety of drinking (from Irish pub to wine cellar), dancing, shopping and shows. Other amenities include four waterfall-filled pools complete with sandy beach and volleyball courts, three wedding chapels and a floor of honeymoon suites, the top-of-the-line Michael's Salon, a spa, and access to the Rio Secco golf course, a half-hour away.

The Rio's casino is huge, sprawling for two blocks, and the predominant colours are green ($25) and black ($100): at weekends, it's hard to find $10-minimum blackjack. Smaller-stakes gamblers should aim for the lower-limit tables in the outlying areas of the casino; or better yet, walk across the street to the Gold Coast. Poker is also on offer – the Rio hosts the annual World Series of Poker (p31) – but it's a tough room filled with locals. A shuttle bus runs between the Rio and the Strip (9am-1pm daily).

Eating & drinking

Café Martorano

NEW *221 8279*. **Open** 6pm-2am Thur-Sat. **$$$**. **Italian**. Map p137 A3 ⑫

Vegas newcomer Steve Martorano might not be a celebrity chef just yet, but it's not for want of trying. Quite the showman, Martorano performs double duty in this 2007 arrival, working the kitchen before switching to the decks; he spent time as a DJ in his native Philadelphia before turning to Italian food. Part restaurant and part club, it's a favourite spot with visiting celebs.

Carnival World Buffet

777 7777. **Buffets** *Carnival World Buffet: Breakfast* 7-11am Mon-Fri; 7.30-10.30am Sat, Sun. *Brunch* 10.30am-3.30pm Sat, Sun. *Lunch* 11am-3.30pm Mon-Fri. *Dinner* 3.30-10pm daily. *Village Seafood Buffet: Dinner* 4-10pm Mon-Thur, Sun; 4-11pm Fri, Sat. **$$**. **Buffet**. Map p137 A3 ⑬

A favourite among locals, the pioneering Carnival World Buffet journeys the planet for its food. It's an idea that several other casinos have since copied, but no one has yet topped the Rio's inter-continental spreads, which take in everything from lasagne to Peking duck. The separate Village Seafood Buffet offers sushi, oysters and lobster, as well as a surprising range of meat dishes, and there are literally dozens of choices of cakes and pastries.

Gaylord

777 2277/www.gaylordlv.com. **Open** 11.30am-2.30pm, 5-11pm daily. **$$**. **Indian**. Map p137 A3 ⑭

The best in-casino Indian restaurant in Las Vegas is also, the last time we checked, the only in-casino Indian restaurant in Las Vegas. Still, that's not to underplay the quality of the cooking at Gaylord, which remains higher than you might expect. Although the food does seem to have been toned down for an American audience, and prices are high, it retains a reassuring hint of authenticity. The decor is pleasing, and service is both friendly and efficient.

Lucky Strike Lanes

NEW *777 7999/www.luckystrikelv.com*. **Open** 11am-3am daily. **$$**. **Bar**. Map p137 A3 ⑮

By removing the glaring lights, reflective lanes and dirty foot smell, and adding loud music, buxom waitresses and higher prices, Lucky Strike has effectively eradicated the blue-collar cafeteria image of bowling. The bar and food menus are creative and tasty, with cotton-candy martinis, sliders, and mac and cheese bites. Even league play is a desirable prospect: at the time of writing, the winning team were due to be rewarded with a trip to the Bahamas.

Nightlife

Chippendales

1-888 746 7784/777 7776. **Shows** 8pm Mon, Tue, Thur, Sun; 8pm, 10.30pm Fri, Sat. No under-18s. Map p137 A3 ⑯

Ladies, why let the guys have all the fun in Vegas when these chiselled male specimens can gyrate for your pleasure? Equal parts theatricality and sensuality, this time-tested father of all male revues makes for the perfect bachelorette, birthday or divorce party setting. The performers won't let you just sit back and passively take it all in; arriving drunk and uninhibited ensures a much better time.

Rio's Masquerade Show in the Sky p139

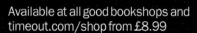

Arts & leisure

Penn & Teller
1-888 746 7784/777 7776. **Shows**
9pm Mon-Thur, Sat, Sun. No under-5s.
Map p137 A3 ⑰
Burly man-mountain Penn Jillette and
the mute, mono-monikered Teller are
the reservoir dogs to most other magicians' ocean's eleven: edgy, angry, and
always seemingly on the verge of
going off. They've become scourges of
the Magic Circle by showing their
audiences how tricks are done, but
they deserve equal credit for the pzazz
with which they pull off the illusions
they don't get round to explaining.
The closing bullet routine is the only
part of the show that falls flat, but the
rest of the evening is very entertaining indeed. Bonus: stick around after
the show for the inevitable autograph
signings, and you may well hear
Teller speak.

Tony 'n' Tina's Wedding
1-888 746 7784/777 7776.
Shows 7pm daily. **Map** p137 A3 ⑱
In this inventive, interactive show,
ticket-holders become wedding guests
taking in the nuptials and reception of
an Italian-American couple coping
with eccentric families, a pregnant
maid of honour, a drunk priest and
more. The set-up is just hokey enough
to make you want to brush up on your
singing and dance moves (think
'YMCA'). But once dinner is served
(an Italian buffet, natch), you'll want
to hightail it like a groom on the business end of a shotgun.

Other venues
Sight & museums

Las Vegas Springs Preserve
NEW *333 S Valley View Boulevard, at
US 95 (822 7700/www.springspreserve.
org).* **Open** *Summer* 10am-10pm daily;
Autumn-Spring 10am-6pm daily.
Admission $18.95; $10.95 reductions.
Map p137 A1 ⑲

Las Vegas's first eco-aware tourist
attraction looks likely to set the standard for future family-orientated theme
parks. See box p144.

Eating & drinking

Artisan Lounge
*Artisan, 1501 W Sahara Avenue, at
Highland Drive (214 4000/www.the
artisanhotel.com).* Bus 204. **Open**
24hrs daily. **$$**. **Bar**. **Map** p137 C1 ⑳
Gold-framed prints and paintings cover
the walls and ceiling, almost to the point
of absurdity, with empty frames even
suspended in the air, and statues inter-
spersed with shelves of books. Somehow,
it works. A unique amalgam of lodge,
bar and gallery, the Artisan is arty
Vegas's living room away from home.
Thanks to the lack of gambling, it's also
one of the quietest lounges in town.

Bourbon Street Cabaret
*Orleans, 4500 W Tropicana Avenue,
between S Decatur & S Valley
View Boulevards (365 7111/*

Penn & Teller

The green desert

The tables are turning against Sin City's culture of excess. Just three miles west of the Strip a new attraction is attempting to challenge Vegas's hitherto-held reputation for frivolous behaviour. It's the **Las Vegas Springs Preserve** (p143), a $250-million theme park showcasing the area's natural history and promoting futuristic sustainable living.

The Springs Preserve stands on the site of the city's humble beginnings, long before it got all fabulous and even before its official birthdate of 1905. Big Springs, as this spot was formerly known, is where the first settlers came to collect water.

Opened in June 2007, the Springs Preserve has exhibits on the area's wildlife, geology and pre-colonial culture. In addition, the 180-acre park is what creators like to call an 'eco-island', offering the growing metropolis a Central Park-style green space. The site showcases a prized collection of sustainable architecture: seven buildings on the site are expected to be certified as LEED Platinum, an honour bestowed upon only a handful of structures by the US Green Building Council. What's more, it shows how the futuristic technology actually works.

The centrepiece of the complex is the Desert Living Center, which promotes all aspects of 'green living'. It includes a Sustainability Gallery full of practical advice for homeowners and a meandering 'Inside Out' display that shares the energy-saving secrets of the structure itself – from the walls' straw-bale insulation to roofing rigged to catch rainwater.

If all this sounds a little bit too worthy, don't worry: along with the botanical gardens and hiking trails, there are dozens of hands-on, family-friendly exhibits, including an IMAX-style cinema. Outside is an open-air amphitheatre, where Jewel performed for the park's christening. And across the way, there's an eco-friendly Wolfgang Puck restaurant, proving that saving the planet needn't mean forgoing the finer things in life.

www.orleanscasino.com). Bus 103, 104, 201. **Open** 6pm-3am Tue-Sun. **$$. Bar. Map** p137 A5 ㉑

Local bands play a mix of rock, pop, Latin and disco in this small lounge six nights a week. It's styled like a French Quarter courtyard and adorned with wrought-iron decorations, with grand pianos suspended overhead. There's usually a two-drink minimum in effect.

Brendan's Irish Pub

Orleans, 4500 W Tropicana Avenue, between S Decatur & S Valley View Boulevards (365 7111/www.orleans casino.com). Bus 103, 104, 201. **Open** 5pm-1am Mon-Thur; 10am-2am Fri-Sun. **$$. Bar. Map** p137 A5 ㉒

The scene is fairly generic for an Irish pub with sports bar leanings. But while the setting is a little bland, the entertainment on weekends spices things up, with everything from Irish bands to zydeco troupes on the agenda. The bands' daffy groupies are sometimes even more of a lark than the music.

Golden Steer Steak House

308 W Sahara Avenue, between Las Vegas Boulevard South & S Industrial Road (384 4470/www.goldensteerlv. com). Bus 204. **Open** 5-11pm daily. **$$$. Steakhouse. Map** p137 C1 ㉓

The enormous (and, yes, golden) steer that signposts this old-school steak place on Sahara also advertises its decor. Discreet it certainly is not: think updated bordello crossed with an Old West saloon and you're almost there. But the steaks are classic: large, juicy and perfectly grilled, albeit served at prices that could stun a cow at 20 paces. Sinatra and Dino both ate here; four-plus decades later, it remains vintage Vegas at its most unreconstructed.

Shopping

Adult Superstore

3850 W Tropicana Avenue, at S Valley View Boulevard (798 0144). Bus 104, 201. **Open** 24hrs daily. **Map** p137 A5 ㉔

There are four branches of this locals' favourite, but this is the biggest of

them. The magazine and video sections are devoted to virtually every fetish and fantasy that's legal in Nevada, and there's an unequalled selection of toys, fetish gear and sexy food items.

David's Bridal

2600 W Sahara Avenue, at S Rancho Drive (367 4779/www.davidsbridal. com). Bus 106, 204. **Open** 11am-9pm Mon-Fri; 10am-6pm Sat; noon-6pm Sun. **Map** p137 B1 ㉕

Off-the-rack gowns at reasonable prices in a variety of styles are this store's speciality. There are also tons of accessories, including frocks for the bridal party and dyeable shoes.

Nightlife

Red Room Saloon

3101 W Sahara Avenue, between I-15 & S Valley View Boulevard (257 9663/ www.vegasredroom.com). Bus 204. **Open** 24hrs daily. No credit cards. **Map** p137 B1 ㉖

In truth, the Red Room is less of a club and more of a bar; witness the round-the-clock opening hours and video poker machines. But it merits mention here for its roster of DJ nights; chief among them is Soul Kitchen, Edgar Reyes's progressive house Thursday-nighter. There are also DJs on Wednesdays and Saturdays (indie and '80s); music starts around 11pm.

Arts & leisure

Century Orleans 18

Orleans, 4500 W Tropicana Avenue, between S Decatur & S Valley View Boulevards (227 3456/www.cine mark.com). Bus 103, 104, 201. **Map** p137 A5 ㉗

This 18-screen cinema complex ushered Las Vegas into the cineplex era with such amenities as stadium seating and THX-equipped auditoria. Although it isn't as chic as its chief competitor, the nearby Brenden Las Vegas 14 at the Palms (p139), it's remained one of the valley's most beloved movie theatres. Every so often, the roster includes a major studio-sanctioned art flick.

LAS VEGAS BY AREA

Golden Nugget Pool p148

Downtown

LAS VEGAS BY AREA

As if to prove that life does indeed go in cycles, Downtown is once again on the rise after decades in the doldrums. This is where Las Vegas was born, but the place has been on the slide for a while, having been gradually usurped by the mega-resorts on the Strip over the last 50 years. Downtown's slow but steady renaissance encompasses its formerly tired casinos (exhibit one: the **Golden Nugget**), but is also punctuated by new developments, such as the **Holsum Design Center** (p161) and the establishment of monthly art fest **First Friday** (p29).

Binion's

128 E Fremont Street, at N Casino Center Boulevard (reservations 1-800 937 6537/front desk & casino 382 1600/www.binions.com). Bus Deuce & all DTC-bound buses. **Map** p147 B2.

Opened by Benny Binion as Binion's Horseshoe in 1951, this Fremont Street relic competes with the Flamingo and Caesars Palace for the title of the most iconic hotel-casino in Vegas history. Certainly, it's been one of the most influential. Binion, a fabulous character and a fairly unpleasant man, was arguably more responsible than any other individual for the tone of 21st-century gambling in the city; it was Binion who abolished table limits for the first time, and Binion who effectively established the World Series of Poker here in the early 1970s.

So much for the past. After the Horseshoe stumbled into financial disrepair under the auspices of Binion's daughter Becky Behnen, the property fell into corporate hands (first Harrah's, then MTR Gaming) and it's not been the same since. The Horseshoe name

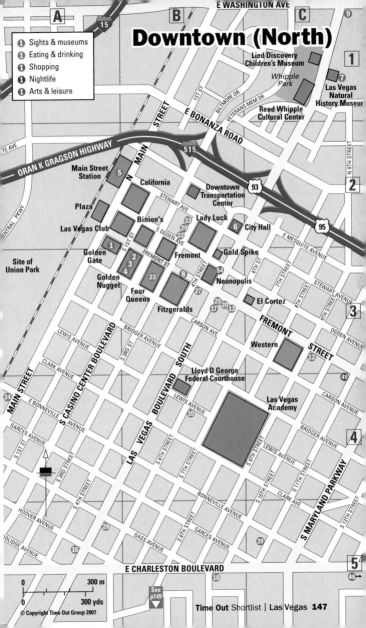

Downtown (North)

E WASHINGTON AVE

Legend:
- ① Sights & museums
- ① Eating & drinking
- ① Shopping
- ① Nightlife
- ① Arts & leisure

A | **B** | **C**

Lied Discovery Children's Museum

Whipple Park

Las Vegas Natural History Museum ⑦

Reed Whipple Cultural Center

E BONANZA ROAD

ORAN K GRAGSON HIGHWAY

Main Street Station ⑤

California

Downtown Transportation Center

Plaza

Binion's

Lady Luck

Las Vegas Club

Golden Gate ①

② ③ ④

Golden Nugget

Four Queens

Fremont ⑥ City Hall

㉝ ㉙ ㉒

Gold Spike

Fremont ⑧

㉓

㊃ Neonopolis

FitzgerIn alds ㉑

㉕ ⑳ ⑬
⑰

El Cortez

FREMONT STREET

Site of Union Park

LEWIS AVENUE

BRIDGER AVENUE

Western ⑫

CLARK AVENUE

Lloyd D George Federal Courthouse

LEWIS AVENUE

Las Vegas Academy

⑩

㊾

E BONNEVILLE AVENUE

GARCES AVENUE

㉔

HOOVER AVENUE

㉓

COOLIDGE AVENUE

⑯

BONNEVILLE AVENUE

㊴

E CHARLESTON BOULEVARD

⑱ ㊻

See p149

0   300 m
0   300 yds

© Copyright Time Out Group 2007

Time Out Shortlist | Las Vegas **147**

has been lost to history, while the World Series of Poker has decamped to the Harrah's-owned Rio. A recent refurbishment of the casino has sapped all atmosphere from the space, leaving this historic property as just another Downtown grind joint. Shame.

When the Binions owned Binion's, you found savvy, renegade dealers in its casino. But dramatic modifications have occurred since the change in ownership. Only four crap tables remain from what was once the centre of the dice universe. The blackjack pits have also shrunk, replaced by some newfangled poker derivatives that would've rendered Benny Binion apoplectic. Still, the video poker is only half bad; and the poker room is one of the largest in town. The race book occupies a former lounge in the West Horseshoe; the sports book is in a separate part of the casino.

Eating & drinking

Binion's Original Coffee Shop is still pretty decent, and there are excellent views from the 24th-floor Binion's Ranch Steakhouse, but otherwise there's not much here.

Golden Gate

1 E Fremont Street, at S Main Street (reservations 1-800 426 1906/front desk & casino 385 1906/www.golden gatecasino.net). Bus Deuce & all DTC-bound buses. **Map** p147 A2.

Being the oldest and smallest of anything aren't normally qualities about which a Vegas property brags, but the Golden Gate manages to pull it off. Having celebrated its 100th birthday in 2006 (it's been known as the Golden Gate only since 1955; it was opened as the Hotel Nevada), this 106-room property appears positively quaint alongside the flashy Golden Nugget, the enormous brash Plaza and the garish Fremont Street Experience. Owned by likeable local maverick Mark Brandenburg, who's shown little inclination to drag his place into the

modern world, this is old Vegas at its most appealingly basic.

The Golden Gate is an old-time, no-frills, family-owned casino, navigated by a multitude of wheelchair-required small ramps. The carpet's worn, the tables and machines are packed like sardines, and the bosses brook no nonsense. From the far dice table closest to the deli, you can make a dash for the famous 99¢ shrimp cocktail between rolls. The comps here are liberal: play $10 blackjack for an hour and ask for the coffeeshop for two.

Eating & drinking

Bay City Diner

Open 24hrs Mon, Fri-Sun; 6am-2am Tue-Thur. **$**. **Diner**. **Map** p147 A2 ❶
Like the casino in which it's housed, this is an icon of old Vegas. There's nothing fussy or upscale about the Bay City Diner: it's just a small room serving basic food for 20 hours a day. But it oozes history, from the grainy decor via the predictable menu to the ageing, no-nonsense waitresses. Anyone interested in the city's past should eat here at least once.

Golden Nugget

129 E Fremont Street, at S Casino Center Boulevard (reservations 1-800 846 5336/front desk & casino 385 7111/www.goldennugget.com). Bus Deuce & all DTC-bound buses. **Map** p147 B3.

After two years in the hands of young duo Tim Poster and Tom Breitling, the venerable Nugget was taken over in 2005 by Landry's Restaurants. Many Downtown observers feared that the Texas-based restaurant chain would drain the place of its character, but a $100-million programme of renovations has actually pepped up the place no end. Following the improvements, the Nugget has consolidated its position as the best casino on Fremont Street.

The refurbishments have been dramatic, and almost entirely for the better. The casino floor now feels almost

Downtown (South)

grand, complete with a new poker room and the city's most handsome sports book. A slew of new restaurants have revitalised what had become a fairly tired catering programme. And then there's the fabulous pool area, complete with private cabanas, its own lounge (the Dive Bar, tee hee) and water slides running through a central shark tank. Well, why not?

The elegant marble lobby of the Nugget's casino may seem out of place on Fremont Street, and the high minimums (mostly $10 for craps and blackjack) in the nicely renovated casino are unusual for Downtown. There's a segregated pit for players with larger bankrolls who want to play baccarat and blackjack without the hoi polloi; it's the only high-limit pit Downtown.

However, there are also good selections of slot and video poker machines from low to high denominations. The sports book was relocated to where the buffet used to be; it's now full-scale.

Eating & drinking

Golden Nugget Buffet

NEW **Buffets** *Breakfast* 7-10.30am Mon-Fri. *Brunch* 8am-3.30pm Sat, Sun. *Lunch* 10.30am-3.30pm Mon-Fri. *Dinner* 3.30-10pm daily. **$**. **Buffet**. **Map** p147 B3 ❷

Revamped and relocated within the all-new Golden Nugget, Downtown's smartest buffet more than delivers the goods that its reputation demands of it. The new room isn't as cosy, but the high quality of the food more than

Neon Museum p152

compensates. The offerings are near the top of the Vegas food chain, especially the carvery and the excellent desserts.

Rush Lounge

NEW Open noon-4am daily. **$$**.
Lounge. Map p147 B3 ❸
Before 2007, 'contemporary' wasn't an adjective that applied to the Golden Nugget casino. However, it's just about the most accurate description for its upscale new Rush Lounge, swathed in sexy reds, browns and horizontal stripes. It's a rare find among the Downtown casinos, not least because it prefers table games to video poker.

Vic & Anthony's

NEW Open 5-11pm daily. **$$$**.
Steakhouse. Map p147 B3 ❹
Modelling itself as a classic Vegas steakhouse, with a live Maine lobster tank, masculine decor and attentive service, Vic & Anthony's manages to make a meal in a new restaurant feel like a step back in time. Start off the experience with a strong cocktail and a tray of fresh Blue Point oysters, then move on to mains of various seafood dishes, grain-fed beef or lamb and veal chops. A smart start to a vintage Vegas weekender.

Main Street Station

200 N Main Street, at E Stewart Avenue (reservations 1-800 713 8933/front desk & casino 387 1896/www.mainstreetcasino.com). Bus Deuce & all DTC-bound buses. **Map** p147 A2.
Main Street Station is the nicest Downtown casino that's not called the Golden Nugget. Themed as a fin-de-siècle delight (check out the gaslamps that front the property), the casino is filled with antiques of all kinds, not all of them Victorian. Teddy Roosevelt's Pullman car is here, now a chic smoking lounge; a carved oak fireplace from Prestwick Castle in Scotland and a set of doors from an old London bank are also on display; and chunks of the Berlin Wall sit in the men's room. Accessible yet smart, upscale (for Downtown) yet fun, this isn't the most charismatic property, but it's likeable all the same.

Main Street's casino offers a good selection of slots and video poker, three-card poker and low limits at the tables; $5 single- and double-deck blackjack dominates and the crap tables offer 20x odds. An illuminated sign over the roulette area depicts a single-zero wheel, but the wheel itself contains two zeros.

Eating & drinking

The choice might be small, but it's all good stuff. Its name a nod to a railway theme that's delineated in fairly tasteful fashion, the Pullman Grille deals in surf and turf favourites. It's fine, but the Triple 7 Brew Pub remains a better bet, the well-above-average burgers and sandwiches acting as perfect stomach-lining for the very decent beers brewed on site. Many locals swear by the Garden Court Buffet: the room is beautiful, the selections are excellent and the prices ($10.99 for dinner) are most definitely right.

Triple 7 Brew Pub

Open 11am-7am daily. **$$.**
Bar. Map p147 A2 **⑤**
The Triple 7 serves fair beer and above-par bar food, and has an unbeatable $1-a-drink happy hour. But the real reason to visit this microbrewery is to gawk at the multi-million-dollar collection of antiques and collectibles, which even extends to the restroom: gentlemen are able to express their opinion on communism by relieving themselves on a portion of the Berlin Wall.

Plaza

1 N Main Street, at E Fremont Street (reservations 1-800 634 6575/front desk & casino 386 2110/www.plaza hotelcasino.com). Bus Deuce & all DTC-bound buses. **Map** p147 A2.
This iconic Downtown property opened as Jackie Gaughan's Plaza, but Jackie is long Gaughan (he now owns El Cortez) and the Plaza is currently owned by the Tamares Group (which also owns the Vegas Club; p180). Even so, the Plaza retains a resolutely old Vegas feel, from the majestically over-the-top lighting beneath the shelter outside its main entrance to the unpalatably smoky casino floor and the resolutely downmarket buffet.

In truth, it's a fairly shambolic place that could really use a little TLC. Still, the prices are right, and the rooftop swimming pool is an appealing extra.

The casino teems with 1,200 slot machines. In the pit, gamblers can play $1 craps or $5 blackjack. Seven-card stud, Texas hold 'em and Omaha hold 'em poker are played in the card room, where limits are low and the players are more gentlemanly than on the Strip. But if you really want to gamble on the cheap, the keno lounge is for you: the Plaza is the only place in the US that offers double keno (simultaneous action on two boards) with games starting at 40¢, a bargain, despite the rotten odds. The bingo room is on the third floor.

Eating & drinking

While it retains a certain vintage Vegas charm and serves a creditable steak, the best things about the second-level Center Stage restaurant are the views straight down Fremont Street afforded from its window seats. The other eating options here are pretty much as you might expect: a round-the-clock diner, a super-cheap buffet (dinner is just $8.99) and a food court holding a handful of global chains.

Other venues

Sights & museums

City of Las Vegas Galleries

Bridge Gallery, 2nd Floor, City Hall, 400 E Stewart Avenue, at Las Vegas Boulevard South (229 6383/www.arts lasvegas.org). Bus Deuce & all DTC-bound buses. **Open** 8am-5pm Mon-Fri.
Admission free. **Map** p147 B2 **⑥**
The City of Las Vegas puts a great deal of thought into the shows it stages: satisfying exhibits by serious artists from across the US, many of which demonstrate a decidedly academic bent. Expect anything from painting, sculpture and photography to drawing and contemporary installation.

Las Vegas Natural History Museum

900 Las Vegas Boulevard North, at E Washington Avenue (384 3466/www.lvnhm.org). Bus 113, 208. **Open** 9am-4pm daily. **Admission** $7; $3-$6 reductions. **Map** p147 C1 ❼

This small but enthusiastically run museum doesn't offer much in the way of bells and whistles. The Marine Life Room features small sharks in a large tank, the Wild Nevada Room has exhibits on the flora and fauna of Nevada and the Young Scientist Center has some interactive displays. However, the five roaring, robotic dinosaurs, among them a vast T-rex, are a big draw. They're so life-like that kids are liable to be genuinely petrified.

Neon Museum

Fremont Street, between Las Vegas Boulevard South & Main Street (387 6366/www.neonmuseum.org). Bus Deuce & all DTC-bound buses. **Open** 24hrs daily. **Admission** free. **Map** p147 B3 ❽

There are 11 restored neon signs dotting Downtown, in so-called 'outdoor galleries' along or just off Fremont Street. The old Hacienda horseman is riding high again, and the long-defunct Nevada Hotel continues to help light up the night, alongside smaller signs devoted to the Aladdin casino, the Flame Restaurant, the Chief Hotel Court and the Anderson Dairy. The museum has also put several signs on display at the Old Las Vegas Mormon Fort Historic Park (right), including the shapely Arabic 'A' from the old Sahara.

In 2009, the Neon Museum plans to convert its Neon Boneyard (currently a resting place for retired vintage neons; open to tour groups by appointment only) into a full-scale museum of historic Vegas signage. The landmark lobby from the old La Concha hotel, one of the city's great Googie structures, has been rescued and moved up the boulevard, ready to serve as the visitor centre, gallery and gift shop for the museum when it opens.

Old Las Vegas Mormon Fort Historic Park

500 E Washington Avenue, at Las Vegas Boulevard North (486 3511/www.parks.nv.gov/olvmf.htm). Bus 113, 208. **Open** 8am-4.30pm Mon-Sat. **Admission** $3; $2 reductions; free under-6s. No credit cards. **Map** p147 C7 ❾

Built by a group of Mormon missionaries in 1855 and then left to become part of the Las Vegas Ranch, this is Vegas's pioneer settlement site, the oldest Euro-American structure in the state and an example of what Vegas was like before the railroad arrived. Though only remnants of the original structure remain, restoration and reconstruction have brought the compound back to life, and knowledgeable guides are on hand to answer any questions you may have.

Eating & drinking

André's

401 S 6th Street, at E Lewis Avenue (385 5016/www.andresfrenchrest.com). Bus Deuce, 206. **Open** 6-11pm Mon-Sat. **$$$. French. Map** p147 B4 ❿

Check out the expense-account crowd at this Downtown institution, with patio dining that's oh-so-New York. Chef and owner André Rochat (also of Alizé; p136), a local legend of sorts, serves French haute cuisine accompanied by a world-class wine cellar (though with few bargains). The Monte Carlo branch even has a plush cigar and cognac lounge.

Art Bar

1511 S Main Street, at Utah Avenue (437 2787). Bus Deuce, 206. **Open** 2pm-6am daily. **$. Bar. Map** p149 B3 ⓫

Cheap drinks and an offbeat style (there's an entire room of velvet Elvi) have helped the Art Bar become the most successful Downtown bar to open in recent years. Owned by wacky but loveable Elvis impersonator Jesse Garon, it's packed every weekend with artists, punks, average Joes, vagrants

Old Las Vegas Mormon Fort Historic Park

and the occasional suspiciously driven intellectual, sipping scotch and taking advantage of the free Wi-Fi.

Atomic Liquors

917 E Fremont Street, at S 9th Street (384 7371). Bus Deuce & all DTC-bound buses. **Open** 7am-11pm daily. **$.** No credit cards. **Bar**. **Map** p147 C3 ⑫
Founded in 1935 and located at the sketchy end of Fremont, this is a gem, from its cut-to-the-chase sign – 'Liquor' in huge white neon – to the cast of crims, bums and chancers who sup here. If you're looking for trouble, you came to the right place. However, although even the bartenders suggest that it's not the place for unaccompanied ladies, most of the barflies are harmless enough.

Beauty Bar

517 E Fremont Street, at Las Vegas Boulevard South (598 1965/www. beautybar.com). Bus Deuce & all DTC-bound buses. **Open** 9pm-2am Mon, Tue, Sun; 5pm-2am Wed, Thur; 5pm-4am Fri; 9pm-4am Sat. **$$.** **Bar**. **Map** p147 B3 ⑬
The New York version of this chain made famous the 'martinis and manicures' concept featured on *Sex and the City*; a shame, then, that cosmetology laws forbid manicures here. The '50s decor was salvaged from the Capri Salon of Beauty in Trenton, NJ, with lighting from Vegas's old Algiers hotel; it's matched by delightful themed cocktails, such as the Platinum Blonde and the Red Head. Bands and DJs entertain more or less nightly.

Chicago Joe's

820 S 4th Street, between E Gass & Hoover Avenues (382 5637/www. chicagojoesrestaurant.com). Bus Deuce, 206. **Open** 11am-10pm Tue-Fri; 5-10pm Sat. **$$.** **Italian**. **Map** p149 C1 ⑭
The kind of no-frills, fair-prices locals' favourite that everyone loves, CJ's – located in a tiny 1932 brick house – has lasted 30 years, thanks to its solid southern Italian cooking and regional specialities (Chicago spicy lobster), and its homey, authentic but quirky setting. Joe's is far removed from the $50 pasta joints on the Strip, and that's the whole point.

Dino's

1516 Las Vegas Boulevard South, at W Utah Avenue (382 3894/www. dinoslv.com). Bus Deuce, 206. **Open** 24hrs daily. **$.** No credit cards. **Bar**. **Map** p149 B3 ⑮

The sign on the side, advertising this as 'The last neighborhood bar in Las Vegas', is hyperbole. Still, this loud dive offers an upbeat mix of hipsters, freaks, drunks and, on the karaoke nights hosted by Elton John doppelgänger Danny G (Thur-Sat), off-key crooners and wannabes. Bar regulars compete to join the Drunk of the Month Club.

Doña Maria's

910 Las Vegas Boulevard South, at E Charleston Boulevard (382 6538). Bus Deuce, 206. **Open** 8am-10pm daily. **$$. Mexican. Map** p147 A5 ⑯
The prices are good and the location is central, but Doña Maria's is very popular with the city's large Mexican community for one reason above all others: the loud and occasionally boisterous place offers some of Vegas's best Mexican food. The *tamales* (spicy chopped meat and ground corn, served in a corn husk) are the real draw, but the *tortas* (sandwiches) and fiery salsas help keep the place busy.

Downtown Cocktail Room

NEW *111 Las Vegas Boulevard South, at E Fremont Street (300 6268/www. downtownlv.net). All DTC-bound buses.* **Open** 4pm-2am Mon-Thur; 7pm-2am Fri-Sun. **$$. Bar. Map** p147 B3 ⑰
Despite its name, this chic, upscale bar will make you forget you're in Downtown; or, at least, Downtown Las Vegas. Perhaps the most casually dramatic addition to the area, done out in deep, sexy reds and sheer curtains you can close for added nook privacy, this understated lounge will put you in the mood to leave with a date even if you didn't come in with one. DJs entertain nightly, though the music is generally pitched at conversation-friendly levels.

Esmerelda's

1000 E Charleston Boulevard, between E Charleston Boulevard & S Maryland Parkway (388 1404). Bus 109, 206. **Open** 11am-9pm daily. **$. Latin American. Map** p147 B5 ⑱

There are a few Mexican dishes on the menu, a nod to the origins of its clientele. But the real reason to visit this unprepossessing storefront eaterie is for its range of calmer but still hearty Salvadorean specialities. Chow down on a *pupusa* or two, a flat corn tortilla stuffed variously with cheese or any number of different meats. Subtlety isn't a strong point of the kitchen here, but you'll leave replete.

Florida Café

Howard Johnson, 1401 Las Vegas Boulevard South, at W Charleston Boulevard (385 3013/www.florida cubancafe.com). Bus Deuce, 206. **Open** 8am-10pm Mon-Thur; 7am-11pm Fri-Sun. **$. Cuban. Map** p149 C3 ⑲
A rather scruffy-looking motel at the wrong end of Las Vegas Boulevard provides the unlikely setting for the most popular Cuban restaurant in Las Vegas. This isn't subtle food, by any means, and nor is it especially healthy. But don't let that stop you – as comfort cooking goes, it's just exotic enough to stand out from the pack. Try a Cuban sandwich if you're not absolutely ravenous.

Griffin

NEW *511 E Fremont Street, at Las Vegas Boulevard South (382 0577). Bus Deuce & all DTC-bound buses.* **Open** 5pm-4am Mon-Sat; 9pm-4am Sun. **$$. Bar. Map** p147 B3 ⑳
Though it's at street level, this putatively Brit-styled joint on Fremont Street is the place to go medieval. Windowless with an eerie but romantic glow fed by candlelight and fireplaces, the new but old-feeling Griffin doubles as an after-work beer pub and a late night indie-rockin' haunt. Tattooed hotties pull Stellas while a dollar stirs T-Rex and the Smiths from the juke.

Grill on Charleston

NEW *Holsum Design Center, 229 W Charleston Boulevard, between Las Vegas Boulevard South & I-15 (380 1110/www.lvgrill.com). Bus 206.* **Open** 11am-2pm, 5-10pm daily. **$. Italian. Map** p149 B2 ㉑

Downtown Cocktail Room

Great minds

Architect Frank Gehry comes to Vegas.

While the Strip's architecture has lately been getting some of the recognition it deserves, the built community beyond the Boulevard is all too often overlooked, if not completely ignored. In Las Vegas, invisibility is an even tougher problem to address than taste. So when, in 2006, Frank Gehry announced he would be designing a building in Las Vegas, people noticed.

Even more surprising than Gehry's arrival was the project itself (the Lou Ruvo Alzheimer's Research Center), its purpose (better understanding of the human mind) and its Union Park in Downtown, the city's soon-to-be-built-from-scratch urban core). The $60-million building will have a front section defined by an orderly mass of blocks, with a chaotic tumble of steel and glass to the rear. Love, hate or just be plain baffled by it, the building is tipped to become the city's first world-class structure that isn't tied to tourism when it opens in 2008.

Lou Ruvo Alzheimer's Research Center president Dr Zaven Khachaturian has claimed that the institutes's wealthy founder Larry Ruvo 'is Lorenzo the Magnificent, and Frank is Michelangelo... They are setting the stage for a total transformation, another renaissance.' Judging from the regenerative powers of Gehry's buildings in Bilbao and Los Angeles, Las Vegas has everything to gain.

This little spot in the Holsum Lofts started out American, but new management brought an Italian slant to the menu in mid 2007. It's off to a good start with fuss-free Italian classics (such as caprese and freshly-baked pizza), plus imported beers and an all-Italian wine list.

Hogs & Heifers

NEW *201 N 3rd Street, at E Ogden Avenue (676 1457/www.hogsand heifers.com). Bus Deuce & all DTC-bound buses.* **Open** 1pm-4am daily. **$$**. No credit cards. **Bar**. **Map** p147 B2 ㉒
'Is that the sound you make when he takes you from behind?' yells a classy maven in boots from her roost on top of the bar. To some onlookers, Hogs & Heifers isn't pretty or fun; still, those onlookers seem to fall in the minority. The schtick here is similar to Coyote Ugly, but less choreographed and more raunchy. Arrive on your Harley or bring along some red for your neck if you're fixin' to fit right in.

Hugo's Cellar

Four Queens, 202 E Fremont Street, at S Casino Center Boulevard (385 4011/ www.fourqueens.com). Bus Deuce & all DTC-bound buses. **$$$**. **American**. **Map** p147 B3 ㉓
One of Vegas's original fine dining establishments, Hugo's old traditions are still good ones: pampering wait staff, a tableside visit from the famous salad cart, a solid wine list and a rose for the lady. The menu is vintage Vegas gourmet rather than fusion; heavy on the meat and seafood (steak and lobster are the stars), and just what you'd expect for dessert (cherries jubilee, bananas Foster).

Ice House Lounge

650 S Main Street, at E Bonneville Avenue (315 2570). Bus Deuce, 105. **Open** 10am-2am daily. **$$**. **Bar**. **Map** p149 A4 ㉔
To locals hoping for a Downtown renaissance, the Ice House (built by the site of the city's original ice house) seemed like a mirage: a $5-million free-standing art deco-style building across

the way from a weekly rental motel and a porn shop. It hasn't quite worked out that way, and the place never really hums outside of happy hour. Still, it remains something of a looker, and a good place to take in a game on the big-screen TVs.

Kabob Korner

NEW *507 E Fremont Street, at Las Vegas Boulevard South (384 7722/ www.kabobkornerlv.com). Bus Deuce & all DTC-bound buses.* **Open** 10am-11pm daily. **$**. **Middle Eastern**. **Map** 147 B3 ㉕

A tidy, unassuming storefront bang in the middle of fast-rising Fremont, Kabob Korner is a family-run and relatively inexpensive boite. It serves a broad menu with something for everyone; burgers, subs and pitta sandwiches, as well as Halal-certified selections (try the tikka and kebab dishes). This stretch of Fremont Street is fast filling with increasingly fashionable bars, but this agreeably basic enterprise remains its best eating option at present.

Luv-It Frozen Custard

505 E Oakey Boulevard, at Las Vegas Boulevard South (384 6452/www. luvitfrozencustard.com). Bus Deuce. **Open** 1-10pm Tue-Thur; 1-11pm Fri, Sat. **$**. No credit cards. **Desserts**. **Map** p149 B3 ㉖

This little shack doesn't look like much, but it dispenses the most moreishly delicious desserts in the city. Frozen custard looks like ice-cream and even tastes a bit like ice-cream, but it's richer and smoother than anything either Ben or Jerry could conjure. Now run by Greg Tiedemann, whose grandparents opened the business in 1973, Luv-It offers four flavours a day, served in cups, sundaes and shakes. A Western sundae's a good start, but you can't go wrong with any of it.

Mickie Finnz Fish House

NEW *425 E Fremont Street, at Las Vegas Boulevard South (382 4204). Bus Deuce & all DTC-bound buses.* **Open** 11am-2am daily. **$$**. **American**. **Map** p147 B3 ㉗

Part of a Fremont Street triple treat since 2007 (along with Irish pub Hennesseys and upscale Brass), this vaguely tiki spot is perfect for the laid-back Downtown crowd. Don't let the name trick you into thinking that seafood is the main staple: although the grilled fish tacos really are delicious, the menu also offers a large selection of bar food and snacks (nachos, burgers, pizzas) intended to lay a good foundation for the drinking later on. There's also live music at weekends (from local bands), which veers from the unfortunate to the unexpectedly good.

Potato Valley Café

NEW *801 Las Vegas Boulevard South, at Gass Avenue (363 7821/www.potato lasvegas.com). Bus Deuce, 206.* **Open** 8am-4pm Mon-Fri. **$**. **American**. **Map** p147 A5 ㉘

The first western outpost for this urban business lunch mini-chain (the other two are in Annapolis, MD, and Washington, DC) features oven-roasted jacket potatoes as a main course. And you won't want much more besides – when they're topped with everything from Cuban chicken to broccoli and blue cheese, they work a treat, albeit a very carb-heavy one. Less calorific options include a decent selection of sandwiches and salads.

Sidebar

NEW *201 N 3rd Street, at E Ogden Avenue (384 2761/www.sidebarlv.com). Bus Deuce & all DTC-bound buses.* **Open** 5pm-midnight Mon-Thur; 5pm-2am Fri, Sat. **$$**. **Bar**. **Map** p149 B2 ㉙

Shake up vintage Vegas appeal with 21st-century style and you have Sidebar, a louche spot attached to the Triple George steakhouse (p159). Martinis are the speciality, drunk to a soundtrack provided by a pianist and with picture windows looking out to 3rd Street in the foreground. An ideal place to while away a few hours, perhaps with a discussion of the difference between gentrification and revitalisation in the Downtown area of Las Vegas.

LAS VEGAS BY AREA

Triple George & Sidebar

El Sombrero

807 S Main Street, at E Gass Avenue (382 9234). Bus Deuce. **Open** 11am-4pm Mon-Thur; 11am-8.30pm Fri, Sat. **$. Mexican. Map** p149 B1 ㉚

The oldest continuously operating non-casino eatery in the city approaches its 60th birthday much as it neared its 50th: with a shrug. Curiously, gloriously oblivious to the last two decades of Strip development, this small hut continues to dispense unflashy but hearty Mexican peasant food to its patrons, many of whom have been coming here for years. Definitely a better bet than its rival Casa Don Juan just down the street.

Thai BBQ

1424 S 3rd Street, at Las Vegas Boulevard South (383 1128). Bus Deuce. **Open** 11am-10pm daily. **$$. Thai. Map** p149 B3 ㉛

Despite its gritty locale, Thai BBQ remains one of the best Thai eateries in town. The friendly and helpful service makes choosing from the large menu of Thai specialities simple; the hearty portions of such classics as pad Thai are worth the trip. Highlights include papaya salad, excellent satay, and rich and spicy beef noodle soup.

Tinoco's Bistro

103 E Charleston Boulevard, at S Main Street (464 5008). Bus 206. **Open** 11am-3pm, 5-10pm Mon-Sat. **$$. Italian. Map** p149 B2 ㉜

The arty industrial space was recently expanded to meet demand (especially at lunch time), and the menu was slightly revamped, but chef Enrique Tinoco's urban bistro remains an Arts District gem. Delicious continental fare features (crab-stuffed shrimp on risotto, veal picatta, and more) and the own-made soups are a must.

Triple George

NEW *201 N 3rd Street, at E Ogden Avenue (384 2761/www.triplegeorge grill.com). Bus Deuce & all DTC-bound buses.* **Open** 11am-4pm Mon; 11am-10pm Tue-Thur; 11am-11pm Fri; 4-11pm Sat. **$$$. American. Map** p147 B2 ㉝

A lunch haven for business suits but an evening haunt for more casually clad Downtowners, this subtly chic art deco room was conceived as a San Francisco-style chophouse, with a central wooden bar surrounded by several private dining enclosures. The steaks, seafood and chops are good, but it's the Louis salads and own-made soups that are the real highlight here. A valiant, upmarket addition to the area.

Shopping

Attic

1018 S Main Street, at E Charleston Boulevard (388 4088/www.atticvintage .com). Bus 105, 106, 108, 207. **Open** 10am-5pm Mon-Sat. **Map** p149 B1 ㉞

Its claim to be the largest vintage store in the world is as silly as the $1 admission charge (refundable on purchase, but that's not the point). Despite this, and its high prices, the Attic is still the best vintage store in Vegas. The ground floor has homewares and custom-made clothing; shoes and accessories are upstairs.

Charleston Antique Mall

307 W Charleston Boulevard, at S Western Avenue (228 4783). Bus Deuce, 104, 105, 108, 206. **Open** 10am-6pm Mon-Sat; 11am-5pm Sun. **Map** p149 A2 ㉟

Formerly part of the Red Rooster Antique Mall, the old 7-Up bottling company has been restocked and renovated with 35 vendors. If you like the look of that old tiki bar, snap it up: the good stuff goes fast.

D'Loe's House of Style

220 E Charleston Boulevard, at S 3rd Street (382 5688/www.houseofstylethen andnow.com). Bus Deuce, 105, 106, 108, 204. **Open** noon-6.30pm Tue-Sat. **Map** p149 B2 ㊱

Mario D'Loe cut his teeth as a costume designer for Vegas shows before filling this store with finds from the 1960s and '70s. A few blocks away is Valentino's Zoot Suit Connection (906 S 6th Street, at E Charleston Boulevard, 383 9555), which offers similar vintage fare with the emphasis on eveningwear.

Epic Shoos

NEW *1209 S Main Street, at W
Charleston Boulevard (388 4343/
www.epicshoos.com). Bus 206.*
Open 11am-7pm Tue-Sat; noon-6pm
Sun. **Map** p149 B2 ③⑦

Todd Burden, owner of hipster clothing boutique Still (p120), opened this
cool sneaker shop in 2006. It specialises in the freshest brands (BBC, Creative
Recreation) and old-school favourites
(Nike, Reebok). Drop by on First
Fridays (p29) for new-release parties.

Funk House

*1228 S Casino Center Boulevard, at E
Colorado Avenue (678 6278/www.the
funkhouselasvegas.com). Bus Deuce,
104, 105, 108, 206.* **Open** 10am-5pm
Mon-Sat. **Map** p149 B2 ③⑧

Cindy Funkhouser's ever-growing collection is especially strong in late 1950s
and early '60s pieces, and there's a wide
variety of glass, jewellery and toys.
One of the best antiques stores in town,
the Funk House is also ground zero for
First Friday (p29).

Gamblers Book Club

*630 S 11th Street, at E Bonneville
Avenue (382 7555/www.gamblersbook.
com). Bus 105, 106, 108, 207.* **Open**
9am-5pm Mon-Sat. **Map** p147 C5 ③⑨

The world's largest distributor of gambling books, be they coffee-table tomes,
industry histories or tips on beating the
system. If you don't just want to read,
there are also cards, chips and gam-
bling-related software for sale.

Gamblers General Store

*800 S Main Street, at E Gass Avenue
(382 9903/www.gamblersgeneralstore.
com). Bus Deuce, 105, 106, 108.* **Open**
9am-6pm daily. **Map** p149 B1 ④⓪

This well-stocked shop is packed with
gift ideas for that special gambler in
your life. There's something to suit all
budgets, from a single casino chip cost-
ing a couple of coins to vintage video
poker machines. Along with the collectibles are pretty much everything
you need to play any of the casino
games, including a library of 'how to'
gaming books.

Las Vegas Paper Doll

NEW *Holsum Design Center, 229 W
Charleston Boulevard, at Grand Central
Parkway (385 7892/www.lvpaperdoll.
com). Bus 206.* **Open** 10am-6pm Mon-
Sat. **Map** p149 B2 ④①

Owner Anne Kellogg's passion for
paper is evident in this beautiful
stationery and gift boutique inside
the historic Holsum bread building.
Someone's birthday? Here's where to
find the card, the gift and the paper in
which to wrap it. The eclectic stock of
magnets, books, cards, jewellery and
baby goods are the direct result of
Kellogg's keen eye for design.

Las Vegas
Premium Outlets

*875 S Grand Central Parkway, at W
Charleston Boulevard (474 7500/www.
lasvegaspremiumoutlets.com). Bus 105,
106, 108, 207.* **Open** 10am-9pm Mon-
Sat; 10am-8pm Sun. **Map** p149 B1 ④②

For brand-name bargains, you can't
beat a discount mall, where stores sell
last season's stock at a fraction of its
original price. This excellent outdoor
outlet mall is geared to the higher end
of the fashion market. Labels on site
include Armani, Dolce & Gabbana,
Brooks Brothers, Lacoste, Theory and
Ralph Lauren, to name but a few.
Twenty-five new shops and a new parking garage, all scheduled for autumn
2007, will up the ante still further.

Modify

*8 E Charleston Boulevard, at S Main
Street (384 6555/www.modifylv.com).
Bus Deuce, 104, 105, 108, 206.* **Open**
1-7pm Wed-Sat. **Map** p149 B2 ④③

This mid-century modern boutique
specialises in Danish modern and
space-age lighting, rugs, pottery, tex-
tiles, books and custom pillows from
vintage fabrics. Hipster brands Diesel
and Urban Outfitters kitted out their
stores with this stuff.

New Rock Boots

*804 Las Vegas Boulevard South,
at E Gass Avenue (614 9464). Bus
Deuce.* **Open** 11am-8pm Mon-Sat.
Map p149 C1 ④④

The ultimate makeover

The regeneration of a low-key Vegas icon.

Gallery P

If Oscar Goodman leaves a lasting legacy from his spell as mayor of Las Vegas, it looks set to be the urban renaissance of Las Vegas's downtrodden Downtown. Complete with entertainment and arts districts, office and medical parks, mixed-use projects, a sports arena and – gasp! – a Vegas version of Central Park, the area around the Fremont Street Experience will soon be unrecognisable.

There's no better example of this kind of regenerative redevelopment than the **Holsum Design Center** (formerly the Holsum Lofts; www.holsumlofts.com), which opened in May 2005 at the intersection of W Charleston Boulevard and Grand Central Parkway. Conceived by developer Jeffrey LaPour, it's a key example of Vegas regenerating itself from within, still relatively rare in a city that usually prefers to demolish and start again from scratch.

The series of structures that the centre inhabits, just across the street from the gigantic World Market Center and the Las Vegas Premium Outlets, were known as

the Holsum Bread Buildings until very recently. Constructed in 1954, it was a fully functioning bakery until 2002, distributing more than 230 different varieties of baked goods to outlets across southern Nevada at its peak. The buildings were as popular for their iconic neon signage as for the aroma of freshly baked bread that wafted through the neighbourhood. Its status within the local community inspired LaPour Partners to renovate the group of white stone buildings rather than raze them.

The overhaul has been dramatic. Today, Holsum houses a collection of art galleries (Contemporary Arts Collective, Gallery P), interior design outlets (the **Lynn Peri Collection** [p163], Bergamo Fabrics, Central Kitchen & Bath) and speciality shops (**Las Vegas Paper Doll** [left], the Dressing Room). It's become a hub for the city's burgeoning arts scene, and is especially lively during Downtown's monthly arts festival, **First Friday**. But, most importantly, it connects Las Vegans to a piece of their city's history.

Cross John Fluevog's edgy style with the Doc Martens aesthetic, stir in the 1970s rock 'n' roll style of Kiss, and lo: New Rock Boots. Decorative touches such as buckles, straps, flames and skulls make the boots popular with punks, goths and bikers, but there's also a wide selection of stilettos.

Red Rooster Antique Mall

1109 S Western Avenue, at W Charleston Boulevard (382 5253). Bus Deuce, 104, 105, 108, 206. **Open** 10am-6pm Mon-Sat; 11am-5pm Sun. **Map** p149 A3 ⑮

A labyrinth of cluttered rooms and individually run stalls, with racks of dusty magazines holding shelf space next to $100 antique bottles. There's fabulous casino memorabilia: ashtrays, chips and postcards.

Toys of Yesteryear

2028 E Charleston Boulevard, at S Eastern Avenue (598 4030). Bus 110, 206. **Open** 11am-3pm Tue-Sat. **Map** p147 C1 ⑯

Forget the dice clocks and gambling chips: this tiny shop has old-fashioned toys and collectibles for adults as well as children, including Kewpie dolls, *Star Wars* figures, books and cast-metal toys.

Williams Costume Company

1226 S 3rd Street, at W Colorado Avenue (384 1384). Bus Deuce, 105, 108, 206. **Open** 10am-5pm Mon-Sat. **Map** p149 B2 ⑰

The only place in town that carries sufficient ancient Egyptian, Renaissance gentry and Elvis costumes to dress the bride, groom and all the guests in your chosen theme. Nightly rental is $50 to $100, plus deposit.

Nightlife

Backdoor Lounge

1415 E Charleston Boulevard, at S 15th Street (385 2018). Bus 206. **Open** 24hrs daily. **Map** p147 C5 ⑱

The artfully named Backdoor Lounge caters to Latino guys and their admirers. It's like any other Las Vegas bar during the week, but plays things up for the weekend with dance parties, drag shows and beauty contests.

Bunkhouse Saloon

124 S 11th Street, at S Fremont Street (384 4536/www.bunkhouselv.com). Bus 109, 207. **Open** 24hrs daily. **Shows** times vary. **Map** p147 C4 ⑲

The Bunkhouse is all about contrasts: though no longer a country bar, it has kept the animal heads and cowboy paraphernalia, but the place packs with hipsters in skinny pants throwing back Pabst Blue Ribbon every weekend. The venues's stage showcases a variety of live music, from blues and punk to indie rock and electronica, every night.

Snick's Place

1402 S 3rd Street, between E Charleston & E Oakey Boulevards (385 9298/www.snicksplace.com). Bus Deuce, 206. **Open** 24hrs daily. No credit cards. **Map** p149 B2 ⑳

Ask longtime gay Las Vegans where they first began meeting other similarly inclined men, and they'll probably mention Snick's, the oldest LGBT watering hole in the city. Sure, it's seen better days, but it still boasts a loyal following.

Arts & leisure

Archinofsky Gallery

1551 S Commerce Street, between W Utah & W Wyoming Avenues (no phone/www.archinofsky.com). Bus Deuce, 105, 108, 206. **Open** 6-10pm First Friday; noon-3pm Sat; by appt. **Map** p149 B3 ㉑

Located inside the Commerce Street Studios, Archinofsky showcases worthwhile exhibits by emerging US artists, of photography and occasionally sculpture. It's a must-visit on First Fridays, when art enthusiasts might also venture a gander at the other funky establishments in the same building.

Dust

1221 S Main Street, at E California Street (880 3878/www.dustgallery.com). Bus Deuce, 105, 108, 206. **Open** noon-5pm Wed-Sat. **Map** p149 B2 ㉒

When Dust opened a few years back, it breathed real life into Downtown's art scene. Today, together with the neighbouring G-C Arts (below), it provides the area's heartbeat. Rotating every six weeks, shows include everything from design abstraction to figural painting, from artists in New York, Los Angeles and Las Vegas. It's all good.

G-C Arts

1217 S Main Street, at E California Street (452 2200/www.gcarts-lv.com). Bus Deuce, 105, 108, 206. **Open** 10am-6pm Tue-Sat. **Map** p149 B2 ⑤③
The town's first blue-chip gallery, G-C is where serious collectors go for original and limited edition works by Ruscha and Rauschenberg, as well as fine art objets by Koons et al. Director Michele Quinn has a New York pedigree, and it shows.

Galaxy Neonopolis 14

Neonopolis, 450 E Fremont Street, at Las Vegas Boulevard South (383 9600/www.galaxytheatres.com). Bus Deuce & all Downtown buses. **Map** p147 B3 ⑤④
Galaxy's Downtown cinema is part of the erstwhile Neonopolis entertainment centre, making it a perfect choice for avoiding crowds. Hipsters looking to kill some time before the area's bars start filling up can catch one of the CineVegas Screening Series' two weekly features. Parking (and validation) are available underneath the Neonopolis mall.

Lynn Peri Collection

NEW *Holsum Design Center, 229 W Charleston Boulevard, at Grand Central Parkway (366 9171). Bus 206.* **Open** 11am-5pm Tue-Sat. **Map** p149 B2 ⑤⑤
This gallery showcases some wall-based artwork and a variety of appealing examples of functional design objects perfect for imaginative home decorating. It's one of the stand-outs in the Holsum Lofts, a renovated bread bakery now home to a variety of gift stores, design businesses and gallery spaces (see box p161).

S² Art Group Atelier

1 E Charleston Boulevard, at S Main Street (868 7880/www.s2art.com). Bus Deuce, 105, 108, 206. **Open** 9am-5pm Mon-Fri. **Map** p149 B2 ⑤⑥
S² reproduces fine art lithographs and sells them at various venues, among them the three Jack Gallery locations at Mandalay Bay, the Venetian and the Fashion Show Mall. The 19th-century French and German presses turn out reproductions of posters by Mucha and Toulouse-Lautrec, vintage film ads and other old favourites, as well as contemporary works. Visitors can watch the presses while touring the large selection of prints.

SEAT (Social Experimentation & Absurd Theatre)

Arts Factory, 103 E Charleston Boulevard, at S Casino Center Boulevard (736 9673/www.godsex andbowling.com/seat.html). Bus Deuce, 206. **Map** p149 B2 ⑤⑦
The mixed-media performances produced by avant-garde theatre company SEAT are somewhat bizarre and occasionally a little controversial. However, they do hang together with surprising cohesion, and the company has garnered a reputation as one of the most jarring and hilariously imaginative in Las Vegas.

Trifecta Gallery

Arts Factory, 103 E Charleston Boulevard, between S Main Street & Casino Center Boulevard (366 7001/ www.trifectagallery.com). Bus Deuce, 105, 108, 206. **Open** noon-4pm Wed-Fri; noon-2pm Sat; or by appt. **Map** p149 B2 ⑤⑧
Tiny Trifecta is the labour of love of Las Vegas artist Marty Walsh, whose masterful, nostalgic paintings memorialise mid-century modern appliances and other artefacts. She also has an ingenious curatorial eye, and alternates showings of her own work with pieces by talented emerging painters. With shows that regularly sell out, Trifecta is the place for serious art collectors on a budget.

Area 51

Worth the Trip

East of Las Vegas

Hoover Dam

On US 93 east of Boulder City (1-866 730 9097/494 2517/www.usbr.gov/lc/ hooverdam). **Open** 9am-6pm daily (last tour 5.15pm). **Admission** *Tour* $11; $6-$9 reductions.

Without the Hoover Dam, much of the development in the Southwest would not exist. The dam controls the Colorado River, providing electricity and water to nearly 20 million people in Nevada, California and Arizona, making it possible for cities and farmland to flourish in one of the driest, hottest and most inhospitable regions of the world.

Building the dam was a mammoth task. First, the Colorado had to be temporarily diverted so the dam wall could be constructed. A vast army of 16,400 workers – the project was built at the height of the Depression – laboured day and night for four years, finishing in February 1935. It's 726 feet (221 metres) high and, at the base, 660 feet (200 metres) thick, and weighs 6.6 million tons. Its reservoir is 110 miles long and 500 feet (150 metres) deep.

The car park (parking $7) and the visitors' centre are on the Nevada side of the Arizona–Nevada border, a 30- to 45-minute drive south from Vegas on US 93. Much of the dam is closed to visitors, but a worthwhile tour does operate every day; as part of it, you'll see films and exhibits detailing the dam's creation. Try and get there early to beat the crowds.

En route, you'll go through Boulder City, built in 1931 to house the workers at the dam. Built as the first 'model city' in the US, it was never intended to be a permanent settlement. However, it got a second wind during World War II and is now flourishing, despite being the only town in the state in which gambling is illegal. There's more on the

Hoover Dam

area at the Boulder City/Hoover Dam Museum (294 1988, www.bcmha.org, $1-$2) within the Boulder Dam Hotel.

Lake Mead

Alan Bible Visitor Centre, on US 93 East of Las Vegas (293 8990/www.nps. gov/lame). **Open** 8.30am-4.30pm daily. **Admission** $5/car (valid for 5 days).

Around ten million visitors come to Lake Mead's 550 miles of shoreline each year to sail, fish, swim, water-ski, camp and generally enjoy the pleasures of an oasis in the desert. Wholly artificial, the lake was created when the Colorado was blocked by the Hoover Dam. It's an incongruous sight, a large blue splodge surrounded by barren mountains and canyon tops. Located only about 20 minutes from the Strip, the lake is the centrepiece of the huge Lake Mead National Recreation Area.

Lakeside Scenic Drive (Highway 146) and Northshore Scenic Drive (Highway 167) skirt the western and northern sides of Lake Mead for 60 miles. The route isn't very scenic, but it's the access road for five concession-operated marinas along the Nevada shoreline. All have ranger stations, grocery stores and some form of restaurant; some also have swimming beaches, picnic sites, motels, showers and gas stations.

The best way to explore the lake is by boat. There are numerous secluded coves, sandy beaches and narrow canyons accessible only by water, and the warm, clear lake is ideal for swimming: the water temperature averages 78°F (26°C) in spring, summer and autumn. You can hire a boat from the marinas; expect small fishing boats to cost around $20-$40 for two hours or $60-$120 per day.

North of Las Vegas

Extraterrestrial Highway & Area 51

SR 375, accessible via US 93 north of Las Vegas.

A few are here to plane-spot the military aircraft that roar overhead. A handful are on their way north to Ely. But the reason most people are ploughing up and down Highway 375, roughly 130 miles north of Las Vegas, is its

Death Valley National Park

now-official nickname, and what reputedly rests just west of the road. This is the Extraterrestrial Highway, and it borders the famously sinister Area 51.

No one gave the Nellis Air Force Range much thought until the 1980s, when physicist Bob Lazar claimed he had worked here on alien spaceships. He also spoke about dry-bedded Groom Lake, allegedly the centre of government investigations into alien life. After the numbered grid square in which the base sits on maps of the test site, it's become known as Area 51. The US government refuses to acknowledge the existence of Area 51, which only fans the conspiracists' flames.

There's not much to see, but do take care: someone somewhere is watching your movements. Don't cross into the military zone: you'll be arrested, questioned and fined. The border is not marked on maps and is often hard to detect: it's defined by orange posts, some topped with silver globes, and occasional 'restricted area' signs, but no fence. The only town on the roads is Rachel, a scruffy collection of houses and huts that's home to around 100 people. This number is swelled by tourists staying at the Little A'Le'Inn (1-775 729 2515, www.aleinn.com), a slightly shabby motel-bar-restaurant combo stocked with cheaply made, dearly priced alien ephemera.

Valley of Fire State Park

On Highway 169, north-east of Las Vegas (397 2088, http://parks.nv.gov/vf.htm). **Open** 8.30am-4.30pm daily. **Admission** $6.

Bounded by the grey limestone Muddy Mountains to the south and west, and located a 50-mile drive north-east of Las Vegas on I-15, Valley of Fire was the first state park in Nevada, and is still one of its most breathtaking. The main attractions are the red sandstone formations, created from sand dunes deposited 135 to 150 million years ago and sculpted by wind and water into bizarre, anthropomorphic shapes: look for Elephant Rock and Seven Sisters along Highway 169, the east–west road through the park. A two-mile loop road runs past some of the most dramatic rock formations.

NEXT
3 MILES

Hiking is permitted, but there are few marked trails, and all are very short. Get a trails map from the visitors' centre (see below). The road north from the centre offers a panoramic view of multicoloured sandstone at Rainbow Vista and ends at the White Domes picnic area. An easy trail from Rainbow Vista leads to spectacular rocks at Fire Canyon.

West of Las Vegas

Death Valley National Park

Death Valley Visitor Center, Furnace Creek, Death Valley National Park (1-760 786 3200/www.nps.gov/deva).
Open 8am-5pm daily. **Admission** $20/car (valid for 7 days).

Enlarged and redesignated a national park under the 1994 Desert Protection Act, Death Valley is now the largest national park outside Alaska, covering more than 5,156 square miles. It's also one of the hottest places on the planet. Air temperatures regularly top 120°F (49°C) in July and August, and are 50% higher on the ground.

After the two and a half-three-hour drive from Vegas, head for the Death Valley Visitor Center. Stop in for advice on current weather and road conditions and take the opportunity to fill up at one of the park's three expensive gas stations. However, if you've entered the park on Highway 190, you'll pass two of the most amazing sights en route to Furnace Creek. Some 5,475 feet (1,669 metres) above sea level, Dante's View is a great place from which to first survey the park's otherworldly landscape. And three miles south of Furnace Creek lies Zabriskie Point, recognisable from its ragged, rumpled appearance.

There's more to see further south. The Devil's Golf Course is a striking, scrappy landscape formed by salt crystallising and expanding; a few miles further is bleak, eerie Badwater, just two miles as the crow flies from Dante's View but more than 5,000 feet (1,500 metres) lower. This is the lowest point in the Western Hemisphere, 282 feet (86 metres) below sea level.

Heading north from Furnace Creek, you'll see the eerie Devil's Cornfield, the frolic-friendly Sand Dunes, which rise and dip in 100-foot (30-metre) increments, and the luxurious Scotty's Castle; built in the 1920s for Chicago millionaire Albert Johnson, it was named after Walter Scott, his eccentric chancer of a friend. Rangers tell the tale on 50minute tours (hourly 9am-5pm, $11).

If you want to stay the night, try the Furnace Creek Inn (1-888 297 2757, 1-760 786 2345, www.furnacecreekresort.com), built in the 1930s and still a charming, cultured place to stay and eat. The Furnace Creek Ranch (same phone & URL) has 200 rather more basic motel-style rooms and cabins.

Mount Charleston

Off Highway 156.
It's true: you can jet-ski near Las Vegas in the morning and snow-ski in the afternoon. A mere 45 minutes northwest of the city lies the Spring Mountain Recreation Area; commonly known as Mount Charleston, it's dominated by Charleston Peak, the highest

point in southern Nevada. In the winter, you can ski and snowboard at Lee Canyon; in summer, hike the forested slopes, far cooler than the city.

There are two roads into the area, both off US 95. Nearest to Las Vegas is Highway 157 (Kyle Canyon Road), which ascends prettily through winding canyons and wooded slopes to the Mount Charleston Hotel, a rustic-style lodge with a huge lobby and an open fireplace. The road continues west for another few miles, past a small park office (872 5486, closed Mon & Tue in winter), and terminating at Mount Charleston Lodge. Here, you'll find a 24-hour bar, restaurant, riding stables and some delightful log cabins.

The US Forest Service prefers hikers to stick to designated trails, but there are numerous unmarked hikes around Mount Charleston (take a compass and a trail guidebook). The six-mile Bristlecone Trail has good views over limestone cliffs and bristlecone pines; the short trail to Mary Jane Falls is both more strenuous and more rewarding, with a 900-foot (270-metre) climb to a waterfall. The mother of all hikes is the 18-mile round trip to Mount Charleston Peak, a difficult and demanding trail that's often not clear of snow until July.

On your way to Mount Charleston, stop off at Floyd Lamb State Park; it's the former site of Tule Springs Ranch, where prospective divorcees waited out their six-week residency requirement in the 1940s and '50s. Located 15 miles from the city (though now surrounded by sprawl), its lush lawns, shady cottonwoods and four lakes make it a popular picnicking and fishing spot. Avoid weekends if you don't like crowds. However, during the week, it's a serene spot: not even the swankiest Strip hotels can match the peacocks that wander around the white ranch buildings.

Red Rock Canyon & around

Off Charleston Boulevard/Highway 159, west of Las Vegas (515 5361/ www.nv.blm.gov/redrockcanyon). **Open** *Visitor centre* 8.30am-4.30pm daily.

Scenic drive Apr-Sept 6am-8pm daily; Oct, Mar 6am-7pm daily; Nov-Feb 6am-5pm daily.

Just 20 miles from Vegas is one of Nevada's most beautiful spots. The cool, deep-cut chasms of the Red Rock Canyon National Conservation Area make it a popular for hiking year-round, while climbers come from all over to enjoy some of the best rock climbing in the US.

Part of the Spring Mountains, Red Rock Canyon has at its centre a nearly sheer escarpment of Aztec sandstone, the remnant of ancient sand dunes that covered the area 180 million years ago. The red and cream Calico Hills are more rounded, as they're not protected from erosion by a higher limestone layer.

Native Americans first used Red Rock Canyon in about 3500 BC. Evidence remains in the form of rock art (etched and painted pictographs), as well as arrowheads and ceramics. More than 45 mammal species now inhabit the park, among them mountain lions, coyotes, kangaroo rats, mule deer and the legendary desert bighorn sheep.

Stop first at the visitors' centre for information and a map, before exploring the one-way, 13-mile scenic drive through the canyon. The road gives access to numerous hiking trails and three picnic sites. Some trails are not marked clearly and require some scrambling; take a map (available at the visitors' centre) and a compass.

The 2.5-mile Calico Tank trail from Sandstone Quarry is a good introduction to the Calico Hills at the start of the drive. Just above the tank is a fine view (smog permitting) of the valley and the Strip's casino monoliths. Other good short hikes include Ice Box Canyon and Pine Creek Canyon. For further details of the scores of other trails, pick up a copy of the BLM's trail leaflet.

Just south of Red Rock on Highway 159 is family-friendly Bonnie Springs Old Nevada (875 4191, www.bonnie springs.com), a mock Wild West town, with gunfighting cowboys, authentic-looking saloons and daily hangings (call ahead; times vary by season). It's rather dilapidated but good fun.

Essentials

The Strip

Hotels

Nothing stays the same for long in Vegas, and so it proves with the city's hotel industry. The boom in the market has caused new developments to sprout up like daisies (or, in some cases, weeds), complementing the constant growth, redevelopment and improvement of the existing resorts.

The industry is always building something new: a 1,000-room tower, a 4,000-seat theatre, a 100-unit mall (the latest trend). And hotel-casinos that don't expand are quick to change; it's a case of adapt or die. If you've not been to Vegas for four or five years, the changes will be noticeable. But even if you were here six months ago, you'll still see something new.

Most visitors to Las Vegas stay where the action is: a hotel-casino. All have casinos, restaurants, bars and assorted entertainments, plus amenities that range from the predictable (pools, malls) to the exceptional (zoos, rollercoasters).

The majority of hotel-casinos are located on the Strip, but there are, of course, hotels in other parts of town. A handful of big resorts are located just off the Strip, chief among them the **Hard Rock** (p121) and the **Palms** (p135). Downtown, the hub of Las Vegas until the 1950s, can't compete with the Strip in the glamour stakes, but you'll find bargains galore.

Money matters

Las Vegas has more rooms than anywhere in the world: upwards of 130,000. However, with 40 million visitors a year, it needs them.

Rates fluctuate wildly depending on the date: the same room can quadruple in price from one night to the next. You'll often find

ESSENTIALS

exceptional deals midweek and/or during off-season. At weekends, though, prices skyrocket, and a two-night minimum is in effect almost everywhere. Steer clear of major conventions; for a full list, see www.lvcva.com.

For one night in a double room, expect to pay about $40-$100 in a budget hotel-casino, $70-$200 for a mid-range operation, and upwards of $150 in a first-class property. In addition to these basic rates, rooms are subject to hotel tax (11 per cent Downtown, nine per cent elsewhere). You can book either by phone or online with almost every property.

South Strip

Excalibur

Listing p48. **$$**.
Housed in two towers behind the castle façade, the Excalibur's small rooms have none of the elegance of the hotel's adjacent sister resorts, the Luxor and Mandalay Bay. But a handful of spacious Parlor Suites have guest bathrooms, dining and living areas; with bold colours, dark wood furniture and wrought-iron fixtures, they're nowhere near as shabby as those at Circus Circus.

Four Seasons

3960 Las Vegas Boulevard South, at W Hacienda Drive (reservations 1-800 819 5053/front desk & casino 632 5000/www.fourseasons.com/lasvegas). Bus Deuce, 104, 105. **$$$$**.
The first boutique hotel to open on the Strip remains the most popular. It has its own private driveway, entrance, lobby, valet and crack concierge staff, as well as an award-winning spa, landscaped gardens surrounding a secluded pool, restaurants and lounges. The twist is that the 424 rooms and suites are located in the Mandalay Bay resort, though they're accessed by private elevators. Guests may use Mandalay Bay's facilities, as well as those within Thehotel at Mandalay Bay (p173).

SHORTLIST

Future favourites
- Encore (p178)
- Palazzo (p177)
- Trump International (p178)

Recent revamps
- Go rooms at Flamingo (p175)
- Golden Nugget (p178)
- Mirage (p175)

Out-and-out luxury
- Bellagio (p174)
- Four Seasons (p171)
- Wynn Las Vegas (p178)

Best on a budget
- Artisan (p182)
- Golden Nugget (p178)
- Palace Station (p183)

Family-friendly
- Excalibur (p171)
- Four Seasons (p171)
- Luxor (p172)

Hottest pools
- Caesars Palace (p174)
- Hard Rock (p181)
- Mandalay Bay (p172)
- Palms (p183)

Strip bargains
- Bill's Gamblin' Hall & Saloon (p174)
- Carriage House (p181)
- Excalibur (p171)

Casino-free hotels
- Artisan (p182)
- Platinum (p181)
- Thehotel at Mandalay Bay (p173)

Dining variety
- Bellagio (p174)
- MGM Grand (p172)
- Venetian (p177)

On-site spas
- Bathhouse at Thehotel at Mandalay Bay (p173)
- Qua at Caesars Palace (p174)
- Spa at Wynn Las Vegas (p178)

ESSENTIALS

Thehotel at Mandalay Bay

The guestrooms are large and luxurious, especially the large marble bathrooms with sunken jacuzzis. Extra points are garnered for service: complimentary cocktails greet guests upon arrival; repeat guests have room keys waiting for them at valet; and families will find rooms child-proofed and stocked with age-appropriate amenities (nappies for babies, PlayStations for older kids). Chilled water and towels are laid on for joggers.

Luxor

Listing p50. **$$**.
Only around half of the Luxor's 4,407 guestrooms are actually located in the pyramid. These Strip-fronted rooms offer great views and are accessed by special elevators called 'inclinators', which rise, like enclosed ski lifts, at an angle of 39°. However, there are compensations if you don't get hooked up with a pyramid room: the guestrooms in the towers, just behind the pyramid, are larger, and were refurbished in 2006.

Mandalay Bay

Listing p53. **$$$**.
All the 2,791 guestrooms and suites at Mandalay Bay were remodelled in 2007 with a contemporary look and additional amenities: lofty pillow-top beds with triple sheeting, 42in plasma-screen TVs, iPod docks and high-speed net access. Bathrooms come with 15in LCD TVs and giant tubs. Larger suites command excellent views – of the Strip or the surrounding mountains.

MGM Grand

Listing p58. **$$$**.
The 5,044 rooms (including 751 plush suites) in the main building of the MGM Grand are mostly done out with art deco-styled furnishings, designed to evoke backlot bungalows from Hollywood's glamour age. They manage it pretty well, too, though you suspect Clark Gable and Louise Brooks would sooner be down the street at the Wynn. A fourth-floor guest services desk functions as an additional concierge, a massive plus in this huge hotel.

ESSENTIALS

However, the real luxury is elsewhere on the premises. First to arrive was the Mansion, with 29 handsomely appointed and even more handsomely priced villas. In 2005, the hotel added 51 Skylofts, vast and chic two-storey accommodations designed by Tony Chi that remain among the town's more fashionable temporary addresses. And then there's the Signature, a luxurious condo-hotel development with three 576-suite towers. Rooms have jacuzzi tubs and balconies; guests also get access to private pool areas, among other perks.

Monte Carlo
Listing p64. **$$$**.
The Monte Carlo's tri-tower set-up contains 3,002 rooms, including 259 suites. The standard rooms exhibit a comfortable, Old World feel, with cherrywood furniture and plump furnishings. The decor gets progressively more opulent the further up the price scale you climb.

New York New York
Listing p65. **$$$**.
NYNY's rooms are concealed behind (but not in) an assortment of towers and skyscrapers. The rooms are done nicely, in art deco-styled woods with black accents, and are well maintained. Although they're pretty small, they're bargains in comparison to some of their Strip competitors, especially during the week. Check when you make your booking that the Manhattan Express doesn't rumble by your window, or you'll be continually disturbed by the squeals of riders.

Thehotel at Mandalay Bay
3950 Las Vegas Boulevard South, at W Hacienda Avenue (reservations 1-877 632 7800/front desk 632 7777/ www.mandalaybay.com). Bus Deuce, 104, 105. **$$$**.
The rooms at Thehotel are all suites, decorated in rich colours and furnished with chairs and beds that manage to be both stylish and extremely comfortable. Most suites have high-speed internet, a nod to the business travellers who choose this hotel for its absence of gambling. The restaurants, shows and

Four Seasons p171

gaming at Mandalay Bay are a corridor away, but the handsome hotel lobby is slot-free. Atop the rooms tower is Alain Ducasse's ultra-posh restaurant Mix (p54), and its attached lounge (p57). The Bathhouse spa (p58) is also excellent. The whole place doesn't feel like Vegas, which, for many guests, is part of the appeal. Recommended.

Tropicana
Listing p69. **$$**.
The original two-storey motor inn buildings surround the pool and are thus conveniently close to it; although they're the oldest at the Tropicana resort, they can be comfortable if you get one with a balcony and pool view. The newer tower rooms are generally better, though they could do with a renovation.

Mid Strip

Bally's
Listing p72. **$$**.
The good-sized standard rooms at Bally's are decorated with a West Coast

Bellagio

casual elegance of bright velvet couches offset by muted earth tones. Of the 2,814 rooms, 265 are suites: the one- and two-bedroom Grand Suites, each with a huge jetted tub, are slightly more contemporary. The 22nd Club offers access to private concierge services and dusk cocktails with gorgeous Strip views.

Bellagio
Listing p74. $$$$.
Bellagio's 3,933 rooms are large and beautifully furnished. The beds all have Serta mattresses, and the spacious, marble-floored bathrooms come with deep-soaking tubs. Flat-screen TVs, electronic drapes and minibars are standard. Atop the Spa Tower, the Presidential suites are ultra-modern; and the nine luxury villas, outfitted with gold and Lalique crystal fixtures, butler service, gyms, steam rooms and private pools, are open to anyone willing to fork out $6,000 a night. The hotel's TV network simulcasts the fountain show music, so you can listen as you watch the dancing water.

Bill's Gamblin' Hall & Saloon
3595 Las Vegas Boulevard South, at E Flamingo Road (reservations 1-866 245 5745/front desk & casino 737 2100/www.billslasvegas.com). Bus Deuce, 202. $$.
You'll be pleasantly surprised by the Victorian wallpaper and paintings, etched mirrors and white lace curtains in the 200 guestrooms, some of which have four-poster brass beds, minibars and whirlpools.

Caesars Palace
Listing p79. $$$.
You'd expect a certain level of variety in a hotel this huge, and so it proves. The standard rooms (billed as 'Classic') are expansive and well maintained, but they aren't decorated in an especially inspiring fashion. If you've got a little cash, it's worth splashing for the 'Deluxe' rooms in the Augustus and Palace Towers, recently upgraded with high-tech facilities and stylishly designed. The suites are fancier still: some have circular beds, in-room saunas, wet bars, living/dining rooms, home theatres, wine grottos, and even steam and workout rooms.

Flamingo
Listing p85. $$.
The standard rooms at the Flamingo are smallish, fairly basic and feel profoundly old-fashioned, despite a

ESSENTIALS

relatively recent renovation. All of which makes the new Go guestrooms a surprise. Designed in a more modern style and done out with flat-screen TVs, iPod-friendly hi-fis and wireless access, they're more inviting than you'd expect from either the other rooms or, for that matter, the rest of the resort. Note that while room rates in all Vegas properties vary from night to night, the differentials at the Flamingo are spectacular even by local standards. Guestrooms can be ridiculously cheap during the week and outrageously expensive at weekends.

Harrah's
Listing p86. **$$.**
The guestrooms and suites in Harrah's three towers are comfortable and festive. Many have minibars, some have jetted tubs. The new deluxe rooms have updated decor and amenities.

Imperial Palace
Listing p88. **$$.**
All guestrooms, from small standard rooms through to the King Suite, recently received much-needed facelifts. Certain rooms come with a jacuzzi-driven 'luv tub'. The best penthouse suites have one or two bedrooms and an extra-large living room.

Mirage
Listing p89. **$$$.**
The 2002 revamp of the Mirage freshened the colour scheme from pale pastels to deeper cranberries and greens, with cane furnishings and crown mouldings. Several years on, the slightly stuffy design is somewhat at odds with the type of crowds the hotel is trying to draw to its bars and restaurants, but the rooms are in good shape.

Paris Las Vegas
Listing p92. **$$$$.**
The smallish guestrooms in Paris Las Vegas are comfortable, prim and stately, decorated in rich Regency style; some are furnished with canopied beds and armoires. The spacious marble bathrooms are outfitted with vanities, a make-up mirror and soaking tubs.

Sun gods

What do you get if you cross a swimming pool with a nightclub? No, it's not a rotten joke: the answer is the hottest summer trend in Las Vegas.

From late April to early September each year, a handful of resorts open their guests-only pools, some of which permit and/or encourage topless bathing, to the same trendy folks who populate Sin City's fabulous clubs and lounges. Beyond these velvet ropes, barely dressed beautiful people frolic in the sun, eating, drinking and dancing the afternoon away.

When it comes to raucous, high-energy fun, the **Hard Rock**'s (in)famous daylight-only Sunday Rehab is the granddaddy of the dayclubs. All suntan oil and water-soaked fun, Rehab is like a pool party at the world's best frat house, set to a house and hip hop beat. When the sun sets, the **Venetian**'s Tao Beach takes over with Sunset Sundays, at which topless sunbathers mingle with runway-worthy ladies sporting pricey resortwear to a loungey, housey soundtrack. And there's a similar scene at the **Palms**, which encourages locals and in-the-know visitors to start the weekend early at a daytime pool party it calls Ditch Fridays.

If you're looking for a pool party that's a little more relaxing and civilised, then you won't have to look very far. Respite can be found at the **Mirage** (Bare) and **Caesars Palace** (Venus), both of which offer top-notch food, relaxing music and, yes, topless sunbathing.

Paris Las Vegas

Planet Hollywood
Listing p96. **$$$**.
The 2,600 movie-themed rooms and suites are done out in what is called 'Hollywood Hip' decor: contemporary shades of rich chocolate and royal purple, Googie-esque carpet and techie amenities such as high-definition plasma TVs. Guests can earn and redeem Starpoints at more than 750 Westin, Sheraton, W, St Regis and Luxury Collection hotels.

Treasure Island
Listing p100. **$$$**.
The 2,885 rooms in TI's 36-storey Y-shaped tower are good enough for the price, decorated in appealing shades of blue and without any undue ornamentation. Many have decent views of the Mirage volcano and the Sirens show below. The 220 suites are spacious, with living rooms, wet bars, two baths, jacuzzis and impressive TVs; they're a good deal if you feel like splashing out but don't want to break the bank.

Venetian & Palazzo
Listing p102. **$$$$**.
The standard suites (there are no regular rooms) at the Venetian are far larger than the Vegas norm. The sumptuously appointed suites underwent renovations during 2007, no doubt to keep them on a par with the Palazzo (due to open next door in 2008). The 12-storey Venezia Tower atop the car park has rooms that are similar to those in the original tower, but that now come with some extra amenities (private elevators, complimentary newspaper delivery, access to the secluded Italian-style pool garden and arboretum). For more exclusivity, the tower's top five floors contain an Old World drawing room-style lounge and speciality baths.

North Strip

Circus Circus
Listing p108. **$**.
After several expansions, Circus Circus now boasts 3,773 spartan rooms, mainly decorated with soft-blue carpeting, pastel bedspreads and upholstery, and dark wood furniture. Of these, the newest are in the West Tower (built in 1997); the cheapest (and oldest) rooms are in the motel-like Manor section. Ask for a south-facing room in the Skyrise Tower for the best view of the Strip. Other amenities include pools and the 399-space Circusland RV Park.

Riviera
Listing p110. **$$**.
The Riviera has five levels of 2,100 rooms, two of them suites. The standard rooms are all in the original tower, while the deluxe rooms (better views) and suites are in the two newer towers. The newer tower rooms are smallish but not cramped, and decorated with dark wood furniture. Half the rooms have views over the pool; the rest face the surrounding mountains. Don't expect much – well, anything – in the way of luxury.

Sahara
Listing p111. **$**.
The 1,720 guestrooms range from standard through three different sizes of suite. They're usually among the cheapest on the Strip, and you get what you pay for. Still, it's a safe and secure operation.

Stratosphere
Listing p112. **$**.
If the guestrooms were in the tower, they would be interesting; as it is, all the Stratosphere's sleeping quarters are in separate buildings below. Some are in the original Vegas World mid-rise; a more recent tower brought the total to 2,444 rooms and suites. There are an overwhelming 13 different types of room, from the smallish standard rooms to the massive Premier Suites. On the eighth floor, there's a big pool and recreation deck.

Trump International
3128 Las Vegas Boulevard South, between Spring Mountain & Desert Inn Roads (www.trumplv.com). Bus Deuce, 203. **$$$$**.

ESSENTIALS

A joint venture between The Donald and Phil Ruffin, Trump's first Vegas property promises to be as posh as sister properties in New York and Florida. When Trump revealed his plans to build a condo-hotel tower here on *The Apprentice*, the condos were all reserved within three weeks. So it was no surprise when, in a subsequent episode, he announced plans to build a second tower a little further down the line.

The 1,200-plus spacious condo guestrooms will feature floor-to-ceiling windows, spa tubs, plasma TVs and, of course, lots and lots of marble. The property is due to open in the first half of 2008; Jack Christie, VP of Sales and Marketing, promises that 'guests will have everything they need to live the Trump lifestyle in Las Vegas', including 24-hour concierge and security services, white-gloved doormen, and the finest in gourmet and casual dining.

Wynn Las Vegas & Encore
Listing p113. **$$$$**.
The Wynn's large and lavish guestrooms offer floor-to-ceiling windows, beds with 320-thread-count European linens, a seating area, a dining table and chairs, flat-screen LCD TVs, spacious bath areas and bedside drapery controls. The suites set a new Vegas standard: some have their own massage rooms, VIP check-in areas, private pools and dining rooms. Don't even get us started on the villas. Due to open in 2008, sister property Encore looks likely to further up the ante.

Downtown

Binion's
Listing p146. **$**.
The majority of Binion's rooms could use some fairly serious regeneration. Eighty of them are from the original casino; the other 286 were added when the hotel acquired the Mint.

Fitzgeralds
301 E Fremont Street, at S 3rd Street (reservations 1-800 274 5825/ front desk & casino 388 2400/
www.fitzgeraldslasvegas.com).
Bus Deuce & all DTC-bound buses. **$**.
There are 638 guestrooms (including 14 suites) in the 34-storey hotel. There have been some modest attempts to modernise the property, including a new business centre.

Four Queens
202 E Fremont Street, at S Casino Center Boulevard (reservations 1-800 634 6045/front desk & casino 385 4011/www.fourqueens.com).
Bus Deuce & all DTC-bound buses. **$**.
The hotel's 690 guestrooms (including 45 suites) have been remodelled, but keep your hopes down. Still, the new flat-screen TVs are a nice touch.

Golden Gate
Listing p148. **$**.
Many of the Golden Gate's original 10ft-by-10ft bedrooms remain open. Although some have been updated with air-conditioning and private baths, most are still characterfully old-fashioned, replete with mahogany doors, plaster walls and tiled bathroom floors. And aside from the addition of a relatively modern key-card system, there haven't been any technological advances here since 1907, when the hotel announced that it had taken control of the first telephone in Nevada (boasting, of course, the number 1).

Golden Nugget
Listing p148. **$$**.
The rooms at the Golden Nugget are not as swanky as some would have you believe; the recent renovations under Landry's were almost entirely limited to the property's public areas (see the extraordinary pool with integrated shark tank). Still, the lodgings here are still pretty decent, and better than those found at any other Downtown property. The three hotel towers contain a total of 1,907 rooms, topped by a number of plush suites (including some spread over two levels). The suites atop the spa tower are in a more modern style, the ones atop the original tower positively old Vegas opulence. Wireless internet is an added bonus.

Condo crazy

How to own a little piece of Sin City.

Platinum

As the city continues to build upwards as well as outwards, Las Vegas Boulevard is lined with high-rise blocks at various stages of development. But one particular type of tower trumps its competitors: the condo-hotel.

The name pretty much explains the concept. Deluxe apartments and studios are sold within the buildings, often in advance of their completion; the buyers can then rent their apartments to visitors on short-term lets. The developer gets upfront funding for his project; the condo buyer gets to make back the not inconsiderable costs of a unit through rental income; and the short-term visitor gets to stay somewhere luxurious and classy, far from the maddening crowds. The first major stand-alone condo-hotel in the city to open was the **Platinum** (p181), which welcomed its initial visitors in 2007. But there are plenty more on the horizon, many of them on the Strip.

At present, the most high-profile of these developments is The Donald's **Trump International** (p178), located just across from Fashion Show Mall. The residential units in this gleaming tower sold out so quickly that reservations were accepted for a second building even before the first was completed (it's due to open in early 2008). The 1,200-plus units went for close to $1,350 per square foot: pricey, sure, but property speculators are convinced that they'll harvest a good return on their investments.

Already grabbing headlines two years before it's scheduled to be completed (late 2009 or early 2010), MGM Mirage's $7.4-billion **CityCenter** (p117) will offer 2,700 residences, from studios to three-bedroom penthouses, in four residential developments named Vdara Condo Hotel, Veer Towers, the Harmon Hotel & Residences and the Residences at the Mandarin Oriental. Again, it's not cheap: the properties should go for between $880 and $1,500 per square foot. However, the plans are stunning, and the location – between the Monte Carlo and Bellagio – can't be beat. What's more, CityCenter hopes to be the largest building in the world to earn LEED certification from the US Green Building Council.

There are several other condo towers under construction, all of which are unconnected to the major Strip hotels and somewhat cheaper than their rivals. **Sky Las Vegas**, **Allure** (both opening in '07) and **Panorama Towers** (one tower already open, with two more to come) have studios available from $575 per square foot. Bargain.

Main Street Station

Listing p150. **$$**.

Themed as a fin-de-siècle delight (check out the gaslamps that front the property), the casino is filled with antiques of all kinds, not all of them Victorian. Teddy Roosevelt's Pullman car is here, now a chic smoking lounge; a carved oak fireplace from Prestwick Castle in Scotland and a set of doors from an old London bank are also on display; and chunks of the Berlin Wall sit in the men's room. Accessible yet smart, upscale (for Downtown) yet fun, this isn't the most charismatic property, but it's likeable all the same. The 430 guestrooms are comfortable, if rather basic.

Plaza

Listing p151. **$**.

The Plaza can usually be relied upon to deliver some of Downtown's cheapest rooms. Once you've stayed in one of them, you'll understand why. All things considered, the lodgings are pretty scruffy and in need of an upgrade.

Vegas Club

18 E Fremont Street, at N Main Street (reservations 1-800 634 6532/front desk & casino 385 1664/ www.vegasclubcasino.net). Bus Deuce & all DTC-bound buses. **$**.

While Downtown drags itself kicking and screaming into the 21st century, the Vegas Club's motel-standard guestrooms remain firmly stranded in 1987. Still, while the decor isn't the height of fashion, the rooms aren't in bad condition, especially compared to those at a few of their more down-market neighbours. The guestrooms in the North Tower are in the best shape, something usually reflected in the prices.

East of Strip

Alexis Resort & Villas

375 E Harmon Avenue, between Koval Lane & Paradise Road (reservations 1-800 582 2228/ front desk 796 3300/www.alexis park.com). Bus 108, 213. **$$**.

Built as an apartment complex and later transformed into an all-suites hotel, Mediterranean-style Alexis is gaming-free, and as a result it's a surprisingly sedate little operation. The two-storey buildings, nestled along winding pathways, house 500 well-appointed suites offering a host of unexpected accoutrements (gas fireplaces, large

Artisan p182

bathrooms and, in some cases, upstairs lofts). But the main selling point? It's right by the Hard Rock (p121).

Carriage House

105 E Harmon Avenue, between Las Vegas Boulevard South & Koval Lane (reservations 1-800 221 2301 ext 65/front desk 798 1020/www. carriagehouselasvegas.com). Bus Deuce, 201, 202. **$$.**

Located next door to Grand Chateau, a new timeshare resort owned and operated by Marriott, the Carriage House is often overlooked by visitors. However, the moderately priced rooms are great value for the location, the best of any hotel not actually on Las Vegas Boulevard South. The rooms and suites are kept in decent shape; even the smallest ones have kitchenettes. Outside, there's a heated pool, a tennis court and a simple sun deck.

Courtyard by Marriott

3275 Paradise Road, at E Desert Inn Road (reservations 1-800 661 1064/front desk 791 3600/www. marriott.com). Bus 108, 213. **$$.**

Las Vegas is the convention capital of the US, welcoming millions of business travellers each year alongside all the tourists. This outpost of the Marriott Courtyard chain is squarely aimed at those here for work purposes, and particularly at those attending events at the Las Vegas Convention Center right opposite the property. All rooms have work spaces and free high-speed internet access, and decor that won't offer any distractions from the job at hand.

Hard Rock

Listing p121. **$$$.**

The casino itself may be like a zoo, but the upstairs guestrooms are remarkably peaceful and minimalist, with mod space-agey furnishings that are sort of *Jetsons* meets the I-Ching. And thanks largely to the fact that the Hard Rock was built very recently, they're also very spacious. Most rooms have been decorated with museum-quality photos of rock stars. Try to get digs overlooking the pool.

Hooters

115 E Tropicana Avenue, between Las Vegas Boulevard South & Koval Lane (reservations 1-866 584 6687/front desk & casino 739 9000/www.hch vegas.com). Bus Deuce, 201. **$$.**

How does the hotel version of Hooters differ from the restaurants familiar across middle America? Simple: instead of a handful of hot female workers in skimpy orange outfits, here there are dozens (200, if you're counting). There are 696 rooms (including 17 suites); the standard ones are comfortable and take a beach-house theme. The pool is paradisical and the spa is a full-service operation with a workout room.

Las Vegas Hilton

Listing p125. **$$.**

Just east of the Strip, the Hilton is perfect for those who want to be close to, but not in the middle of, the action. (The on-site monorail station can connect you to that in a hurry.) The seven room 'levels' each have their own decor, more than just increasingly plush renditions of the standard look. Park Avenue, for instance, is classic Manhattan style, while Classic goes for 1920s Hollywood. Some standard rooms are dark and claustrophobic. In addition to the standard ('deluxe') room, there are six 'levels' of suites.

Platinum

211 E Flamingo Road, at Koval Lane (reservations 1-877 211 9211/front desk 893 0824/www.platinumlasvegas. com). Bus 201. **$$$.**

The second condo-hotel to open in Las Vegas (the first was the Residences at the MGM Grand), this highly impressive property sits within a five-minute walk of the Strip. Free from both gambling and smoking, the Platinum is the perfect refuge for the residents who snapped up many of its 255 suites and now live here part-time, but also great for visitors keen on retaining their sanity while all around them are losing theirs. It's a very well-run operation, retaining a certain urban style in its ground-floor bar, Platinum Restaurant

ESSENTIALS

(p132) and beautifully appointed spa. And the suites themselves are both extremely capacious (the bathrooms in some suites are bigger than guestrooms at a couple of hotels in town) and handsome, done out with high-spec amenities and very comfortable beds. The cannily designed indoor-outdoor pool on the fifth floor is another nice touch in a property that's quietly full of them.

Renaissance

3400 Paradise Road, between E Desert Inn Road & E Twain Avenue (reservations 1-800 750 0980/front desk 733 6533/www.renaissancelas vegas.com). Bus 108, 213. **$$$**.
This 15-storey, 550-room Marriott hotel south of the Las Vegas Convention Center seems all business, with a list of amenities that includes the highest-tech wireless internet (WiMAX), ergonomic desk chairs and even 'Exhibitor Suites'. The hotel has a sophisticated executive level with a lounge, a pool area, spa service, comfy beds with high-end linens and piles of pillows, and flat-screen televisions in every room. The Renaissance is the city's largest non-gaming property, but there is one type of sin on site: Envy (p129), a Richard Chamberlain steakhouse that serves a variety of rich comfort foods from a Kobe filet mignon to truffle mac and cheese, accompanied by a selection of 1,500 bottles of wine.

Westin Casuarina

160 E Flamingo Road, at Koval Lane (reservations 1-800 937 8461/front desk & casino 836 5900/www.star woodhotels.com). Bus Deuce, 202. **$$$**.
The first Westin-branded hotel in Las Vegas is a low-key resort, which is just how the majority of its guests like it. There is a small casino here, and even (though you'll need to look to find it) a cosy little showroom, but the Casuarina is aimed less at holiday-makers and more at the kind of business traveller who wants to get some work done but also wants the bright lights of the Strip within easy reach.

The rooms here are everything you'd expect from a Westin property, which is to say that they're comfortable, handsome (in a discreet way), immaculately maintained and well equipped for the business traveller. And the 'Heavenly Beds' live up to their name.

West of Strip

Artisan

1501 W Sahara Avenue, at Highland Drive (reservations 1-800 554 4092/front desk 214 4000/www.theartisan hotel.com). Bus 204. **$$**.
This boutique hotel, housed rather unexpectedly in a former Travelodge in the shadow of I-15, shares a trait with most Strip resorts: it has a theme. The old-world European decor is inspired by art and artists; paintings, a mix of pieces by local artists and reproductions of iconic works by the likes of Rembrandt and Van Gogh, cover virtually every inch of wall space in the public areas, and even decorate the ceilings. The theme continues in the Artisan Lounge (p143), a late-night hotspot frequented by local hipsters, and in the hotel's dining room. The 64 individually decorated guestrooms and suites are priced a little highly for their location, but they're likeable enough and a good option if you fancy steering clear of the Strip. A spa is scheduled to open in 2007.

Gold Coast

4000 W Flamingo Road, at S Valley View Boulevard (reservations 1-800 331 5334/front desk & casino 367 7111/www.goldcoastcasino.com). Bus 201. **$**.
Boyd Gaming took hold of Coast Casinos in 2006, renaming the Barbary Coast and leaving this spot as the oldest link in Michael Gaughan's chain. So far, it's relying on the same formula for success. The 711 rooms have been upgraded with the seemingly mandatory 32in LCD TVs.

Palace Station

2411 W Sahara Avenue, at N Rancho Drive (reservations 1-800

*634 3101/front desk & casino
367 2411/www.palacestation.com).
Bus 104, 204.* **$**.

The original Station casino has been a favourite of locals for more than 30 years, thanks largely to the popular gaming promotions. But the hotel also draws its share of tourists, due to its close proximity to the Strip. The 1,000-plus cheap rooms and suites are divided between the economy courtyard and the deluxe tower (due to be remodelled in 2007).

Palms

Listing p135. **$$$**.

The rooms at the Palms aren't giant, but many compensate by having great views – and you get to curl up on the same beds as those you would find at the luxury Four Seasons. Two floors of Fantasy Suites include a Hugh Hefner Sky Villa with balcony pool; the Hardwood Suite, a vast playpen with a jacuzzi and a half-court basketball court; the Kingpin Suite, with a pool table and a bowling lane; and an Erotic Suite, with a circular, 8ft rotating bed with mirrored ceiling. The 'What

happens in Vegas' line has surely been uttered more here than anywhere else.

Rio

Listing p139. **$$$**.

The Rio's comfortable mini-suites feature floor-to-ceiling windows, big (32in) televisions and fridges. The full suites, measuring 1,600sq ft (150sq m), come with better sound systems and wet bars. All very pleasing.

Orleans

*4500 W Tropicana Avenue, between
S Decatur & S Valley View Boulevards
(reservations 1-800 675 3267/front
desk & casino 365 7111/www.orleans
casino.com). Bus 103, 104, 201.* **$$**.

The theme at the Orleans is more Disneyland than French Quarter. Still, located very close to the Strip (and within a five-minute walk of the Palms), the Orleans is one of the few casinos at which locals and tourists happily mix in every part of the operation. The rooms aren't especially exciting, but they're kept in good condition and by no means offensively designed. In any case, it's hard to grumble at these prices.

Gold Coast

Getting Around

Arriving & leaving

By air

McCarran International Airport (261 5211, www.mccarran.com) is just five minutes from the south end of the Strip. There are hundreds of internal flights to Las Vegas each week. However, direct international flights are limited. Most flights to and from Europe require passengers to change at an East Coast airport or at LAX.

Public bus routes 108 and 109 run north from the airport: the 108 heads up Swenson Avenue and stops at the Las Vegas Hilton, while the 109 goes along Maryland Parkway. Shuttle buses run by **Bell Trans** (739 7990, www.belltrans.com), **Grayline** (739 5700, www.grayline.com) and **Ritz** (889 4242, www.shuttlelasvegas.com) run to the Strip and Downtown 24 hours a day. Expect to pay $5-$7 for transport to a Strip hotel, slightly more to Downtown.

Taxis can be found outside the arrivals hall. There's a $1.20 surcharge on all fares originating at McCarran; bearing that in mind, expect to pay $10-$15 to get to most hotels on the Strip, or $15-$20 to Downtown (plus tip).

Public transport

The **Citizens Area Transit** bus network (**CAT**; the name may change in the near future) is run by the **Regional Transportation Commission of Southern Nevada** (**RTC**; 228 7433, www.rtcsouthernnevada.com). The **Downtown Transportation Center** (**DTC**) at Casino Center Boulevard and Stewart Avenue is the transfer point for many routes. For a map of the system, see www.rtcsouthernnevada.com/cat/sysmap.

CAT fares & tickets

Most **CAT** routes cost $1.25, or 60¢ for over-62s, 6-17s and the disabled. The exception is the Deuce route along the Strip, which costs $2 or $5 for a 24-hour pass. Use exact change. Transfers are free.

CAT routes

The most useful bus for tourists is the **Deuce**: named as it's a double-decker bus, it travels the length of Las Vegas Boulevard from the DTC in the north to I-215 in the south, stopping in front of all major casinos. It runs 24 hours daily.

Most other bus routes, which operate roughly 5.30am-1.30am, run along the length of a single street. Buses with a route number beginning '1' generally run north–south; those starting '2' run east–west. Below is a list of some key routes.

105 MLK Boulevard/Industrial Road
106 Rancho Drive
107 Boulder Highway
108 Paradise Road
109 Maryland Parkway
110 Eastern Avenue
113 Las Vegas Boulevard (N of DTC)

201 Tropicana Avenue
202 Flamingo Road
203 Spring Mountain Road/Sands Avenue/Twain Avenue
204 Sahara Avenue
206 Charleston Boulevard

Many bus routes, among them the Deuce, 105, 107, 108, 109, 113 and 207, stop at the DTC. Throughout the listings in this book, we have used the shorthand 'DTC-bound buses' to refer to these buses.

Monorails & shuttles

Las Vegas Monorail

699 8200/www.lvmonorail.com.
The pricey and not wholly convenient
LV Monorail runs from the Sahara to
the MGM Grand, stopping at the
Hilton, the LV Convention Center,
Harrah's, the Flamingo and Bally's.
The service runs 7am-2pm Mon-Thur,
and 7am-3am Fri-Sun. The journey
from end to end takes 15 minutes.
Single rides cost $5, with two-ride tick-
ets at $9 and a day pass at $15.

Other monorails

Free, 24hr monorails, separate to the
Las Vegas Monorail, link the Mirage
and TI; and Excalibur, the Luxor and
Mandalay Bay. For all of them, it's
often quicker to walk.

Free shuttle buses

A shuttle bus connects the Rio with
Harrah's on the Strip, just south of
the Aladdin. Nearby, the Palms lays on
a shuttle to and from the Fashion Show
Mall and the Forum Shops. The Hard
Rock runs a shuttle that loops from the
hotel to the Forum Shops, Planet
Hollywood and the MGM Grand.

Taxis & limos

Technically, you're not allowed to
hail a taxi from the street, but there
are **taxi ranks** outside most hotels.
Restaurants and bars are happy to
call a cab for you. Meters start at
$3.20, and increase by $2 per mile. If
you have a complaint, call the
Nevada Taxicab Authority
(486 6532, www.taxi.state.nv.us).

Limousines are a popular way
to get around. The rides vary from
the basic black stretch ($40/hr) to
huge SUVs with hot tubs, disco
balls and the like ($100/hr). Many
limos are available for hire outside
hotels and the airport.

Cab companies

Yellow-Checker-Star (YCS)
873 2000.

Desert *386 9102.*
Whittlesea *384 6111.*

Limousine companies

Bell Trans *385 5466/*
www.bell-trans.com.
Las Vegas Limo *736 1419/*
www.lasvegaslimo.com.

Driving

Las Vegas gets very congested
during rush hours (7-9am, 4-6pm)
and at weekends, when traffic is
horrific in tourist areas after 4pm.
The Strip turns into a virtual car
park when the town is busy. The
nearby parallel streets – Industrial
Road and Frank Sinatra Drive to
the west, Paradise Road to the east
– move faster, and provide access
to several casinos.

For north–south journeys longer
than a block or two, it's often worth
taking I-15, which runs parallel
to the Strip. I-15 intersects with
the east–west US 95 north-west
of Downtown. US 95 connects to
the 53-mile beltway at the edges of
the valley, which leads commuters
around the region.

In general, the speed limit on
freeways is 65mph; on the highway,
it's either 65mph or 70mph. Limits
on main urban thoroughfares
are 45mph; elsewhere, limits are
25mph, 30mph or 35mph.

Unless specified, you can turn
right on a red light, after stopping,
if the street is clear. U-turns are not
only legal (unless specified) but
often a necessity given the length of
the blocks. In Nevada, you can be
arrested for driving under the
influence if your blood alcohol level
is 0.08 or higher (0.02 for under-21s).

Gas is cheaper than in Europe,
but pricey for the US. There are
gas stations by Circus Circus and
across from Mandalay Bay;
stations abound on Paradise Road,
Maryland Parkway, Tropicana
Avenue and Flamingo Road.

ESSENTIALS

The **American Automobile Association (AAA)** provides maps, guidebooks and other useful information. They're free if you're a member or belong to an affiliated organisation, such as the British AA. The Vegas office is at 3312 W Charleston Boulevard; call them on 870 9171 or see www.aaa.com.

Car hire

Most car-hire agencies are at or near the airport. Call around for the best rate, booking well in advance if you're planning to visit over a holiday weekend or for a major convention. When business renters are scarce, though, you should get a good rate, and maybe – if you ask nicely – an upgrade.

Almost every firm requires a credit card and matching driver's licence; few will rent to under-25s. Prices won't include tax, liability insurance or collision damage waiver (CDW); US residents may be covered on their home policy, but foreign residents will need to buy extra insurance. UK travellers should note that rental deals struck with the UK offices of the major firms include insurance.

Car rental companies

Alamo *US: 1-800 462 5266/263 8411/ www.alamo.com. UK: 0870 400 4562/ www.alamo.co.uk.*
Avis *US: 1-800 331 1212/261 5595/ www.avis.com. UK: 0870 606 0100/ www.avis.co.uk.*
Budget *US: 1-800 527 0700/736 1212/www.budget.com. UK: 0844 581 2231/www.budget.co.uk.*
Dollar *US: 1-800 800 3665/www. dollar.com. UK: 0808 234 7524/ www.dollar.co.uk.*
Enterprise *US: 1-800 261 7331/ 365 6662/www.enterprise.com. UK: 0870 350 3000/www. enterprise.co.uk.*
Hertz *US: 1-800 654 3131/ 220 9700/www.hertz.com. UK: 0870 844 8844/www.hertz.co.uk.*

National *US: 1-800 227 7368/261 5391. UK: 0870 400 4581. Both: www.nationalcar.com.*
Thrifty *US: 1-800 847 4389/896 7600/www.thrifty.com. UK: 0808 234 7642/www.thrifty.co.uk.*

Parking

Most hotel-casinos have valet parking, which is convenient, safe and free (apart from the $2-$5 tip as you exit). Self-parking is free at every resort (Downtown casinos require a validation stamp), but the convenience of lots is variable.

Cycling

In a word: don't. Drivers on the three- and four-lane roads simply aren't looking for cyclists.

Walking

Pedestrians are rarely seen off the Strip in Vegas, and even there they face danger from carefree and often careless drivers. The bridges on the Strip help, but it's still tricky. Jaywalking is so potentially deadly that police often issue citations.

The safest places to cross are the overhead pedestrian bridges at key Strip locations. You can find them at Tropicana Avenue, at Flamingo Road, and at Spring Mountain Road near Wynn Las Vegas. Where there are no bridges, closely follow all traffic signals and check both directions twice before stepping into the street.

It's possible to take short-cuts from one Strip hotel to the next, but you're likely to get trapped in a maze of service roads. Don't underestimate distances between resorts: the Strip is longer than it looks. And factor in plenty of time to get out of the resort in which you've been staying, dining, or gambling: you may be as much as a 15-minute walk from the main exit.

Resources A-Z

Accident & emergency

All the hospitals below have a 24-hour ER. The UMC on Charleston is the only hospital that by law must treat all applicants.

North Vista Hospital *409 E Lake Mead Boulevard, between Las Vegas Boulevard North & N Eastern Avenue, North Las Vegas (649 7711/www.north vistahospital.com). Bus 113, 210.*

Sunrise Hospital & Medical Center *3186 S Maryland Parkway, between E Sahara Avenue & E Desert Inn Road, East Las Vegas (731 8000/ www.sunrisehospital.com). Bus 109.*

University Medical Center *1800 W Charleston Boulevard, at Shadow Lane, West Las Vegas (383 2000/ www.umc-cares.org). Bus 206.*

Business

Vegas is the convention capital of the US. The LVCVA is the largest convention facility in the US.

Las Vegas Convention Center *3150 Paradise Road, at Convention Center Drive, East of Strip (892 0711/ www.lvcva.com). Bus 108, 213.*

Credit card loss

American Express *1-800 992 3404/ travellers' cheques 1-800 221 7282*
Diners Club *1-800 234 6377*
Discover *1-800 347 2683*
MasterCard *1-800 622 7747*
Visa *1-800 847 2911*

Customs

On US flights, non-US citizens are given two forms – one for customs, one for immigration – which must be completed before landing. Foreign visitors can import the following items duty-free: 200 cigarettes or 50 cigars (not Cuban; over-18s only) or 2kg of smoking tobacco; one litre of wine or spirits (over-21s only); and up to $100 in gifts ($800 for returning Americans). You must declare and maybe forfeit plants and foodstuffs. See www.cbp.gov/xp/cgov/travel.

UK Customs & Excise allows returning travellers to bring in £145 of goods bought abroad. Citizens of other countries should check the rules in their country.

Dental emergency

The **Nevada Dental Association** (255 4211, www.nvda.org) will make referrals to registered dentists.

Disabled

Strip resorts are fully wheelchair-accessible, though things are harder in older Downtown properties. A few casinos offer games for sight- and hearing-impaired players. Disabled parking is found almost everywhere; buses and many taxis are adapted to take wheelchairs. Contact the **Southern Nevada Center for Independent Living** (889 4216, www.sncil.org) for advice.

Electricity

The US uses a 110-120V, 60-cycle AC voltage. Except for dual-voltage flat-pin shavers, most foreign visitors will need an adaptor.

Embassies & consulates

The nearest foreign embassies and consulates to Las Vegas are in California.

Australia *Suite 3150, Century Plaza Towers, 2029 Century Park East, Los Angeles, CA 90067 (1-310 229 4800/ www.dfat.gov.au).* **Open** 9am-5pm Mon-Fri.

Canada *9th Floor, 550 S Hope Street, Los Angeles, CA 90071 (1-213 346 2700/http://geo.international.gc.ca).* **Open** 8.30am-4.30pm Mon-Fri.

New Zealand *Suite 600E, 2425 Olympic Boulevard, Santa Monica, CA 90404 (1-310 566 6555/www.nzcgla. com).* **Open** 8.30am-1pm, 1.30-4.30pm Mon-Fri.

Republic of Ireland *Suite 3350, 100 Pine Street, San Francisco, CA 94111 (1-415 392 4214/www.irelandemb.org).* **Open** 10am-noon, 2-3.30pm Mon-Fri.

South Africa *Suite 600, 6300 Wilshire Boulevard, Los Angeles, CA 90048 (1-323 651 0902/www.saembassy.org).* **Open** 9am-noon Mon-Fri.

United Kingdom *Suite 1200, 11766 Wilshire Boulevard, Los Angeles, CA 90025 (1-310 481 0031/24hr 1-877 514 1233).* **Open** 8.30am-5pm Mon-Fri.

Internet

Laptoppers can link to free Wi-Fi at 12 branches of the Coffee Bean & Tea Leaf, in the Fashion Show Mall near the Apple Store, and in the city's libraries. For those without a laptop, a few convenience stores have terminals. Public libraries offer free access; five branches of FedEx Kinko's (http://fedex.kinkos. com) have paid-for access.

Opening hours

The casinos, their bars and at least one of their restaurants or coffeeshops are open all day, every day, as are many grocery stores, dry-cleaners and gas stations. On a local level, Vegas keeps small-town hours. Office hours are 9am to 5pm.

Police

In emergencies, dial 911 (free from payphones). For non-emergencies,

there's a police station at 400 E Stewart Avenue, just off Las Vegas Boulevard (795 3111).

Post

For your nearest post office, call 1-800 275 8777 and quote the zip code. General delivery mail (poste restante) can be collected from the Downtown station (to: General Delivery, Las Vegas, NV 89101).

Main post office *1001 E Sunset Road, at Paradise Road, East of Strip (1-800 275 8777).* Bus 212. **Open** 8am-9pm Mon-Fri; 8am-4pm Sat.

Downtown station *201 Las Vegas Boulevard South, between E Fremont Street & E Bonneville Avenue (1-800 275 8777).* Bus Deuce & all DTC-bound buses. **Open** 8.30am-5pm Mon-Fri.

Strip station *3100 Industrial Road, at Stardust Way, West of Strip (1-800 275 8777).* Bus Deuce, 105. **Open** 8.30am-5pm Mon-Fri.

Smoking

In 2007, smoking was banned in most establishments that serve prepared food (casinos and strip clubs were exempt). However, many businesses flouted the law, and it remains a matter for debate whether continued enforcement is possible. Smoking is ubiquitous on casino floors, though a couple have non-smoking areas. A few hotels are entirely smoke-free; most offer non-smoking rooms.

Telephones

The area code for Vegas is 702, within Vegas you only need to dial the seven-digit number. Outside the city, calls are long distance: dial 1, then the area code, then the number. The 1-800, 1-866, 1-877 and 1-888 codes denote toll-free numbers; many are accessible from outside the US, but you'll be charged for your call. Calls to 1-900 numbers will be charged at premium rates.

Most hotels charge a flat fee of between 50¢ and $1 for calls to local and toll-free numbers. Long-distance and international calls can be pricey if direct-dialled from a hotel; you're better off using a US phonecard. Drugstores and convenience stores sell them in various denominations.

Mobile phones

Vegas operates on the 1900 GSM frequency. European travellers with tri-band phones will be fine; all others will need to rent a handset.

Public phones

Payphones are harder to find these days, though casinos still have them. To use one, check for a tone and then put in your change (35¢ for a local call; await an operator for long-distance calls). Operator and emergency calls are free.

Tickets

Ticketmaster (474 4000, www. ticketmaster.com) sells tickets for many events, although the booking fees can be high.

Time

Nevada operates on Pacific Standard Time, eight hours behind GMT (London). Clocks go forward by an hour in late April, and back in late October.

Tipping

Tip limo drivers ($10-$25 per ride), valet parking attendants ($2-$5), cocktail waitresses ($1-$2), housekeepers ($2-$4 a night) and even desk clerks ($10-$20 if you're looking for a better room).

Tourist information

Las Vegas Convention & Visitors Authority *3150 Paradise Road, opposite Convention Center Drive, East of Strip, Las Vegas, NV 89109 (892 0711/www.visitlasvegas.com). Bus 108, 213.* **Open** 8am-5pm Mon-Fri.

What's on

The *Las Vegas Review-Journal* (www.lvrj.com) is a daily newspaper covering local and national stories. 'Neon', the *R-J*'s pull-out guide issued each Friday, has listings for films, shows and restaurants.

Alternative weeklies include the *Las Vegas Weekly* (free, www. lasvegasweekly.com), which is focused on entertainment and *Las Vegas CityLife* (www.lasvegascity life.com) less glossy and a touch more political. Good free magazines include the calm, cultured *Vurb* (www.vurbmagazine.com), which has its eye trained on Downtown, and the more raucous *Racket* (www.racketonline.com), more interested in the city's nightlife. *Q-Vegas* (www.qvegas.com) is the leading media resource for the LGBT community.

Visas

Citizens of 27 countries including the UK, Ireland, Australia and New Zealand do not need a visa for stays in the US of less than 90 days if they have a passport valid for six months beyond the return date and a return (or open standby) ticket. Canadians and Mexicans do not need visas. All other travellers must have visas.

UK travellers should check the US Embassy's website at www.us embassy.org.uk, or call its helpline on 09042 450100 (£1.20 a minute).

ESSENTIALS

Index